PLOTS AGAINST RUSSIA

PLOTS AGAINST RUSSIA

Conspiracy and Fantasy after Socialism

ELIOT BORENSTEIN

CORNELL UNIVERSITY PRESS
ITHACA AND LONDON

First published 2019 by Cornell University Press

Library of Congress Cataloging-in-Publication Data

Names: Borenstein, Eliot, 1966– author.
Title: Plots against Russia : conspiracy and fantasy after socialism / Eliot Borenstein.
Description: Ithaca : Cornell University Press, 2019. | Includes bibliographical references and index.
Identifiers: LCCN 2018041939 (print) | LCCN 2018043657 (ebook) | ISBN 9781501716355 (epub/mobi) | ISBN 9781501716362 (pdf) | ISBN 9781501716331 | ISBN 9781501716331 (cloth) | ISBN 9781501735776 (pbk.)
Subjects: LCSH: Popular culture—Russia (Federation) | Political culture—Russia (Federation) | Conspiracy theories—Russia (Federation) | Paranoia—Social aspects—Russia (Federation) | Post-communism—Social aspects—Russia (Federation) | National characteristics, Russian.
Classification: LCC DK510.762 (ebook) | LCC DK510.762 .B67 2019 (print) | DDC 306.0947—dc23
LC record available at https://lccn.loc.gov/2018041939

For Franny, of course.
And in memory of
Joel Bernstein
(1937–2017)

Of course there's an anti-Russian conspiracy; the problem is that its participants include Russia's entire adult population.

—Victor Pelevin, *Generation P*

CONTENTS

PREFACE

This is an uncomfortable book to write. It is also the book that I've been preparing to write for my entire adult life, although there is no way I could have known it.

The awkwardness stems from an awareness that my position in writing it is thoroughly compromised. The book you have in your hands (or possibly on your screens) is a study of paranoid, conspiratorial, and extremist trends in Russia's media, film, and fiction since the collapse of the Soviet Union. Given the geopolitical climate during this book's gestation (2014–2018), I fear that it will be interpreted as simply an academic variation on the demonization of Vladimir Putin, which has proved both inevitable and unproductive during Putin's third term as president. On the off-chance that *Plots against Russia* should come to the attention of media types in the Russian Federation, accusations of "Russophobia" are as predictable as Russian election results (indeed, my inner "Kremlin troll" could compose the appropriate denunciation in seconds flat). It's one thing for Richard Hofstadter to isolate a "paranoid style" in US politics in the

1960s—he was American, engaged in the sort of internal critique on which a healthy democracy should thrive. To make a similar argument about someone else's culture is to invite accusations of bias and insensitivity.

During my three decades of studying Russian literature and culture, I've been acutely aware of the dangers of exoticizing the Other. In analyzing sexuality, gender, and mass culture, I've learned to question a tendency to be attracted to the bizarre and to try to ground my focus on Russia's fringe phenomena in a larger context that goes beyond the novelty factor. This becomes increasingly more challenging, in particular because of the role of new media in Russian (self-) presentation. The Internet has an insatiable appetite for just the sort of oddities that are something of a Russian national resource. Yet the world does not need the academic equivalent of the "Meanwhile, in Russia" meme.

But this book is also a capitulation to the reality of Russian mass culture in the aftermath of the seizure of Crimea. I have been studying and teaching conspiracy theory for years, yet I was long reluctant to publish my writings on Russian conspiratorial thought out of the concern that I am taking marginal figures and texts too seriously. After all, how accurate would an examination of North American media and culture be based on the writings of Lyndon LaRouche? But the last few years have seen most of the conspiratorial ideas (and their proponents) that I have been studying move from the margins to something resembling the center. Nearly all of it gets airtime on Russian state television (not to mention its ubiquity on the Russian Internet).

This sudden, unexpected relevance of fringe thought is disturbing, and not just for all the obvious reasons. It has been essential for me as a cultural studies scholar and literary critic to carve out a space that is intellectually significant yet fundamentally irrelevant. The field of Soviet Studies thrived during the Cold War, thanks to abundant government funding and the constant appeal to "policy relevance." That is, the justification for studying the Soviet Union (and even such ideologically distant phenomena as, say, the poetry of Alexander Pushkin) was always about gathering and creating knowledge about the enemy. This was extremely helpful when it came to arguing for grants and tenure lines, but it also threatened to reduce all culture to manifestations of Soviet ideology and the presumably malign intent of the men in the Kremlin. As the gloriously irrelevant Russian author Nikolai Gogol once wrote, in the conclusion of his absurd tale about two men named Ivan feuding over nothing of particular value, "It's a dreary world we live in, gentlemen."

Despite the ups and downs in Russian-American relations, one hopes that Kremlinology will have the decency to remain dead. It was always a hermeneutic endeavor of dubious worth, using the Soviet leadership as a screen for the projection of our own values and fears. It also relied on paranoia as a fundamental interpretive strategy ("What does this *Pravda* editorial *really* mean?") So, despite the fact that this book would pass the policy relevance test of a grant application with flying colors, I hope that it can be understood as the result of years of observation rather than a reflexive response to a regime that does look increasingly authoritarian and paranoid. Indeed, the one obviously politically relevant lesson to be gleaned here is that none of the ideological stances that have become so prominent in Putin's third term is particularly new, nor can they simply be ascribed to a Putin propaganda brain trust. Even if a regime looks to outsiders as though it is lost in a world of fantasy, the leaders are nearly always building the fantasy on what they already have to work with—that is, on what the culture readily provides.

Which leads me to my final point: while I am viewing Russian culture and politics through the lens of fantasy, I am not arguing that a fantasy-inflected approach to the world is unique to contemporary Russia. All ideology is fantasy, and the United States is no stranger to fictionally derived worldviews (as the past three decades of American Studies have shown). Every culture, and every cultural moment, produces its dominant myths, and some of these myths might even be true. But the fifteen-plus years of a political culture dominated by the same set of people (to the exclusion of virtually anyone who could be considered the loyal opposition), along with the first tumultuous post-Soviet decade that brought this culture into being, provide a precious opportunity to observe the interaction between apparently idle fantasies about a country's past, present, and future (the ideological fictions at stake here, many of which circulated as low-rent entertainment) and the lurching, stopping-and-starting attempts to articulate an explanatory myth (an ideological "just-so" story) about the country's political destiny (from the bureaucratic fumblings toward a "national ideology" under Yeltsin through the ideological placeholder of "sovereign democracy" to whatever is being formed now). Moreover, all of this is happening in real time.

There is an argument to be made that narrative entertainments ("literary" fiction, bestsellers, films, and television) can yield insight into the broader political culture. To those who greeted the decoupling of literature and ideology in the wake of the USSR, this is a mixed blessing. Thus the subject of my book in many ways recapitulates the evolution of the scholarly field that has produced it, an evolution that (in one of the many Marxist ironies haunting our supposedly post-Marxist world) is largely dialectical. The perceived menace of the Soviet Union lent Russian Studies significance but threatened to reduce the field to pure utility. The collapse of the USSR released the field from its Cold War gilded cage, with great intellectual benefits, but also at real cost. If Russia was no longer considered an existential threat, Russian Studies itself was threatened with extinction. Now we are suddenly relevant again (however briefly); perhaps we can take advantage of this relevance without falling back into the traps of Cold War reductionism.

ACKNOWLEDGMENTS

Writing the Acknowledgments section is always a daunting task, but it is all the more intimidating for a book about conspiracy theories. Will my inevitable omissions be taken as an intentional slight at the orders of my Illuminati masters? Or am I being unforgivably naive in naming names at all? I can only hope that the people involved will forgive me, whether for forgetfulness or breach of confidence.

First I'd like to recognize the support and patience of my colleagues at New York University. In the Department of Russian and Slavic Studies, I begin with Anne Lounsbery, a longtime friend who puts up with my frequent unannounced visits to her office to solicit her opinion on whatever I am trying to transfer from my mind to the computer screen. Irina Belodedova, Jane Burbank, Stephen Cohen, Rossen Djagalov, Diana Greene, Boris Groys, Mikhail Iampolski, Ilya Kliger, Ekaterina Korsounskaia, Michael Kunichika, Evelina Mendelevich, Leydi Rofman, and Maya Vinokour have all been ideal colleagues throughout the whole process. Yanni Kotsonis, Joshua Tucker, and Heather Messina at the Jordan Center have been wonderfully supportive of my efforts on the All the Russias blog, where some of the ideas in this book first took tentative shape.

At the Department of East Asian Studies (EAS), Alejandra Beltran, department manager extraordinaire, made it possible to balance my new commitments to EAS with the ongoing project of *Plots against Russia*, as did her assistants, Candace Laning and Stacy Sakane. My EAS faculty colleagues—Laurence Coderre, Tom Looser, Yoon Jeong Oh, Moss Roberts, Annmaria Shimabuku, and Xudong Zhang—have been delightful interlocutors.

I owe a similar debt of gratitude to Linda Mills in the Office of Global Programs for her unwavering support, and to all the amazing people I work with at Global: Janet Alperstein, Zvi-Ben Dor Benite, Peter Holm, Tyra Lieberman, Nancy Morrison, Gbenga Ogedegbe, and Marianne Petit.

So many friends and colleagues have been supportive during the years this project took shape, and I will do my best to name them all: Amy Adams, David Bethea, Clare Cavanagh, Una Chaudhuri, Robert Davidson, Faye Ginsberg, Helena Goscilo, David Herman, Judith Kornblatt, Natalia Levina, Mark Lipovetsky, Tomislav Longinovic, Yuliya Minkova, Fred Myers, Robin Nagel, Eric Naiman, Crystal Parikh, Jennifer Presto, Stefanie Russell, John Scaife, Eric Sobie, and Ilya Yablokov.

Special thanks go to Bruce Grant, co-editor of my last book, who gently but firmly advised me to set aside my chapter on conspiracy theory and save it for a future project, and to Elizabeth Dunn, who after inviting me to present on conspiracy to the Council for European Studies suggested that this would make a good topic for my next project.

A rough draft of this book originally appeared on my blog plotsagainst russia.org, which gave me feedback from many subscribers and Facebook friends. Special thanks to Deborah Martinsen, who seems as incapable of missing a typo as I am of writing a sentence without them; she emailed me after virtually every blog post and saved the blog from countless errors. I am also grateful for feedback from Tony Anomone, Betty Banks, Elizabeth Beaujour, Nathaniel Borenstein, Angela Brintlinger, Catherine Ciepiela, Sara Dickinson, Luke Ellenberg, Mark Galeotti, Jim von Geldern, Monika Greenleaf, Robin Hessman, Kate Holland, Volha Isakava, Diane Koenker, Joseph Livesey, Maxim Matusevich, Holly Myers, Coassio de Oliviera, Jiri Pehe, Sophie Pinkham, Jonathan Platt, Michele Rivkin-Fish, Randy

Rowe, Marian Schwartz, Brandon Schechter, Valerie Sperling, Yujing Tao, Tony Vanchu, Jose Vergara, and Maria Vinogradova.

Parts of this book took shape at talks delivered at the Council for European Studies, Florida State University, Hamburg University, Macalaster College, Miami University, NYU-Abu Dhabi, NYU-Prague, Stanford University, Trinity College, the University of Colorado-Boulder, the University of Florida, the University of Oregon, the University of Salzburg, the University of Southern California, the University of Tempere, and the University of Toronto. I would also like to thank the Guggenheim Foundation for its support.

In a different form, parts of this book appeared in *Public Books* and *The Huffington Post*. The first draft of the entire manuscript was serialized on plotsagainstrussia.org, and I appreciate the cooperation of Cornell University Press in making this happen, particularly my editors, Roger Malcolm Haydon and Susan Specter, as well as Carolyn Pouncy, whose copyediting skills are truly phenomenal.

Jennifer Smith provided consistent and reliable child care that gave me the freedom to write. My sons, Lev and Louis, put up with the intermittent absences this project required. And I want to take the opportunity to acknowledge the rest of my family—my brothers Seth, Nathaniel, and Joe, my in-laws Anne Marie Reidy-Borenstein, Mari Noruzi, Trina Borenstein, Nita and Anny Lutwak, and my mother-in-law Joan Kosta. My greatest debt of gratitude is, as always, to Fran.

Plots against Russia

Introduction

Russia as an Imaginary Country

You can tell a lot about a community based on what it bothers to censor. By the same token, if you do not know enough about the community doing the censoring, then the choice to ban or expunge looks almost random. A 2011 photo of Hillary Clinton sitting in the Situation Room surrounded by a number of male officials looks inoffensive, at least as an image; an Orthodox Jewish newspaper's excision of Clinton from the picture makes sense only in light of a prohibition on displaying the female form, even one as demurely pants-suited as Clinton's (Associated Press).

Turning to contemporary Russia, the 2015 decision to prevent screenings of the American film *Child 44* looks only somewhat less puzzling. The story takes place at the height of the Stalinist repressions; although there has been a great deal of whitewashing of Stalinism in recent years, pointing out that people were arrested and killed for no good reason is still not forbidden.[1] The plot involves the hunt for a serial killer who has been murdering homosexual men, all closeted by definition; outlawed in Soviet times, same-sex activity is legal in the Russian Federation, and if the serial murder of men who have been engaging in sex with each other on the down-low constitutes "gay propaganda," one wonders how many young people can be expected to take humiliated murder victims as their romantic role models. Could the minister of culture perhaps unconsciously be conflating *Child 44* with a gay rights group that, by pure coincidence, all but shares its name with the film: *Deti-404* (Children-404)? Children-404 advocates for gay teens in a legal climate that renders all such advocacy virtually illegal and takes its name from the error message "404—Page Not Found," usually displayed when a website is no longer live—or, in the case of LGBT-themed sites, closed down by government order. Although there is delicious irony in the juxtaposition of a story about gay victims of predators and an organization dedicated to help a juvenile population that has been redefined as the target of (gay) predators, irony alone gives no cause to ban a film.

Yet banned this film was. Partly, it was a matter of timing: *Child 44* was to be released just three weeks before the seventieth anniversary of the defeat of Nazi Germany, and this particular Victory Day was obviously going to be a monumental celebration (the opening of the 2014 Olympics in Sochi had already set the aesthetic parameters for national historical festivals: solemn commemoration meets Vegas floor show). The Russian Culture Ministry condemned "the distortion of historical facts and original interpretations of events before, during, and after the Great Patriotic War" (Birnbaum). Speaking later to RIA-Novosti, Culture Minister Vladimir Medinsky made a telling connection between the depiction of history and the country's very sense of self: "It is important that we should finally put an end to the endless series of schizophrenic reflections of ourselves" (Birnbaum). According to this view, the film is bad because it is a Western distortion of the Russian past, and because it is a continuation of a Russian debate about the essence and fate of Russia. What looks like a contradiction is actually an inadvertent piece of insight about the current media landscape, in which Russia's own cultural productions have to compete with Hollywood in the creation of an imaginary history for an audience that the elite cannot trust to come to their own conclusions. Indeed, in his condemnation of the (rather obscure) Western fiction that is *Child 44*, Medinsky invokes *The Lord of the Rings*, a narrative that has conquered virtually all national boundaries: the movie, he complains, portrays Russia as "not a country but a Mordor, with physically and mentally inferior subhumans."

The point here is not to defend *Child 44*, which is based on a mediocre novel by a man with a shaky understanding of Soviet reality. In the book, the author, Tom Rob Smith, sets himself a perverse task: to develop generically familiar tales of murder and its investigation against the backdrop of state violence on a massive scale. Smith has clearly read the English-language books about the notorious Soviet-era serial killer Andrei Chikatilo, along with a number of poorly digested potted histories of Stalinism and the gulag. He creates a totalitarian fantasyland based on the one lesson his reading afforded him: the most important thing under Stalin was survival. In his hands, Soviet citizens become cold, efficient survival machines, whose every action is the result of a carefully weighed, logical decision that might be followed by a muted, unemotional discussion. The result is a staggeringly alien one-dimensionality of characterization, as if Dostoevsky's underground man had emerged from his isolation, spent a few years at the London School of Economics repenting his previous irrational ways, and now set out to apply rational choice theory to human behavior. At times, Smith's books depict a fascinating world, but I find myself wishing he had embraced the inherent fantasy of his vision, and, like Gregory Maguire in *Wicked*, moved his meditations on authoritarian regimes to the not-so-merry old Land of Oz.

Why does *Child 44*, whether book or movie, do such a bad job of reproducing Soviet life under Stalin? A number of very simple and plausible answers immediately come to mind: laziness on the part of the filmmakers, the aforementioned faults in the source material, and, most of all, the complete lack of a sense that there is anything in particular at stake. In brief, it's just a movie. But *Child 44* was portrayed as part of a Western plot to slander Russia, presumably by suggesting that homosexuals existed in the Soviet Union before the United States and Europe had the opportunity to exert their pernicious influence. As in the case of the scandal a decade earlier, when Russian legislators were outraged that Dobby, the house elf who debuted in the third Harry Potter film, seemed to display a marked resemblance to Vladimir Putin, Western mass culture provides a useful straw man ("Russian Lawyers"). In each case, the immediate assumption is that nothing is left to chance, and that Hollywood is taking its orders from the White House or the State Department. Russia's fate, it seems, is to be the object of slander and conspiracy at all times. And the purveyors of this conspiratorial worldview see this victimization as a point of pride.

The crux here is far more than the tired question of representation and accuracy, nor should we stop at the simple conclusion that Russian governmental officials during Putin's third term were unnecessarily touchy. Representation suggests something static or iconic and is a category that is too dependent on external, often unverifiable notions of the true essence of the thing represented. If we deal in representations, we can too easily succumb to the dichotomy of "propaganda" vs. "truth," falling into the very sort of paranoid trap that I hope to investigate. Instead, I would frame the questions raised by the *Child 44* incident in terms of narrative and interpretation. Part of the problem is with the narrative that *Child 44* appears to provide, but the larger issue is the narrative into which the making and marketing of *Child 44* are all too easily assimilated. In each case, we find a question of *plot*.

I am by no means the first critic to point out that the English language provides endless possibilities for word play and interpretive flights of fancy based on the multiple meanings of the word "plot" (the events of a story as elaborated in a narrative vs. conspiracy).[2] And if we want to ascribe explanatory power to this lexical coincidence, we must first reckon with the fact that this word play has no equivalent in the language that forms the subject of this book—that is, Russian. The Russian language suggests other tantalizing possibilities, since the word for "plot/conspiracy" (*zagovor*) is closely linked to terms for faith healing and magic spells. Rather than pretend that etymology has some sort of magical interpretive primacy, I prefer to admit upfront that I am simply taking advantage of the possibilities that English vocabulary affords. The focus of this book is both the power of plot/narrative to model conceptions of Russia's identity and fate, and the habits of conspiratorial theorizing that are the building blocks of so many of these stories.

Russia and Other Ideas

A whole host of objections immediately arise. Don't all cultures define themselves in terms of story? Is Russia truly unique in its government officials' concern for the country's image? Is Russian culture being dismissed as "paranoid"? And aren't conspiracy theories popular throughout the world?

My imaginary critics have a point (several of them, actually). On the surface, nothing I have described is difficult to imagine in nearly any other country or culture, and the familiar clichés about the Russian tradition—its logocentrism, for instance—do not get us very far. While there is definitely an argument to be made for conspiratorial thought's deep Russian roots, conspiracy's prominence in the past is not a reliable predictor for the present, let alone the future. Instead, we should consider the difficult historical moment that extends from 1991 to the present day.

Narrative bears a heavy burden of significance during times of turmoil and transition. These are the moments when a country's fate and identity appear to be up for grabs. Even more important, these are the moments when narrative consumers, and even the narratives themselves, treat the nation, its culture, and its people with undeniable self-consciousness. North American readers who remember the 1960s and 1970s, even if those memories are secondhand, should be familiar with the often tendentious stories whose claim to fame resides in their examination of American myth. Take, for example, the familiar plot of the road trip. Thanks to the 1969 film *Easy Rider*, a cross-country journey during this period was, more often than not, a quest to "find America" (a phrase that becomes ironic when translated into Russian, the equivalent of "reinventing the wheel"). Just a little over a decade later, traveling across the country loses its iconic significance. The road trip of *Anywhere but Here* or *Thelma and Louise* certainly means something, but it isn't an ethnographic excursion into America's heart of darkness. Indeed, if we recall that post-Watergate television and cinema, with their self-critical examinations of malaise and crisis, give way to what Susan Jeffords (*Hard Bodies*) sees as a triumphalist mode under Reagan, we might find broad parallels with Russia's cultural scene as it moves from the 1990s to the Putin years.

The years following the collapse of the Soviet Union were notoriously difficult, marked by rising crime rates, plummeting living standards, terrorism, and ethnic violence. But this was also an era that could not shake an identity crisis. The country in which the population had spent its entire lives was gone, and even the basic vocabulary for describing the successor states and their citizens was unfamiliar and unstable. European empires, such as the one brought down by the Russian Revolution, were guided by God and destiny. The Soviet Union was the fulfillment of the promise of human progress, an unprecedented social experiment aligned with the laws of history (a history which Francis Fukuyama was busily declaring officially defunct). The Russian Federation, like its fellow successor states, was a geopolitical accident, whose borders had been set according to the low stakes of internal cartography—hence the problem of Crimea. What, then, was Russia for?

In the debates about Russia and its fate during the Yeltsin era, two terms inevitably recurred: "ideology" and "the Russian Idea." Discussions about the need for a state ideology, without necessarily endorsing Soviet values, took a Soviet philosophical framework for granted: a powerful state must have an ideology, preferably one made explicit by experts and disseminated through the media and educational system. On the surface, such an orientation resembles contemporary Western critique; scholars from Adorno through the poststructuralists have dedicated much of their work to exposing ideological constructs that circulate as "natural" (questions of race, class, and gender in particular). The Western academic Left exposes ideology in Europe and North America as an act of resistance, while the post-Soviet argument in favor of ideology is in part an act of resistance against a perceived onslaught of *foreign* ideology (individualism, consumerism), and in part an affirmation that a consciously elaborated ideology both creates and binds communities. In any case, the "ideology" argument had numerous obstacles to overcome, starting with the burdensome connotations of the term itself.

The Russian Idea had a much more attractive provenance. As the country's publishing industry—and, therefore, readers—rediscovered the heritage of Silver Age (prerevolutionary twentieth-century) culture and philosophy, a wealth of books arrived on the shelves with a seven-decade delay, but with an accompanying sense of relevance and immediacy that they would more than likely have lacked had they been part of the cultural conversation during Soviet times. One of the many post-Soviet success stories of Russian prerevolutionary philosophy is the revival of Nikolai Berdyaev, especially his most famous work, *The Russian Idea* (1946). Both a history of Russian philosophy and a polemical analysis of Russian philosophy, *The Russian Idea* argued that Russian identity depended on a sense of messianic mission, eschatological purpose, and communitarian cohesiveness.[3] Berdyaev is helpful not to argue for or against the relevance of his particular notion of the Russian Idea, but rather to note his importance in propagating the *idea* of the Russian Idea as a discursive structure.

The Russian Idea continues to exert a great deal of power as an idea, but in terms of any practical utility, it reached its nadir in 1996, when Yeltsin established a commission of experts to develop a new Russian Idea in the course of a year. The commission's unsurprising failure, along with the impossibility of resolving disagreements about the Russian Idea in any diverse public forum, is less a matter of intellectual incapacity than it is a sign that the search was being conducted in the wrong place. Russia's identity was being effectively negotiated and renegotiated in popular and elite *narrative*. The Russian Idea suggests something static—an image of a country's purpose or future. Ideology sounds equally disassociated from the passage of time—a set of principles and goals that do not, on their own, tell a story. Yet it is in the form of story, of narrative, that collective fantasies about Russia's destiny take on their most compelling shape. And, as with most ideological fictions, their fantasies are effectively transmitted to the extent that the stories encoding them capture their audience's attention.

For the purposes of the present study, these fantasies play out in four categories of text

(1) Narratives that do not make Russian identity/fate their primary theme, but which nonetheless can be mined for evidence of broader cultural trends. Such texts acquire significance primarily as a function of their number; that is, a broad-based reading of multiple narratives is required to reach even tentative conclusions. This was the approach I used in parts of my previous book, *Overkill*, and that I apply only sparingly here.

(2) Narratives in which reflections on Russia and its role in the world are among the dominant concerns. That is, fictional works in prose, film, or television that are self-consciously preoccupied with the Russian theme, and that in turn demand a similar preoccupation on the part of the audience.

(3) Political/philosophical tracts about Russia and "Russianness." While these works take the form of nonfiction (whether in prose

or as documentaries), they are actually most effectively treated as unintentionally Borgesian experiments in fictional nonfiction. Their power comes not from the persuasiveness of their constituent ideas but from the appeal of the story they tell about Russia and its enemies.

(4) The discussion and presentation of current invents in the news media and online.

Framing these questions in terms of fantasy means steering discussion away from the limited question of historical accuracy (the question raised by *Child 44*). One of the more dismal points of commonality between theories of postmodernism and the empirical experience of ideological debates in the blogosphere and on social media is the growing irrelevance of the verifiable fact. If facts actually solved arguments, the Internet would be a vastly different place, with no room for animus about, say, global warming or vaccine safety. Debunking a fallacy is less a tool for persuasion than it is a rite of solidarity performed by and for the faithful.[4]

The narratives discussed over the next several chapters are persuasive in that they tell a persuasive story. Both a right-wing tract and a dystopian novel offer their reader a portable, imaginary Russia that may or may not ring true. Each describes a fantasy world whose effectiveness depends on its congruity with its audience's prior understanding of the world around them, an understanding that is always already conditioned by earlier fantasy narratives.

What I am calling for is a deliberately perverse reading of these texts as exemplars of what looks like the wrong genre. I want to treat realist fiction about the contemporary world either as if it were historical fiction about an imagined past, or fantasy about an imaginary world that bears a striking resemblance to contemporary Russia. When writers turn to a different era (or, for that matter, an exotic land), they can labor under a burden of fidelity that is far more onerous than when setting a work in a default, amorphous present. While historical fiction can be composed in a variety of literary styles, it is instructive that one of the first questions to come to a naive reader's mind is that of accuracy: Can I trust a given portrayal of the past? And if I can't, why should I continue to read it? For such a reader, fiction about the past should be both informative (letting us know what a given time was "really" like) and confirmative (maintaining verisimilitude in part by not straying too far from the reader's expectations of the period). On the surface, this looks like conventional realism, but it also resembles what is known in fantasy and science fiction circles as "world building": constructing an elaborate fictional setting that feels both "lived in" and parceled out. The reader should intuit that there is much more world available than just the part contained in the text. Casual fans of Tolkien can easily sense that *The Lord of the Rings* has a vast prehistory, while true devotees can avail themselves of the books' multiple semifinished prequels, which dole out exhaustive fictional historical knowledge and deep aesthetic disappointment in equal measure.

From Second World to Secondary World

The conspiratorial fantasies examined here are only sometimes explicitly fantastic in form. The Russian adaptation of the hit British television series *Life on Mars*, whose twenty-first century protagonist wakes up after an accident to find himself in the body of his father in the Brezhnev era, is an example of the "portal quest" fantasy, in which a traveler from "our" world finds himself in a magical land. Calling the late socialist USSR "magical" is, admittedly, a bit of a stretch, but the rosy nostalgia that has come to surround the "era of stagnation" and the Soviet Union's status as capital of the Second World, along with the unexplained mechanism by which the hero makes his journey, suffuses the entire series with a sense of the fantastic. As Farah Mendlesohn writes in *Rhetorics of Fantasy*, "When we think of portal fantasies, we commonly assume that the portal is from 'our' world to the fantastic, but the portal fantasy is about entry, transition, and negotiation." This process of negotiation is one that can lead to insights about both worlds, not just the "other" one.

The portal quest guarantees an external perspective to the fantasy world; Narnia's delights unfold largely in the consciousness of its visitors. Such stories sharply contrast with the other most common form of fantasy narrative, which Mendlesohn calls "immersive." Here there is no external perspective. As a result, the fantastic in these tales is almost entirely in the minds of the reader. Frodo may be unequipped to deal with orcs, and the inhabitants of George R. R. Martin's Westeros may have grown skeptical about the existence of dragons and the walking dead, but in each case, the characters live in a world where the impossible is defined differently than it is in ours. Frodo does not know that he lives in a fantasy world, but Dorothy is acutely aware that she is visiting one.

By extension we can posit that all fiction, including the default realism of most popular and literary fiction, exists in a variation on Tolkien's idea of the "secondary world"—one that is internally consistent but operates according to different rules from our "primary" world. In realism, the secondary world is constructed to mimic the primary world as closely as possible, and yet it is still a world that is constructed rather than simply found, posited rather than given. Casual discussions of fantasy genres engage in a simple but flexible taxonomy that distinguishes various sub-genres and even specific texts according to a simple metric: just how much magic do they contain? Epic fantasy can range from great gobs of magic (as in Tolkien) to relatively little (Martin's *Game of Thrones*) to virtually none (Mervyn Peake's *Gormenghast*), while urban fantasy can combine the veneer of contemporary realism with quasi-Manichaean metaphysics (Sergei Lukianenko's *Night Watch* novels), show a mundane world shadowed by various mythological or magical other worlds (almost anything by Neil Gaiman), or exploit the cognitive dissonance inspired by the casual acceptance of one, perhaps two, elements of the traditionally supernatural in an otherwise recognizably mundane world (the early entries in Charlaine Harris's Southern Vampire series, which inspired HBO's *True Blood*). Realism, then, is just a special subcase of fantasy that allows no magic whatsoever, a secondary world that tries its best to pass for primary.

For most purposes (and most readers), the constructed nature of the realist secondary world is unimportant. This changes to the extent that the plot seems contrived or the characters' behavior incomprehensible. But it also changes if the text has a satirical function or serves as social criticism; referring the reader to a social injustice or societal foible requires that the reader will actually recognize the problem as relevant or possible. Ideological, tendentious, or political fictions are immersive fantasies whose secondary world attempts to pass for the reader's primary world; they are successful when they get their readers not merely to suspend disbelief (understood as a prerequisite to successful fantasy since the days of Samuel Taylor Coleridge) but to adopt the belief posited by the fantasy and, if only briefly, reconsider their primary world in terms of the lessons of the secondary. And, as with all immersive fantasies, the lack of an external viewpoint or reader surrogate goes only so far; when we close the book or turn off the screen, we realize that we, like Bilbo, have gone there and back again. As readers, we have traveled to this secondary world whose primary difference from the one in which we live lies in its sheer legibility. The Russia narratives reprocess the primary world, producing an imaginary version that, unlike life, comes equipped with a user's manual. These narratives explain why the world is the way it is and sometimes indicate what is to be done to change it. The Russia narratives move seamlessly from the descriptive to the prescriptive.

And this is what unites the Russia narratives in both their fictional and nonfictional forms. The nonfiction version may claim to be enumerating facts on the path to the revelation of truth, but its purchase depends on its ability to create a cohesive simulacrum of Russia and its place in the world. The nonfiction, like the fiction, is deeply committed to world building. But where nonfiction plays down its resemblance to fiction for the purposes of persuasion, the fiction plays down the polemical in favor of the fictive and the entertaining. In the Russia narratives, the forms of fiction and nonfiction are not in opposition to each other, but rather represent two ends of a spectrum on which the narrative travels.

Epic Fail

The political/philosophical tract about Russia's fate is a laboratory that develops so many of the components found in fiction. Samuel R. Delany provides a helpful framework for us when he chooses to define science fiction and fantasy not in terms of subject matter (robots or unicorns) but grammatical mood, on the very level of the sentence: various flavors of science fiction are conditional/subjunctive (they tell of things that could happen but have not, or things that could have happened but did not), while fantasy is their grammatical opposite (it tells of things that could not happen, could not have happened, and never will) (Delany, 10–12). Ideological tracts erase the difference between the conditional/subjunctive and the indicative, passing political fantasy off as a faithful description of Russia's past, present, and possible future.

Fantasy and science fiction as alternative historical moods to the indicative of default realism help us understand the project undertaken by Dmitry Bykov in his wonderfully perverse *Living Souls* (ZhD): in terms of technology and realia, the novel takes place either in the very near future or an indeterminately flexible present, but it is a present that appears to be a distorted version of our own: after all, since when is Russia a nation whose aboriginal population has receded from view while an age-old conflict between the Varangians (i.e., the Vikings) and the Khazars (i.e, the Jews) turns into full-fledged war? The novel centers on the repeated conquests of Degunino, a small town inhabited by the natives and presenting no real intrinsic value. Nearly all the main protagonists are involved in some form of miscegenation, which, by the end of the novel, may have led to the birth of the Antichrist.[5]

Closer examination shows that *Living Souls* is the present-day extrapolation of a centuries-long alternate history. As a popular genre, alternate history usually poses the question "What if a particular crucial historical turning point had been resolved in another fashion?" (hence the most popular subtype of alternate history, often boiled down to the two-word statement "Hitler wins").[6] Bykov's "what if" is ideological, or rather, a burlesque on ideology instead of a direct engagement with it: what if the blood-and-soil rantings of extreme Russophile nationalists such as Grigorii Klimov, the Eurasianist ethnic fantasies of Lev Gumilev and Alexander Dugin, and Arthur Koestler's oddly racialized, obsessive identification of European Ashkenazi Jewry with the vanished Khazars were all not simply ideology (i.e., fantasy) but identifiable elements of factual history?

Bykov does what fantasy authors have been doing for decades, if not centuries: he writes about the fantastic (what could not happen, or what could not have happened) as if it were the actual (what has happened, and what is happening right now). In so doing, Bykov exploits the tension that such fantasy fiction can provide: by taking ideological fictions at face value (describing them as if they were simply accepted reality), he naturalizes them and denaturalizes them at the same time. The world of *Living Souls* becomes plausible, to the extent that we live in it for hundreds of pages without becoming hopelessly lost, but is so open to magic, prophecy, and the supernatural that the novel's conditional believability only reminds us of equal feats of verisimilitude: Dugin's, Klimov's, and Koestler's ideas become real, but only to the extent that Narnia becomes real, or Middle Earth proves internally consistent. *Living Souls* inflates ideology as entertainment and thought experiment but deflates it as a worldview, showing ideology to be just another internally consistent, well-wrought fantasy.[7] The implication is that Dugin may be fun to read, but implementing policies based on his writings is analogous to dressing up as Frodo or Gandalf and learning to speak Elvish.

When writers engage in this sort of ideological cosplay, they are nearly always collapsing time. Certainly, every futuristic utopia or dystopia inevitably bears the mark of its moment of composition; in the aftermath of the British enclosure of farmlands, Thomas More's *Utopia* reflects on agriculture in a way that Yevgeny Zamyatin's *We* and George Orwell's *1984* do not. Yet so many of the most noteworthy recent fantasies about Russia's future are remarkably backward-looking. In addition to Bykov's focus on Khazars and Varangians in *Living Souls*, we also have the revival of the policies and mores of Ivan the Terrible in Vladimir Sorokin's *Day of the Oprichnik* and Mikhail Yuriev's *Third Empire*; the resurgence of serfdom in Tatyana Tolstaya's *The Slynx*, and the resurrected threat of a Fourth Reich in both the multivolume Ethnogenesis series of young adult novels and, less centrally, in the future history Dmitry Glukhovsky began in the transmedia juggernaut *Metro 2033*.[8] Glukhovsky's underground postapocalyptic Moscow subway even has a union of ring line stations calling itself the "Hanseatic League," while the Sokolniki (red) line has become the overdetermined home of diehard Bolsheviks. Geography may or may not be destiny, but it is an indispensable accessory.

All of this leaves room for a tedious historiographic debate: should Russian history be understood as a set of cyclical, recurring patterns whose regularity can be used for predicting the country's future? Or is this merely an ideological construct (as well as a possible self-fulfilling prophecy)? Whether or not Russia is doomed to repeat its past, we, fortunately, are not doomed to repeat this debate. Instead, what is important is the persistent habit of seeing such patterns, of interpreting Russian history as if it were all part of a legible plan. Such a habit does more than just foster a sense of pessimistic resignation; it insists on the power of history for both the future and the present, rendering history always immanent.

Alternate history is a powerful tool in the conspiracist arsenal, allow-ing conspiracy to become *the* story of Russia, something of a postmodern national epic. Scholars of Russian literature will recall the Neo-Classicist preoccupation with the national epic in the eighteenth century: it was the one element of the classical constellation of genres that Russia could not provide. Certainly, Russia had folk epics, and, like most Slavic epics, these were stories of defeat rather than triumph. But there was no single unify-ing story that could serve as a cultural point of origin. Ironically, as soon as one contender appeared (*The Igor Tale*) it was haunted by accusations of forgery. Russian literature is hardly the poorer for it: would anyone really trade Pushkin or Dostoevsky for a Slavic *Beowulf* or *Chanson de Roland*? But the Russian conspiratorial narrative offers a story that always reaffirms Russia's role as the hero of history while emphasizing its status as the world's victim or offended party.

Alternate history would then be a deliberate falsification that threatens to undermine the very foundations of a commonplace Russian self-perception. But in fact, the goal of alternate history is the opposite. Alternate history, by essentially lying about the nation's past, is an attempt at strengthen-ing Russian cultural and historical legitimacy. If history, understood as inevitably recurring patterns, takes on the function of national myth, the replacement of reputable history with out-and-out mythology ends up telling an even more compelling story than could be supplied by mere facts.

Again, this is the sort of mythmaking that is easier to spot in its natural habitat of pure speculation: one expects to hear about the origin of the world in sacred texts (the Garden of Eden), mythology (Odin's construc-tion of the world from the corpse of Ymir), and epic fantasy (the forma-tion of Middle Earth by squabbling gods). Yet this obsession with origins is also found in myth's more prosaic counterpart, utopia (where, often as not, politics and law take the place of divinity and magic). The radiant future of utopia is usually preceded and predicted by a Golden Age, with the point of origin and endpoint serving as bookends for the story of a fallen humanity reclaiming and reinterpreting paradise as part of a secular future history. The communist "withering away of the state" mirrors a posited primitive communitarianism; feminist utopia reinscribes a prehis-toric matriarchy; and the imagined triumph of the white race reenacts an equally confabulated primordial Aryan purity. The imaginary origin legitimizes the imaginary endpoint.

Alternate history serves a similar function, but, in the cases discussed in this book, at a more local level. The broader, international category of alternate history as entertainment is another matter, since the sheer novelty of a different historical outcome can be a sufficient source of textual pleasure. Russia has no shortage of this sort of story, but the high stakes for the Russia narratives become clear when alternate history makes the species jump from novels preoccupied with the rearrangement of historical fact to pseudoscholarship whose organizing principle is the replacement of fact with fiction and the dismissal of all traditional scholarship as conspiratorial fabrication.

In this, as in most things, Russia is not unique in producing conspiratorial counterhistories. But, again, the current historical moment is crucial. Since the dismantling of the USSR, counterfactual narratives have flourished, and none more than the New Chronology product spearheaded by the renowned mathematician and stupendous crackpot Anatoly Fomenko. Following in the wake of a series of less-known attempts at chronological revisionism, Fomenko claims to have proven mathematically that history as we know it is a vast falsification. His New Chronology is to history what Young Earth Creationism is to paleontology: all of human experience has unfolded in a hypercompressed timeline. Prehistory began in the ninth century CE, Christ was born in the eleventh century, and the New Testament was written before the Hebrew Bible. Fomenko takes every opportunity available to him to combine a supposedly ancient city even with a more recent counterpart. Thus Jerusalem was actually Constantinople, and "ancient" Greece was really medieval Greece.[9]

When summarized, the scope of Fomenko's historical revisionism is misleading. The purpose of Fomenko's thirty-volume work is to make Russia the hero of history. Marco Polo visited Yaroslavl, and the Scythians, Huns, Cossacks, Ukrainians, and Belarusians are simply parts of a mammoth Russian Horde. The title of a 2009 book composed with his frequent co-author Gleb Nosovsky puts it best: *Christ Was Born in Crimea. And That's Where the Mother of God Died, Too.*[10] As with so much of the tendentious fiction to be examined here, *Christ Was Born in Crimea* would take on new significance after Putin's national-authoritarian turn (along with skyrocketing sales). This is not to suggest that Putin and his advisers were turning to pulp fiction and lunatic fringe pseudoscholarship for direct inspiration, but rather that the margins of mass culture were a comfortable home for ideas that would later move to the mainstream. At the very least, it is a reminder that the policies of Putin's third term, the seizure of Crimea, and the demonization of Ukraine did not appear out of nowhere.

Fomenko's revisionism has roots going back to Soviet times (which, if we follow his mathematical contortions, probably took place during the first half of 2002). Russia, we should remember, invented the radio, baseball, and even *The Wizard of Oz*. But before we laugh dismissively at Fomenko's ravings, it's worth noting that the attempt to resituate history within local and recent national boundaries looks rather . . . American. Christ's birth in Crimea fits rather well with the Mormon claim that he visited North America after the crucifixion. And Fomenko's assertion that Christopher Columbus was a Cossack may argue for a Russian claim to the New World, but it also reminds us of the problematic character of the entire Columbus story: "discovering" a continent where people had been living for centuries.[11]

As world power latecomers, Russia and the United States share a tendency to see themselves as the heroes of history—and to spin conspiracy theories at the drop of a hat. But where the United States blunders forward in the narcissistic self-confidence of a people unconcerned with the past, Russia has historically been troubled by a preoccupation with origins and legitimacy. Fomenko's narcissism is neurotic, and it forms the basis of a counterhistory that must be seen as compensatory. Whenever possible, Fomenko's alternate history rejects the very category of the Other. To call Fomenko's project imperialist would be an understatement, as he subsumes territorial aggrandizement to semiotic expansionism. For Fomenko, the whole world is Russian.

Welcome to the Deserters of the Real

Much of the discussion so far has revolved around terms that are simultaneously common enough not to require definition and so theoretically loaded as to demand a statement of allegiance to one of several possible critical approaches. The continued invocation of fantasy, along with the use of "imaginary" in this chapter's title, requires the help of that most unhelpful of thinkers, Jacques Lacan. Lacan's poststructuralist revision of Freudian psychoanalysis is brilliant in its scope, vexing in its terminology, and thoroughly confounding in its prose. Rather than get bogged down in Lacanian arcana, I want to briefly consider the conceptual triad that took on increased prominence throughout his career: the Imaginary, the Symbolic, and the Real. While these ideas are rooted in Lacan's elaboration of the Mirror Stage and its relation to the Oedipal, we have little need to engage with the Mirror Stage for the purposes of the present study. Still, the Lacanian emphasis on developmental stages—and early childhood in particular—has a presumably unintended benefit: Lacanian thought finds remarkable illustrations in children's entertainment and fairy tales, a coincidence that I hope to leverage in the explanation that follows.

The Imaginary is related to the portable self-image that we all carry with us once we enter into language and subjectivity. If we close our eyes, we have an image of ourselves that only partially aligns with exactly how we look at the present moment, since we are not actually looking at ourselves from the outside at all times. The existence of the Imaginary in one's mind has little relation to one's actual existence in everyday life; instead, the Imaginary is the set of prefabricated images and notions against which we *compare* what we experience and see in real life. The Imaginary allows us to identify and to misidentify. If we see an animal and identify it as a dog, we are recognizing the Imaginary notion of the dog as it maps onto the actual dog. But if we are the human characters in the 2002 Disney movie *Lilo & Stitch*, we misrecognize an alien genetic experiment as a dog because a dog is the closest available referent we can apply to this only vaguely doglike creature. Only in the sequels can the humans unfailingly identify other alien genetic experiments, because Stitch has now provided an Imaginary model for them.

The Imaginary is essential precisely because it enables recognition, but it is limited because that very recognition is literal and reductive. The Imaginary allows for one-to-one matching, and its projection of templates onto the Real has distinct implications for paranoia. But this literalism is a dead end, much as the Oedipal child's fixation on the actual mother and *only* the mother threatens to turn the Family Romance into an unwinnable, endless Cold War. The Imaginary fosters a false sense of identity between the thing represented and its imagined representation, an inflexible resistance to substitution. Steven Spielberg's *A.I. Artificial Intelligence* (2001) turns this inflexibility into the stuff of tragedy: a couple whose terminally ill child is kept in suspended animation decides to compensate for its loss by acquiring David, an android built to function as a young child. But both David and his adopted mother, Monica, suffer from a deficit of supplementarity and substitution; when the mother's biological child is suddenly cured, she does not have room in her heart for both. By the same token, David has been designed with a limitation that makes no sense as science fiction but is emotionally powerful for the fable at the heart of the movie: David can only ever form an attachment to one person throughout his entire existence. Once he has bonded with Monica (somehow, Monica's husband is not an issue here), he is doomed to love and need only her. Thousands of years later, David still longs for Monica and can never be happy without her. David's robotic love is entirely Imaginary; unlike an ordinary child, he cannot transfer his affections to someone else, cannot engage in the sorts of symbolic substitutions that generally mark adult, nonincestuous love.

It is the Symbolic that allows (indeed, requires) abstraction and substitution. Lacan's Symbolic Order encompasses practices, customs, laws, and traditions—the very systems that structure our understanding of the real without having a specific physical manifestation to wholly embody it. The Symbolic assumes a distinction between, say, the laws of a country and the physical copy of the constitution that elaborates the laws, or between the economic value of two different denominations of currency and the physical reality of the actual bills. Anyone who has ever used a credit card to buy something online implicitly understands this sort of abstraction: though we carry credit cards with our account numbers on them, it is the numbers themselves that matter, not the plastic on which they happen to be printed. Virtually nothing inheres to the materiality of the card. The Oedipal boy's progress toward (heterosexual) adulthood is all about accepting the Symbolic, giving up a sexual claim on the mother in favor of substitution by another woman and the attainment of the father's place in the triangle. Again, Disney comes to our rescue here, in that one of the recurring themes of feature cartoons for children is the creation of a new family to take the place of a broken one (*Lilo & Stitch, Up, Brother Bear*).

The Symbolic is also the precondition to any understanding of alterity: it is the Symbolic that demands a structuring of the self in relation to the Other. The Imaginary can only create the lower-case other, the alter ego that is merely a projected version of one's imagined fantasies about another being. This is the "imaginary capture" that Lacan says can be countered only by the "supremacy of the symbolic over the imaginary." The Symbolic Order is the set of laws and rules that make a community of Others possible, the "pact" linking "subjects together in one action" (Lacan, 1–7).

Both the Symbolic and the Imaginary fail to fully apprehend the the third and final category: the Real. The Real is that which precedes all language and signification, that which language and the Symbolic can only approximate but never grasp. Intense physical pain, for instance, or severe trauma break down both orders and bring us closer to the primal state, which, once we have entered into language, we can no longer properly conceive: the state of pure, unmediated physicality. The Real is, quite literally, unspeakable, because, once spoken, it ceases to be the Real; the mediation of language turns it into the Imaginary or the Symbolic.

Where, then, does this admittedly oversimplified Lacanian triad map onto "Russia as an imaginary country," and how does it connect to the conspiracy and paranoia that are the subject of most of the rest of this book? If we look back at the main categories of texts treated here—fictional narratives whose prime concern is Russia itself, poetical/philosophical tracts, and the news media/blogosphere—the concepts of the Symbolic and the Imaginary have some *taxonomic* value. Many, but not all, of the tracts are founded on a reductive approach to geopolitics that can easily be assimilated to the Imaginary: Russia, America, the West, all become reified and caricatured as entities with essential, unchanging cores, an essentialism that is Imaginary *par excellence*. Indeed, all essentialism could be termed Imaginary by definition, an assertion that probably covers this very statement about essentialism. The Russian media's framing of world affairs in the past several years, in eagerly appropriating the terminology of Eurasianists, nationalists, and conspiracy theorists, actively insists on an Imaginary understanding of Russia and its perceived enemies. This understanding replicates the primary flaw of the Imaginary approach to the Other, in constructing an other that is based on one's imaginary understanding of self. Thus the state media caricature of the United States and the State Department requires that the US government and politics be structured as vertically as the state media presents Russia: every political expression or opposition to Putin's government (whether within Russia or without) was part of Obama's master plan.

The fictional narratives oscillate between the Imaginary and the Symbolic, thereby reflecting the tension between ideology and artistry. In the case of prose fiction, the more committed the text is to actually being a novel, the more likely that the Imaginary systems of the tracts used as sources become subject to productive Symbolic play. Bykov's *Living Souls*, in this scenario, turns out to be a novel that plays with the Imaginary conceptions of Dugin and Koestler (among many others), complicating them through juxtaposition and novelistic expansion. To switch metaphors for a moment, Bykov is taking two-dimensional figures and making them move through a three-dimensional space.

The conspiratorial "Russia narratives" examined in this book are symptoms of a disease of the Imaginary, a dogged insistence not only on the integrity of the Imaginary constructs at stake ("Russia," "the Jews," etc.), but on the argument that the creators and consumers of these narratives have themselves bypassed the deceptions of the Imaginary and truly reached the Symbolic. Conspiracies, in Russia as elsewhere, are second-order simulations, models of the world whose truth value lies in the assertion of their esoteric nature. Conspiracies purport to be the deep structure buried beneath a deceptive, superficial representation of the world; belief in them requires superimposing the conspiracy on the presumably random, disordered world of the Real. The conspiratorial model, which will be treated in more detail in chapter 1, is not a pure substitute for the Real—it is not virtual reality, but something closer to augmented reality: the goggles that helpfully display explanatory information about the objects in the viewer's field of vision.

Huge Tracts of Land

The Russia narratives are conspiratorial in the sense that all narratives are: the ordering of mere events (story) into a coherent set of connected motifs, trends, and patterns (plot) always suggests a guiding hand, whether that be the hand of God, the invisible hand of the market, the laws of history, or simply (and most commonly) the author's concerted efforts to create a narrative that will make sense to the reader or viewer.[12] Even the experimental cinema of Andy Warhol or Alain Resnais, or the *nouveau roman* of Alain Robbe-Grillet, only remind the audience of the author's guiding role through its demonstrative abdication. We are back at the linguistic coincidence built into the English word "plot."

But the Russia narratives are also a special case of conspiratorial thought. Again, it is not the only case, and the prominence of conspiracy in Russian culture is not unique. No doubt one can argue for a conspiratorial basis to a variety of national cultures, with the United States being no exception; indeed, if there is anything that proves this point, it is American exceptionalism. But the Russian case should prove useful for a general understanding of conspiracy, and the application of conspiracy studies to postsocialist Russia should be equally productive.

The first, and perhaps most obvious, feature of the Russia narratives is that they place Russia squarely at the center of modern world history. The only reason this might surprise Americans, and perhaps the French and Germans, is that they think this spot has already been occupied by none other than themselves. It is in the nature of a great power—whether current, aspiring, or fading—to adopt such a worldview, because history rewards confirmation bias; presumably, it would require more effort for Liechtenstein to cast itself in a similar heroic role.

But it is also worth noting the crucial role played here by geography. Not by actual geography; there is no claim here about the role of the steppe or the forest in the formation of the Russian "national character," or worse, the "Russian soul" or "Russian mentality."[13] What is remarkable, though, is how many plotters behind the Russia narrative want to do precisely that. Both Eurasianism and *pochvenichestvo* (a kind of nationalism both metaphorically and etymologically rooted in the soil) elevate geography to ideology. Berdyaev famously compares Russians and Jews as two competitors for messianic status as nations, but the two could not be more different when it comes to geography. The Jewish diaspora, as opposed to Zionism, makes nationhood and the national idea portable, hence modern, while Russia has tended to look on emigration with skepticism, if not hostility.[14]

Thus in the postmodern, postindustrial age of global capital and transnational cultures, the Russia narratives push in the opposite direction. They implicitly fight the forces of deterritorialization with *reterritorialization*.

This is why the attempts by intellectuals associated with the Russian journal and website *Snob* to develop the category of the "global Russian" seem so radical; the global Russian (usually identified as such in English rather than Russian) lives "where they feel like" and can be comfortably Russian in virtually any part of the world (Gessen, "Iskusstvo")

By contrast, the pull of the motherland is more often cast in spiritual or metaphysical terms.

Indeed, emigration itself, whether cast as betrayal or simple "brain drain," often features in the fantasy of anti-Russian conspiracy. Witness Putin's July 2015 condemnation of Western foundations that "hook" children on "grants" to get them to leave home and work for the benefit of foreigners, who presumably cannot do without Russia as a source of intellectual as well as natural resources (Gelaev). The plot against Russia at the heart of the Russia narratives nearly always involves attacks on multiple levels of Russianness. Values and spirituality, economic and military power, and cultural autonomy are the abstract analogues to the more tangible realms of vulnerability: natural resources, borders, and territorial integrity/sovereignty.

The Russia narratives rely on a powerful identification between the people and the land, one that exploits facile geographical metaphors to create an image of national character or "soul": broadness and expansiveness, like the vastness of the country's physical space; extremes of feeling/passion, like the extremes of the weather; and an intermittent emphasis on pagan holdovers in an Orthodox Christian country—reverence for "Moist Mother Earth," for instance.[15] Again, none of these assertions can be evaluated beyond the standard of cherry-picked, anecdotal evidence, but verification is not the point. The point is the myth.

The other major component of the myth is more explicitly conspiratorial, in that it posits the story of Russia as alternations between greatness and betrayal. These two concepts simultaneously appeal to national pride while explaining away national failure. Conspiracy, after all, is a ready answer to an eternal question: why are things so bad? In this case, the answer is that we (our land, our resources, our people) are so valuable that evil enemies are plotting against us. And, as is so often the case with conspiracy, there is valid historical evidence that can be made to fit with this assertion—not least among them the "Tatar Yoke," Napoleon's invasion, and World War II. Conspiracy weaves these discrete historical events into a long-term pattern. If we go back to our discussion of fantasy and world building, along with the problem of the Imaginary, we can say that conspiracy takes these events and uses them as building blocks of a story about an Imaginary Russia whose entire history ends up looking as if it were constructed of only these sorts of events. This Imaginary, conspiratorial Russia is, in fact, holographic or fractal in its nature: every component piece of it looks the same.

For its adherents, conspiracy does more than simply "explain" Russia. More often than not, conspiracy serves as a myth of origin: the Soviet Union was founded/betrayed by Jews, for instance, or Jews were the ones who hooked Russians on vodka (White, 183). Americans and their agents destroyed the USSR; the Masons have been guiding Russian history. As we shall see, conspiratorial narratives tend to be all-encompassing, easily assimilating new data or plot points. For the conspiracist, conspiracy becomes *the* story of Russia, something of a postmodern national epic. The Russian conspiratorial narrative offers a story that always reaffirms Russia's role as the hero of history while emphasizing its status as the world's victim or offended party.

Throughout Putin's third term, politicians and academics in Russia debated the desirability of adopting a single Russian history textbook for the entire country. After two decades during which civil society organizations and liberal historians had moved toward the development of a menu of textbook options, a unified text would be only one of many steps toward reviving elements of the Soviet educational system (which was hardly a model for curricular pluralism). It also resonates with Culture Minister Medinsky's lament quoted at the beginning of this chapter: we've spent too much time entertaining conflicting, often negative, interpretations of Russian history. As Medinsky himself said about the proposed textbook, "A fifth-grader's head is not the place for pluralism" (Ivanova, "Mediinyi"). Professional historians have been taught to distrust coherent narratives for decades, at least since Hayden White's publication of *Metahistory* (1973). The push for a single history textbook reflects a desire to see both history and the study of history as the result of a reliable, guiding hand (Tsyrlina-Spady, "Patriotism," 41–58; Whitehouse, "Historical Thinking" 15–28).

Allegories of Rereading

The search for a single, legible history as Russia's master narrative links back to the Russian Idea (or rather, the *idea* of the Russian Idea), employing itself in that most paranoid of classical forms, allegory. At issue are the interpretive strategies deployed to make sense of Russian history and culture. Mikhail Epstein, eschewing the simplicity of the Russia Idea, establishes the metaphysics underlying twentieth-century Russian politics and thought by categorizing Russian Marxism as a form "ideocracy," a term Jaroslaw Piekalkiewicz had previously applied to a wide variety of "totalitarian" regimes.[16] Epstein is most interested in the Platonic roots of Soviet ideocracy; he implicitly follows the Russian dystopian tradition inaugurated by Yevgeny Zamyatin's *We*, in which the totalitarian future is tantamount to Plato's Republic run by a mad philosopher king (Epstein, "Ideas"). Where he is most exorcized over such a state's antipathy to true philosophy and intellectual inquiry, I am intrigued by the links between ideocracy and the habit of reasoning that Plato's *Republic* encourages most obviously in its most famous chapter: the Allegory of the Cave.

Plato's Allegory is doubly allegorical: it instructs readers to see earthly reality as manifestations of a higher essence (the Theory of Forms), while also encouraging them to see stories as the encoding of an esoteric if readily comprehensible truth. Stories, it seems, are not just stories. Granted, the Allegory is labeled as such, thereby distinguishing it from other stories that might not lend themselves to allegorical interpretation, but the entire conceit of *The Republic* is based on the same analogical reasoning as the Allegory of the Cave: we spend hundreds of pages talking about justice in a city in order to understand justice in the individual soul. Ideocracy encourages a similar habit of interpretive displacement, transforming the mundane into the visible signs of the Idea and its master narrative. In the Soviet case, this transformed allegorical reading into something of a reflexive response. To see this, we need only follow the example of the perestroika era and look back to the 1920s.

The first decade of Soviet power had long been a site of nostalgia for Russian intellectuals, since it constituted a brief interval of creative freedom bracketed by tsarist censorship on one side and Stalinism on the other. Cultural historians focus on the ideological battles that characterize

the 1920s, between hardliners who wanted to create a purely socialist culture and "fellow travelers" who, while sympathetic to the Soviet
project, wanted art and culture to remain relatively autonomous. These
debates, however, are a strange phenomenon, and focusing on their actual
content ("the new man," "the new world," etc.) ultimately distracts us
from their substance. Throughout the 1920s, the emerging Soviet subject
was learning the key intellectual habit of ascribing political or ideological
significance to everyday phenomena (food, housing, sex, shopping). Stephen Kotkin famously argues that, under Stalin, Soviet citizens learned to
internalize the vocabulary and tropes of the Soviet project: "the ways of
speaking about oneself became refracted through the lens of Bolshevism"
(221). My point is that the far less disciplined 1920s paved the way for
this linguistic mastery by inculcating the *deep structure* of Bolshevism:
ideocracy and allegorical thinking.

In his proclamation of the primacy of Socialist Realism, Andrei
Zhdanov identified *ideinost'* as one of the movement's pillars. Translated
roughly as "ideological commitment," the word is literally "idea-ness,"
suggesting less ideology per se than the commitment to the simple fact
of an idea. *Ideinost'* is Epstein's ideocracy, not as a top-down oppressive
structure but as a hegemonic discourse in which the crucial role of the idea
is accepted as a given. As I have discussed at length elsewhere, the best
expression of the pitfalls of *ideinost'* is found in Yuri Olesha's 1927 short
novel, *Envy* (Zavist') (Borenstein, "Defying Interpretation"). In *Envy*,
the resentment felt by a young loser, Nikolai Kavalerov, and his recently
adopted mentor, the failed inventor and inveterate romantic Ivan Babichev,
is directed at Babichev's brother, Andrei, the successful director of the
city's public cafeterias and creator of a new variety of super-sausage, as
well as Andrei's disciple, the soccer star and future engineer Volodya
Makarov. For decades, readers and critics have responded to this book in
essentially allegorical terms, seeing this rivalry as the prosaic manifestation of the higher struggle between the forces of the Old World and the
builders of the New. It turns out, however, that this allegorical reading
comes to us prepackaged by the characters themselves, who complicate
(and in some cases, ruin) their interpersonal relationships precisely by
treating them in terms of this Manichean conflict. If the book does offer
an example of the "new man," it is not just Volodya: it is nearly every
character we encounter. Even Kavalerov, who sees no place for himself in

the new Soviet society, is a disciplined subject of emerging Bolshevism, in that he has accepted its ideological premises.

Envy exposes the dangers of allegorical thinking, of the interpretive hypertrophy that refuses to leave the everyday alone. Certainly, there is comfort in living in a world in which everything is endowed with meaning. But that meaning always points away from the world. Epstein, along with many other critics, faults the Soviet utopian project for its emphasis on the future at the expense of the present; not only is the present important only to the extent that it creates the future, but all present misery is justified in the name of an unrealized, and probably unrealizable, future. Andrei Platonov dramatized this problem brilliantly in *The Foundation Pit*: the workers spend the entire book digging the pit for a grandiose building to be constructed at a later date but instead prove to be simply digging their own vast, communal grave (the replacement of the proposed gargantuan Palace of Soviets with an outdoor public swimming pool is a real-life analog to Platonov's tale). This dynamic (sacrificing the present for the future) is a displacement in time, but it is conditioned by a prior displacement in signification—the meaning of an experience is shunted further down the semiotic chain from signifier to signified. A more graphically inclined critic might map the temporal and semiotic displacements on the same grid, with the "real experience" as point of origin for two rays forming a 90-degree angle—one for time, the other for meaning.

Allegorical thinking is a structure that requires neither sincerity nor credibility; it does not matter whether listening to bootleg Western rock in the 1950s and 1960s was indicative of a desire to betray the motherland, nor does desultory participation in a Komsomol meeting entail a belief that the group's activity is advancing the cause of socialist construction. But it is a way of thinking that assumes meaning to be intrinsic to the daily world even as it points to something external. In this light, we can see the repeated refrain of the late 1980s and 1990s about wanting to live in a "normal" country as, among other things, a rejection of the allegorical imperative. The 1990s are commonly treated in terms of the absence of ideology (the idea of the idea), of a time of moral incoherence, but all of these features are also a breakdown of allegorical thought, a breakdown that would prove temporary.

In the first two terms of Putin's presidency, as well as during the years when he and his prime minister, Dmitry Medvedev, switched jobs for the length of another presidential term, the rejection of the 1990s did not translate into the wholesale adoption of ideological and allegorical thinking. Even as the country's media lost most of its independence from the state, the government's interventions in the culture were limited. But when Putin returned to the presidency for a third term in 2012, he faced a country whose people had become more willing to express public dissatisfaction, whether through street protests, online satire, or direct challenges to the legitimacy of the carefully catered (i.e., rigged) national elections. In his third term, Putin doubled down on the notion of Russia as the keeper of traditional Christian values, as opposed to a Europe led astray by liberalism and political correctness. Russia was now under siege by the combined efforts of Europe and the United States to isolate the country strategically and ruin it culturally. Conspiracy, which had been slowly moving out of the margins, was now mainstream.

The Map Is Not the Territory

Conspiracy insists on mistaking the Imaginary for the Real, turning history into fantasy, and reading everyday life as allegory. For the researcher, conspiracy's tendency to float free of reality is liberating, in that the questions of historical or statistical accuracy that are crucial to historians become a second-order problem. The burden is not the proper representation of Russia, but the careful representation of Russia's misrepresentation in the country's own media, art, and politics. Still, the fantastic nature of conspiracy is also daunting. On one hand, there is the danger of unconsciously adopting the interpretive strategies of hardcore conspiracy theorists by seeing conspiracy theory everywhere, while on the other, the sheer inventiveness of conspiracy theory, combined with its omnivorous habit of bringing everything into its scope, threatens to make the entire subject unmanageable.

But manage we must. I make no pretense to account for every conspiracy theory that has had any currency in Russia, or even in the post-Soviet period.[17] Although such a catalog would be fascinating, an emphasis on conspiracy's multiplicity would do little to further the aims of the present study. The six chapters that compose this book are thus a compromise between the chronological and the thematic, as well as between large- and small-scale conspiratorial thought. The first chapter looks at some of the most prominent accounts of the nature of conspiracy theory in order to suggest an approach of my own, one that allows for both Michael Barkun's syncretic "superconsipracies" that try to explain absolutely everything and the ways in which conspiracy might be viewed in terms of smaller, memetic units. Most important for the rest of the book will be this chapter's assertion that conspiracy should be seen as a mode or a short-term subject position, which allows us to set aside questions of sincerity and cynicism.

Chapter 2 has the broadest historical scope, going back to *The Protocols of the Elders of Zion* and forward to the beginning of the twenty-first century. It is also the chapter that is most concerned with large-scale conspiratorial narratives, which develop within two overlapping frameworks. The historical/metaphysical framework is the apocalypse: most of these theories are about, if not the end of the world, then the end of whatever iteration of the Russian state exists at the time. The narrative/generic framework is melodrama, which elaborates conspiracy as a set of compelling dramatic tropes that continually point back to the high moral stakes of the conflict described.

Chapter 3 turns to the ideological construct that underlies most of these conspiracies: Russophobia. Russophobia provides the motivation for the various evildoers, foreign and domestic, who wish Russia harm, while serving double duty as an existential threat that is supposed to rally readers and viewers around an all but vanished post-Soviet Russia while emphasizing Russia's primacy on the world stage.

Chapters 4 through 6 are devoted almost entirely to the twenty-first century, turning to three of the pillars of contemporary Russian conspiratorial culture. The first of these, discussed in chapter 4, is the creation of a Western enemy whose assault on Russia is both ideological and ideologically motivated: that enemy is liberalism itself. When Russia is redefined as the last redoubt of "traditional values," the country faces the twin threats of political correctness and "gender ideology," best embodied by the LGBT community's insistence on its own rights.

By shifting attention to the current rhetoric of "zombification" (brainwashing), chapter 5 examines the metaconspiratorial discourse that not only disqualifies any oppositional views but reduces virtually all arguments to a cynical game of manipulation and capitulation. At its core, zombification is a theory of media and media consumption that treats all information as propaganda, casting doubt on the very notion of individual subjectivity.

Chapter 6 is a study of the war in Ukraine, which began in 2014 and was still simmering as of this writing. The center of nonstop Russian media attention, the Ukrainian conflict is, among other things, a renegotiation of a national sense of self and other, as well as a case study in the rhetoric of propaganda and "zombification" discussed in the previous chapter. It also brings the "Russia narratives" back into focus by looking at the interplay between reality and fantasy in the conflict's presentation. The actual war was the culmination of years of fantasizing about Ukraine as the last battlefield (Armageddon) for the neverending struggle between Russia and the United States.

US-Russian relations are also the focus of the conclusion, which brings in the ongoing media battles about alleged collusion between Donald Trump's team and Russian intelligence agencies. This is the point at which plots against Russia meet plots against America, a superconspiracy that only reinforces the Russocentric conspiratorial worldview sustained by the Russian media.

By the end of this book, the reader will, I hope, have learned many things. But "the Truth" is not among them. In a time when it is increasingly difficult to convince anyone to revisit a particular belief, it is essential that we understand the beliefs themselves—that we know where they come from, how they circulate, and why they are so appealing.

1

CONSPIRACY AND PARANOIA

The Psychopathology of Everyday Speech

> I have neither the competence nor the desire to classify any
> figures of the past or present as certifiable lunatics.
> —RICHARD HOFSTADTER, "THE PARANOID STYLE IN
> AMERICAN POLITICS" (1963/1964)

Known Unknowns

After spending enough time on the Russian Internet, flipping channels on state television, leafing through extremist newspapers, or simply reading the latest action-packed potboilers, it's easy to come to the conclusion that Russia is under siege, from within as well as from without. The country's apparent enemies include Muslims, Communists, oligarchs, the Central Intelligence Agency (CIA), the Federal Security Service (FSB), Georgians, Ukrainians, a rainbow coalition of "color revolutionaries," homosexuals, Harvard University, and let's not forget the Jews (because, trust me, no one else has). The building blocks of conspiracy may change—or, more likely, simply increase in number—but their possible combinations and permutations are limitless only on the level of small details.

If it seems that I'm picking on Russia, I hasten to point out that anyone with a Facebook friend who watches Fox News can testify that the United

States is hardly immune to syncretic conspiratorial thinking. After all, this country has, on two separate occasions, elected a gay Kenyan Muslim black separatist socialist secular antichrist (proving yet again that for a black man to succeed in America, he has to overachieve). The fact that he was succeeded in office by a man who praises Alex Jones's *Infowars* and *The National Enquirer* while hyping nonexistent voter fraud threats speaks for itself.

So Russia is not alone when it comes to conspiracy. Indeed, we could see the growth of conspiracy theory in both Russia and the United States as yet another manifestation of a decades-old rivalry: which country can outperform the other in conspiracy theory production? The rise of conspiratorial thought in the United States is a well-studied, and sadly relevant, phenomenon, and this chapter directs readers to the literature on the topic. Russia's multiple brands of conspiracy are far less familiar to an English-speaking audience, but the country has not been idle: for at least fifty years, Russia (along with the Russophone diaspora) has been a reliable provider of conspiratorial narratives, overfulfilling virtually any conceivable paranoid plan with Stakhanovite zeal.

I use the hackneyed metaphor of the Soviet shock worker advisedly, since it has been decades since Russia could be accused of the hyperproduction of anything besides oil. Or at least, of anything tangible. In a marvelous essay titled "Labor of Lust," Mikhail Epstein demonstrates that any failure to produce factories, heavy machinery, and weapons on the scale demanded by the various five-year plans was easily remedied by a proliferation of images and texts (i.e., discourse) *about* factories, heavy machinery, and weapons. In the symbolic realm, Russia/the Soviet Union was a powerhouse of productivity, an indefatigable manufacturer of simulacra and simulation.

Conspiracy, however, is more than mere simulation. It takes all the various mythemes available to it and turns them into a persuasive narrative; that is, conspiracy is a kind of discursive *bricolage*. Even this formulation is not entirely satisfactory, since it looks at conspiracy on too large a scale. The basis of all the mythemes and tropes that form a conspiracy theory is a much more fundamental substance: information. Conspiracy is a disease of information, and a communicable disease at that. A better word, though, would be disorder, if it weren't for the fact that conspiracy's relation to information is to take what is dis-ordered and express it as a surfeit of order. It is a disorder of signal to noise, in which all noise is construed as signal.

Conspiracy does what centuries of crackpots' failed attempts at perpetual motion machines could not: conspiracy fights entropy without increasing entropy. Operating according to an inversion of the Second Law of Thermodynamics, conspiracy concentrates all information into an increasingly orderly system. Trying to define "conspiracy theory" is a thankless and ironic task. Thankless, in that there is a vast body of literature on the subject that must be addressed. Ironic, in that the term "conspiracy theory" is so familiar as to be part of *common* knowledge, while the philosophy of the conspiracy theory is based on the idea of *hidden* knowledge. We know a conspiracy theory when we see it, but what we know is that it is an argument that there is something we don't know because we can't see it. It is the unknown that we know everything about.

Or at least we think we do. But the literature on conspiracy theory has been growing since Karl Popper's 1945 *The Open Society and Its Enemies* (1945); though the topic is always current, the field is already older than most people who will read this book. Popper saw conspiracy as a deeply flawed approach to history and sociology, an approach he called "The Conspiracy Theory of Society": "It is the view that an explanation of a social phenomenon consists in the discovery of the men or groups who are interested in the occurrence of this phenomenon (sometimes it is a hidden interest which has first to be revealed) and who have planned and conspired to bring it about."

Popper's essay, while initially influential, has receded in importance in recent decades. As Charles Pidgen sees it, part of the problem is that Popper's definition is overreaching: it claims that believers in conspiracy theories think conspiracy is *always* the explanation for *any* given phenomenon. Pidgen writes: "If this is the theory, Popper is right to deny it. It is ridiculous to suppose that every social phenomenon is the product of a conspiracy. But by the same token it is a thesis that nobody believes" (20). And, in keeping with recent revisionism that takes issue with previous blanket condemnations of conspiracy theories, Pidgen finds that Popper is too skeptical: after all, conspiracies can and do happen, and believing in the ones that are true is therefore quite rational.

Popper's hostility toward conspiratorial thought is to be expected as part of a book called *The Open Society and Its Enemies* (a title that has a whiff of the paranoid about it). The title also reminds us that Popper's discussion is part of a much larger project to which conspiracy is only tangential. It is no surprise, then, that his definition is unsatisfactory to those who have chosen conspiracy as their primary object of study; he and Pidgen disagree at least in part because they are talking about different things.

This also means that Popper's understanding of conspiracy functions better outside academia, since it closely resembles what we might call a folk definition of conspiracy theory: a conspiracy theory is the result of crazy people always assuming that nothing happens by accident, and that sinister plotters are behind all significant historical events. In any case, Popper would be eclipsed by the man who made conspiracy theory both a household word and a credible academic topic: Richard Hofstadter.

A Paranoid Style Guide

Richard Hofstadter delivered his now-famous talk, "The Paranoid Style in American Politics," at Oxford on November 21, 1963, the day before the Kennedy assassination.[1] Such fortuitous timing really should be the basis of its very own conspiracy theory, but to the best of my knowledge, no one has gone looking on the grassy knoll for signs of a Hofstadter connection. Published a year later in *Harper's Magazine*, it would serve as the anchor to an essay collection of the same title in 1965. Though now widely criticized by conspiracy scholars, it is still their most frequent point of departure. While Hofstadter's essay is unquestionably valuable on its own terms, its time of origin and publication are part of the reason "The Paranoid Style" is still the center of gravity in conspiracy studies: it coincided with the US conspiracy's primal scene, the Kennedy assassination, and was thoroughly engaged with the hysterical political climate that followed.[2]

Hofstadter's essay, while examining a trend he saw in more than one time period in US history, was a response to Barry Goldwater's campaign for the presidency, a campaign with strong support from the anticommunist fringe John Birch Society. Goldwater's campaign was widely seen as extremist, a term that the candidate himself did not entirely disavow (as he said when accepting the Republican nomination, "Extremism in the pursuit of liberty is no vice!"). Whatever one might think of Hofstadter's broader claims, the election of Donald Trump demonstrates how timely his essay has become once again.

It is Hofstadter who brought "conspiracy" and "paranoia" into the contemporary political and cultural lexicon. This is due in no small part to Hofstadter's eloquence and clarity, but also, once again, to timing: whether or not a "paranoid" style was perennial in American history, it seemed self-evident in the mid-1960s. Central to Hofstadter's paranoid style is "the feeling of persecution," which is "systematized in grandiose theories of conspiracy," along with a tendency to see the enemy as a "perfect model of malice":

> The distinguishing thing about the paranoid style is not that its exponents see conspiracies or plots here and there in history, but that they regard a "vast" or "gigantic" conspiracy as the motive force in historical events. History is a conspiracy, set in motion by demonic forces of almost transcendent power, and what is felt to be needed to defeat it is not the usual methods of political give-and-take, but an all-out crusade. The paranoid spokesman sees the fate of this conspiracy in apocalyptic terms. (Hofstadter)

Thus Hofstadter, like Popper before him, proposes a model of conspiracy theorizing whose persuasiveness is based on an intelligent restatement of an idea that immediately appears obvious (but that readers might not have come up with on their own). Hofstadter restates what we already know but may not be aware of knowing.

Since Hofstadter's time, a number of scholars (most notably Peter Knight, Jack Z. Bratich, Brian L. Keeley, and Michael Barkun) have developed much more sophisticated models of conspiracy theories, thanks to the insights of modern media theory, poststructuralism, and cultural studies, not to mention the thematic primacy of conspiracy in post-Hofstadter mass culture. After paying deference to Hofstadter, they all take issue with his chosen term: the paranoid style.

Paranoia is so frequently linked with conspiracy theories in the media and mass entertainment that it is difficult to imagine decoupling the terms. Given the clear overlap between the two concepts, their pairing may have been inevitable, but it was Hofstadter who brought the language of popularized psychoanalysis to the world of popular politics. This move is largely responsible both for his essay's success and its harsh criticism by subsequent scholars. Hofstadter is quick to disavow any suggestion of psychological diagnosis in his use of the term "paranoid":

> I call it the paranoid style simply because no other word adequately evokes the qualities of heated exaggeration, suspiciousness, and conspiratorial fantasy that I have in mind. In using the expression "paranoid style," I am not speaking in a clinical sense, but borrowing a clinical term for other purposes. . . . When I speak of the paranoid style, I use the term much as a historian of art might speak of the baroque or the mannerist style. It is, above all, a way of seeing the world and of expressing oneself. (Hofstadter)

In other words, "paranoid" for Hofstadter is essentially a metaphor, and one that fits perfectly with the term's use in ordinary conversation ("You're just being paranoid"). The scholars who have come after Hofstadter were educated in a milieu that takes metaphor seriously, treating it with justifiable suspicion (if not paranoia).

Chief among the complaints against Hofstadter is that, in fact, this metaphor is by no means innocent. As Bratich puts it, Hofstadter "pathologized" both the conspiracy theory and the conspiracy theorist: such terms as "the paranoid style" or "political paranoia" are "in essence more sophisticated ways of calling someone a crackpot" (5). Knight finds the "paranoia" analogy to be tautological: "what is paranoia, if not a propensity to believe in conspiracy theories?" ("Making Sense," 17). Keeley concurs: "To label a conspiracy theory 'paranoid' is merely to restate the claim that it is unwarranted; it is not evidence for rejecting it" (118).

Keeley sees the "paranoid" label as an unfounded, and perhaps irrelevant, diagnosis of an individual: "To attempt to reject conspiracy theories on the grounds of their proponent's mental condition is bogus" (118). Other scholars take this objection further, as an unwarranted characterization not just of the theorist but of the society in which the theorist functions. After all, Hofstadter's primary target is the entire culture. As Knight puts it, "The diagnosis of paranoia—even if it is not individual but collective—still carries with it the suggestion that conspiracy theory is not simply misguided but a sign that society is suffering from an illness that should be pitied and, if possible, cured" (*Conspiracy Culture*, 15).

In a particularly complex argument, Bratich treats the media and scholarly coverage of so-called conspiracy theories within the tradition of the moral panic. He argues that the "conspiracy panic" targets "a particular form of thought (and its potential links to action). The scapegoating of conspiracy theories provides the conditions for social integration and political rationality. Conspiracy panics help to define the normal modes of dissent" (11). Though Bratich himself does not put it this way, the shift from "conspiracy" to "conspiracy panic" is also a transposition of the "paranoid" metaphor: now it is the *experts* on conspiracy who are paranoid about conspiracy theories.

This, in turn, brings us back to Hofstadter, and the peculiar overreaching in his definition of the paranoid style, which, as Dentith puts it, "characterizes conspiracy theorists not as people who see some conspiracies here and there but, rather, as people who think that conspiracies are the motive force in historical events" (9). Perhaps Hofstadter's insistence on the unrelenting paranoid epistemology of the conspiracy theorist (who seems incapable of *not* seeing a conspiracy theory anywhere and everywhere) transforms the conspiracist from a political subject possibly capable of nuance into what Stanley Cohen, founder of the study of moral panics, calls a "folk devil"? (9).

There is a better way to account for a possible relationship between nonclinical paranoia and conspiracy theories. But proposing it requires some familiarity with the alternative frameworks developed since Hofstadter's time. These frameworks are built on a shift in vocabulary that also suggests a shift in discipline: the replacement of psychology with philosophy.

While much of contemporary conspiracy theory scholarship pays less attention to the theorizers and more to the theories, when the belief in a conspiracy theory comes up, the flaw attributed to the believer is generally posited to be epistemological: as Cass Sunstein puts it, conspiracy theorists suffer from a "crippled epistemology." Volker Heins calls conspiracy theorists "hyper-rationalists who do not simply proclaim a truth, but actively track it" (790). Frederic Jameson sees conspiracy as "the poor person's cognitive mapping in the postmodern age" (356), while Mark

Fenster argues that "conspiracy theory works as a form of hyperactive semiosis in which history and politics serve as reservoirs of signs that demand (over)interpretation, and that signify, for the interpreter, far more than their conventional meaning" (95).

It is possible to attribute the problem less to the believer than to circumstance. Victoria Emma Pagan finds that conspiracy theories are "characterized by an epistemological gap caused by the secrecy and silence that shroud the event." In this sense, excessive secrecy is just a way of begging for a conspiracy theory.

Most of these approaches are united by an emphasis on the believer's insistence on seeing connections. "Conspiracy theorists," Keeley asserts, "are some of the last believers in an ordered universe" (116). But it is the work of Michael Barkun that most thoroughly explores this particular understanding of conspiratorial epistemology: "A conspiracist worldview implies a universe governed by design rather than by randomness" (3). Barkun finds this "emphasis on design" expressed in "three principles found in virtually every conspiracy theory": "Nothing happens by accident," "Nothing is as it seems," and "Everything is connected." Where others might find these principles frightening, the conspiracist finds them reassuring, "for it promises a world that is meaningful rather than arbitrary" (4).

Barkun's emphasis on connectivity leads him to think big. In *A Culture of Conspiracy*, Barkun pays particularly close attention to the "superconspiracy": the conspiracy that encompasses all other conspiracies. For Barkun, the essentially syncretic nature of conspiracy theory means that what nonbelievers might dismiss as contradictions are easily assimilated into the conspiratorial logic. What the hapless heroes of Umberto Eco's *Foucault's Pendulum* do as a joke (forging a master conspiracy as a satirical response to the conspiracists whose work they publish), Barkun studies as the ethnography of the digital age.

The superconspiracy is a compelling concept and will have enormous resonance with the Russian material examined in the present study. The alternative I'm presenting is as much micro as macro; while not ignoring connectivity, it dwells on the specific, singular moments of connection. But there is one last question that needs to be addressed before I can make my own case.

What if the conspiracy is real?

Conspiracy and Its Subjects

In the fall of 1986, when I was studying in Leningrad, a friend showed me a Soviet newspaper report that Ronald Reagan's government was selling arms to Iran in order to fund the Contras, the right-wing rebels who were trying to overthrow Nicaragua's socialist government. We both rolled our eyes but admitted to a sense of perverse admiration: you had to hand it to those Soviet propagandists. Every now and then, they displayed a real spark of imagination.

Except, of course, they hadn't. The Iran-Contra Affair—which also involved photogenic colonels, ingénue secretaries, and large amounts of cash—really happened (even if nearly everyone involved got away scot-free). By comparison, Watergate, the go-to scandal of the last three decades of twentieth-century US politics, was straightforward: a set of crimes and cover-ups. Iran-Contra was so baroque that the Illuminati and the underground lizard people would have fit right in, if it weren't for the fact that this particular conspiracy actually happened.

A wholesale dismissal of conspiracy theories does not justify a wholesale dismissal of conspiracies. At some point, what looks like healthy skepticism can turn out to be gullibility. Perhaps the ultimate conspiracy theory would be to posit that some evil entity is deliberately spreading absurd conspiracy theories so as to drown out actual conspiracies in a sea of noise.[3] Keeley addresses this problem head-on, noting that a typically capacious understanding of conspiracies would include surprise parties, which, however unwelcome they may be, hardly qualify as sinister. He has created a special subset of conspiracy theories: the "Unwarranted Conspiracy Theory" (UCT):

> (1) A UCT is an explanation that runs counter to some received, official, or "obvious" account. . . .
> (2) The true intentions behind the conspiracy are invariably nefarious.
> (3) UCTs typically seek to tie together seemingly unrelated events.
> (4) As noted, the truths behind events explained by conspiracy theories are typically well-guarded secrets, even if the ultimate perpetrators are sometimes well-known public figures.
> (5) The chief tool of the conspiracy theorist is what I shall call "errant data."
> Errant data come in two classes: (a) unaccounted-for data, and (b) contradictory data. (116–18)

The UCT is a valiant attempt on Keeley's part, but he himself is the first to find fault with it, admitting that both Watergate and Iran-Contra meet the UCT criteria. The UCT was first proposed in 1999, but it has not caught on with the scholarly community, since it contains an evaluative component that can never be completely validated.

Years later, Lance deHaven-Smith tries to do away with the term "conspiracy theory" in its entirety: "I introduced the concept of State Crime against Democracy (SCAD) to displace the term 'conspiracy theory.' I say displace rather than replace because SCAD is not another name for conspiracy theory; it is a name for the type of wrongdoing about which the conspiracy-theory label discourages us from speaking. Basically, the term 'conspiracy theory' is applied pejoratively to allegations of official wrongdoing that have not been substantiated by public officials themselves."

Like the UCT, the SCAD has yet to catch on, even as it avoids the pitfall of developing a definition based on the truth or falsehood of a given theory. DeHaven-Smith's project is one of reclamation, trying to balance skepticism of conspiracy with skepticism of official claims. But any value the term may have is bracketed by his study's very title: *Conspiracy Theory in America*. DeHaven-Smith presumes the existence and desirability of democracy; what happens when democracy is not an issue? Certainly Russian history is rife with conspiracy theories developed during decidedly undemocratic times.

For our purposes, while it is important to acknowledge the reality of some conspiracies (and the possible reality of others), truth value is not the primary concern. The issue for the Russia narratives discussed in the introduction ranges from the conspiracy theory as habit or default to conspiracy as a mode available for adoption. Therefore, we are looking at the conspiratorial subject position. And that brings us back to paranoia. Narrative is conspiracy. Paranoia is how we read and understand it.

So far, the study of conspiracy has focused on the obvious targets: full-blown conspiratorial narratives and full-time conspiracy theorists. But for most of us, conspiracy and paranoia are part-time jobs. When we call something a conspiracy theory, or when we label someone (nonclinically) paranoid, our primary motivation has less to do with the objective truth of the theory or assertion than it does with our evaluation of a point of view. Can the assertion be treated as implicit evidence of a highly suspicious stance? Does it suggest a possibly excessive emphasis on connectivity and a rejection of coincidence? Can we then assume that the author of the assertion is habitually suspicious, preoccupied with making connections, and dismissive of mere chance? Or, if we turn it around and recall the Iran-Contra example, could it be that both "warranted" and "unwarranted" conspiracy theories are more likely to be uncovered by someone with precisely these habits of mind?

Even the most earnest attempts at rehabilitating conspiracy cannot escape the hygienic impulse to distance conspirators from everyone else. The attempts to decouple paranoia and conspiracy try to free conspiracy from its stigma by entirely displacing it onto paranoia. Part of the problem with our discussion of conspiracy theory and paranoia is that it is predicated on a Cartesian model of the subject, one that presumes an integral self. When we talk about belief in conspiracy or about debunking conspiracy, we implicitly posit a subject who is either thoroughly rationally or wholly irrational. But what if we try to think not in term of subjects but subject positions?

To do so requires that, instead of isolating conspiracy from paranoia, we double down on the connection between the two. What I am proposing is a continuum from isolated instances of suspicion to full-fledged paranoia, a conspiratorial spectrum on which we can all be located, even as those locations may be subject to dynamic change.

The primary components of a conspiratorial outlook are features of human psychology that can generally be considered adaptive and useful: the search for patterns and the assumption of intent. The issue of pattern recognition in conspiracy and paranoia has been raised by a number of scholars, and its role is rather obvious: the urge to connect disparate events into a conspiratorial pattern is akin to the tradition of assigning random stars to constellations. Moreover, patterns once seen are difficult to unsee.

Daniel Dennett argues for the primacy of what he calls the "intentional stance" in the operations of human consciousness and folk psychology:

> Here is how it works: first you decide to treat the object whose behavior is to be predicted as a rational agent; then you figure out what beliefs that agent ought to have, given its place in the world and its purpose. Then you figure out what desires it ought to have, on the same considerations, and finally you predict that this rational agent will act to further its goals in the light of

its beliefs. A little practical reasoning from the chosen set of beliefs and desires will in most instances yield a decision about what the agent ought to do; that is what you predict the agent will do. (17)

Simon Baron-Cohen extrapolates an "intentionality detector," which is key to typical infant development (and whose impairment may play a role in some cases of autism) (38). I would add that both the ability to determine an intentional stance and the tendency to see patterns are inherent to the experience of any narrative—even avant-garde, nonlinear narratives, which exploit the frustration of these very impulses in the audience or reader. At its most benign, paranoia is not psychosis; it is phenomenology. It is a mistake to use politics and the "real world" as a starting point for understanding conspiracy. Conspiracy belongs first to art, then to ideology.

How to Do Things with Plots

In the introduction, I made the case for treating both ideology in general and the various narratives about Russia in particular as if they belonged to the genre of fantasy. Now I'm arguing that conspiracy's natural home is art rather than politics. Is this just perversity for its own sake (not that there's anything wrong with that)? Or is there, as a conspiracy theorist might say, a hidden agenda?

Actually, there are several. The first might be called methodological, but only in the spirit of generosity rather than rigor. Without getting bogged down in the depths of high theory, there was always something productive in Jacques Derrida's insistence on reversing binaries and exploring the result, most notably his assertion of the primacy of writing over voice. As a thought experiment at the very least, such perverse reversals capitalize on estrangement and generate new connections and approaches.

The second would be archeological, and it amounts to recognizing Barkun's contribution to the genealogy of conspiracy, but with a shift in emphasis. As the first half of *Culture of Conspiracy* shows, so many of the tropes of popular theories have their origins in literary and paraliterary texts: *The Protocols of the Elders of Zion* were lifted from a French satire by Maurice Joly and a German novel by Hermann Goedsche. The infamous lizard people best known from the rants of David Icke come from a novel by Edward Bulwer-Lytton, while the connections between alien abduction narratives and low-rent science fiction could not be more clear.[4]

It is the third and final agenda that is most important, in that it circles back to our discussion of intent and belief: what does it mean to take conspiracy theory "seriously"? And, more provocatively, what would it mean to treat conspiracy as unserious: playful, artificial, artistic?

In "Signature Event Context," a polemic with John Searle over ordinary language, Derrida offers a critique of John Austin's Speech Act Theory that, however, indirectly, helps make my case. In *How to Do Things with Words*, Austin initially divides utterances into two categories: constative (statements that can be evaluated according to their truth value, such as "the cat is on the mat") and performative (statements that are best considered as either succeeding or failing in *doing* something ("I sentence you to life in prison") (7–9). After explaining this distinction in exhaustive detail, Austin then concludes that it is not quite accurate: many utterances have truth value and an effective result, as well as an effect on the listener. The sentence "Your hair is on fire!" is either true or false, contains the deep structure of a performative act ("I declare that your hair is on fire!"), and no doubt has an effect on the person to whom it is addressed.

Derrida commends Austin for what he sees as a fundamentally deconstructive move: establishing a binary (performative/constative), showing its limits and contradictions, but leaving the binary available as a nonetheless useful construct despite its problems. But where he takes Austin to task (and where he argues with Searle) is on the question of seriousness: Austin insists that, for an utterance to be evaluated according to its felicity (that is, its effectiveness), it must not be a joke or part of a fictional context. Thus the statement "I now pronounce you husband and wife" has to be made by someone empowered to do so, and in a serious context (and not, for example, on stage).

Derrida's objections are twofold: first, Austin's distinction requires that we evaluate an utterance according to the speaker's intent (which can be unknowable, contradictory, and in any case irrelevant); second and more important for our purposes, it leaves the entire category of playful speech outside the realm of ordinary language. Instead, Derrida argues that playfulness and seriousness are simply another binary in relation to which an utterance can be assessed, and that any theory of language can claim validity only if it allows for play (which he sees as a fundamental part of both speech and writing).

The same holds true for conspiracy theory: since we cannot always be sure of the intent behind the articulation of a given conspiratorial idea, we should be able to address it separately from its seriousness as a political program or political critique. In the Russian context, this releases us from the obligation to determine if a given political actor (including Putin and his top aides) is serious or cynical when indulging in conspiratorial speculation. More generally, we can examine both "sincere" conspiracy and its satire through not just the tropes common to both but also the epistemological stance adopted and/or satirized.

But the most important consequence of the acceptance of play is the recognition of the weakness of the boundaries between the political and the artistic, between conspiracy as argument and conspiracy as entertainment. Here we are back to conspiracy as *plot*, in all the senses of the word.

The Play's the Thing

No discussion of conspiracy in the last two decades is complete without at least invoking *The X-Files*. Over the course of nine seasons (which was at least three seasons too long), Chris Carter's genre-bending hit television show made conspiracy a household name. When it returned after over a decade's absence, it had all the freshness of revelations about NASA's fake moon landings, but it still remains unrivaled as the touchstone for all conversations about conspiracy and popular entertainment. I bring up *The X-Files* not as either the cause or symptom of the mainstreaming of conspiracy and paranoia, but simply as the most legible example of conspiracy as entertainment, in order to get at the question of conspiracy and play. The experience of watching *The X-Files* is all about paranoid subject positions.

As an hour on television, *The X-Files*, like any televised fiction, should make us aware of the conventions of drama. If we start watching an episode of *Law and Order* or *CSI*, we do not expect the culprit behind the evening's murder to be aliens. Indeed, they simply cannot be aliens. If we're watching *The X-Files*, however, aliens are not just possible but plausible. Let's say that we, like so many viewers in the 1990s, enjoy and appreciate both *The X-Files* and *Law and Order*, and we might go from watching one of them at 8:00 to watching the other at 9:00. For the first hour, we are willing to "believe" in aliens (at least within the confines of the story), but for the next, we rule them out entirely. First we're Mulder, then we're Scully.[5]

The point is not that *The X-Files* turns us into true believers in aliens (or that *Law and Order* trains us to think that a criminal case "ripped from the headlines" can be resolved in the course of an hour). More important is the way in which fiction allows and even requires an audience to temporarily adopt a subject position that might otherwise be alien. One could even read all the *X-Files* alien abduction narratives in terms of the infiltration of viewers by an alien subject position, an idea to which we will return in the "zombification" chapter.

Immersion in fiction produces, if not an altered state, then an altered subjectivity. For brief periods of time, we adopt the position of believer in superpowered mutants (*The X-Men*), happy intergenerational romance (*Harold and Maude*), or the efficacy of torture (*24*). A fictional narrative that cannot temporarily convince us of something we might otherwise doubt is a failure; if you spend the entire duration of a musical wondering how it is that all the characters know the lyrics and dance steps, then the musical has not convinced you to inhabit the temporary selfhood of someone who takes these things for granted.

All of this returns us to Derrida's notion of the possibility of play as a precondition for the serious. If we can't believe in a conspiratorial fiction that calls itself fiction, we will never commit to a conspiratorial fiction that calls itself fact. We identify a paranoid subject position in others because we have experienced it ourselves. If we keep conspiracy at a distance, we can see fiction as a laboratory for the careful containment of conspiratorial notions. But if we're less convinced by the epistemological boundaries between fiction and fact, then the circulation of motifs between entertainment and political tracts should come as no surprise.

Moreover, the very conventions of narrative encourage interpretive habits that, in other contexts, look paranoid: the expectation that nothing is random or extraneous, and that the entire story is the result of careful design.

Good readers make good paranoids.

The Conspiratorial Mode

If conspiracy can be a game and paranoia can be playful, we need to broaden our understanding of both phenomena. More and more critics reject the "paranoid" label for conspiracy theorists as a way to fight against a social hygienic impulse ("conspiracy theorists are all raving lunatics wearing tin-foil hats"), but their goal is, more often than not, to rehabilitate discussion of "real" conspiracies by distinguishing them from their lunatic-fringe counterparts. The distinction still comes down to truth (for conspiracy) and sanity (for paranoia). My point is broader: "true" and "false" conspiracy theories share the same basic structure, and all of them function as the predicate for a paranoid subject position.

Moreover, I want to complicate one further category that often frames these discussions: sincerity of intent vs. cynical manipulation. Presumably, at least some of those who espouse a given conspiracy theory are concerned more with the theory's utility than its veracity. Here, too, we have an often unanswerable question of another person's motivations. And here, too, I propose setting aside this question as functionally but not politically irrelevant.

This brings me back to my earlier proposal of a conspiratorial continuum, a paranoid spectrum to locate anything from a discrete utterance to a full-blown narrative. If we can adopt a paranoid stance when enjoying conspiratorial entertainment or, more broadly, when analyzing an artistic text under the assumption that it is a maximally consistent system rather than a set of randomly arranged events, we can adopt (and discard) a similar paranoid stance toward more "serious" matters, such as politics, ideology, or world affairs.

If I seem strangely comfortable with the word "paranoid" when most contemporary conspiracy scholars do their best to avoid it, it is because the word is not attached to a person, at least not as a long-term or permanent attribute. It is not a diagnosis, because there is no person to diagnose. True, the paranoid or conspiratorial subject position does imply a subject, but it is a temporary subject, or a subject at a given moment rather than over a long term. In a distinction that probably works better in Spanish (*ser* vs. *estar*), that subject is not paranoid, but *is being paranoid*.

This is where Hofstadter's notion of a paranoid *style* can be reclaimed. As a style, paranoia does not have to be a long-term attribute or characteristic of an individual subject. But where Hofstadter's unit of measure is an entire text (say, the speech of a particularly radical conspiracy theorist), mine is the sentence itself, or the utterance. I propose treating paranoia not as a style but as a *mode*. This brings paranoia closer to irony, which is, of course, ironic: by rights, irony should be conspiracy's kryptonite.

So what does conspiracy look like when broken down to its smallest units?

Approaching conspiracy only as a system of connections means falling into the trap of conspiratorial thought, reproducing a monomaniacal gigantism (It's all connected! And it's huge!) even when the goal is to debunk. Conspiratorial thought is most recognizable as a system, but its operation and circulation prove far broader—and far messier—when it escapes the boundaries of the systemic. These boundaries are entirely notional, and they result from choosing the full-fledged conspiracy theory as the primary object of study. Returning to the level of the conspiratorial utterance, we exchange the macro view of the system with the micro perspective of the meme.

After more than a decade of social media, nearly everyone knows what a meme is. Or, more to the point, nearly everyone thinks they know what a meme is but is technically wrong. The beauty of the error is that, in misunderstanding memes, people create new evidence in support of meme theory. Coined by Richard Dawkins in *The Selfish Gene* (1976), the word "meme" is meant to cover any unit of information that can be transmitted from person to person (or mind to mind), regardless of the means of transmission (254–56). Dawkins invents meme theory in the service of a much grander goal. Just as Saussure laid the foundations for modern linguistic as essentially the first test case for a then-nonexistent field he called semiotics, Dawkins saw memetics (meme theory) as a way to argue for the larger idea of "universal Darwinism" (248): in any system involving information to be replicated, vehicles for their replication, scarce resources, and the possibility of error, the result will be evolution. In biological terms, he is talking about genes (the information) and biological organisms (the replicators), with evolution resulting from the occasionally imperfect copying of genes from one generation to another, occasionally giving rise to a mutation that will prove useful and be passed on.

In applying Darwinian principles to information and culture, Dawkins is much more modest than most of his predecessors. The only biological drive he posits is the impulse to copy, an impulse we see in basic child development. What actually gets copied (information/culture) is independent of physical biology.

So a meme is simply any unit of information: the opening notes to Beethoven's Fifth Symphony, Bartleby the Scrivener's famous expression of disinterest, or even an obscure sentence written down once three hundred years ago in a book that no one has ever read. Like genes, memes have a reproductive strategy: catchiness. Catchiness is what ensures the survival and transmission of Beethoven's Fifth, while its lack is what ensures that my hypothetical three-hundred-year-old sentences will never have any offspring—that is, copies of themselves written or spoken by others. Information evolves precisely because transmission is riddled with errors, such as mishearing or typos. Bartleby's catchphrase, "I would prefer not to," is sometimes misremembered as "I would prefer not" (a new meme resulting from the old). Elton John never sang "Hold me closer, Tony Danza," nor did Pat Benatar invite listeners to "hit me with your pet shark," but such perceptual errors have doubtless produced new texts and new meanings, not to mention t-shirts.

In common parlance, memes are now simply images, videos, and catchphrases spread throughout the Internet, with the assumption that memes are only a small subset of the information in our cultural ecosystem. The frequent application of the qualifier "viral" reinforces the sense that memes are somehow hostile, foreign, and invasive—promoting a paranoid notion of the meme. The viral metaphor plays into fears of persuasion and mind control (as in Richard Brodie's *Virus of the Mind*) on the basis of a false dichotomy between self and nonself: "viral" memes invade a mind that is otherwise presumed to be integral and impregnable. But meme theory as originally construed posits a much more radical notion of subjectivity: all information, including thoughts, is composed of memes, and even the most banal exchange of information is an exchange of memes. If we recall the observation that surprise parties are technically conspiracies, then "Happy Birthday to You" is just as "viral" as a Nike commercial.

It is worth dwelling on the construction of the "viral" before turning to the role of memes in conspiracy because the viral metaphor, with its implications of malignancy and even agency, threatens to subsume memetics to a fundamentally conspiratorial worldview. My intent, however, is precisely the opposite. Rather than allow a discussion of memes to facilitate paranoia, I want to use memetics to posit the circulation of elements of conspiracy theory in the absence of any real agency at all.

The memes of conspiracy are the familiar tropes, images, and phrases that, over the lifespan of a given theory, reach beyond the initiated, becoming part of the larger discourse. While their dissemination may be the result of agitation by conspiracy partisans, if anything, their spread is facilitated much more effectively by satirists and debunkers. Consider, for example, the following list:

black helicopters
one world government
men in black
new world order
tin-foil hats
The Bilderberg Group
The Trilateral Commission
FEMA camps

At least some of these phrases will be familiar to most readers, including those who are not steeped in conspiratorial lore. Clearly, each phrase can theoretically be used in an entirely neutral context, but they are so thoroughly entangled in a conspiratorial semantic web that their very invocation serves as shorthand for a larger narrative. Whether that narrative is taken seriously or not is, in this instance, unimportant: it is the constituent memes of conspiracy, rather than the theory itself, that most easily reach the largest number of people.

Conspiratorial memes can be an unintentional trap for the speaker who invokes them naively. On September 11 (!), 1990, President George H. W. Bush delivered a speech to Congress laying out his vision of the world in the aftermath of the Cold War, with "the very real prospect of a new world order." A charitable, and plausible, reading of Bush's phrasing would be that the president had no idea that he was employing a phrase that had been circulating in extreme right-wing groups for over a decade; a conspiracist might see the speech as the moment when Bush finally tipped his hand.

Old Jews Telling Jokes: Meet the Elders of Zion

To see how the memes of conspiracy migrate, let us turn to conspiracy theory's original sin: *The Protocols of the Learned Elders of Zion*. The peculiar lineage of the *Protocols* is all the more Russian for its European roots: plagiarized from a decades-old French satire, the *Protocols* became the foundational text for both Russian and global conspiracy theories. Simultaneously cosmopolitan and parochial, the *Protocols* cannot be accepted by their Russian proponents as either Russian (i.e., the creation of the tsarist secret police) or French (the product of shameful literary theft that recapitulates a centuries-long inferiority complex in relation to European high culture).

The story of the *Protocols* is well known, though that has not stopped their circulation as revelatory texts over a century later. Originally published in Russian in 1903, the *Protocols* purport to be the minutes of a meeting of a secret cabal of Jews who are responsible for nearly every aspect of world affairs. Though it was not the first tract to make such an argument, it became one of the most successful; in the United States, Henry Ford sponsored a large print run of the English translation, while in Germany, Hitler's citations of the *Protocols* in *Mein Kampf* heralded their prominence in Nazi propaganda. Over the past few decades, their truth has been widely proclaimed by several leaders in the Arab world, while in the West, the understanding of the *Protocols* as a forgery has inspired a brilliant postmodernist short story (Danilo Kis's "The Book of Kings and Fools"), a bestselling novel (Umberto Eco's *Prague Cemetery*), and a nonfiction graphic novel (Will Eisner's *The Plot*).

Readers who are not diehard antisemites or committed conspiracy theorists are likely to have difficulty taking the *Protocols* seriously as a text. Starting with the book's very premise (the leaders of a top-secret global conspiracy take meticulous notes for their records), the author of the *Protocols* makes little effort to render them plausible. In fact, if the *Protocols* are bad nonfiction, they are much worse when read as the author's fantasy: on top of everything else, the *Protocols* are a crime against fiction. The conspirators prove to be laughably cartoonish villains, with no attempt to give them even a hint of moral complexity. The author simply can't help but make sure that the villains' words reflect an awareness of their own evil as well as an indication of the "good" that they abhor: "The people, under our guidance, have annihilated the aristocracy, who were their one and only defense and foster-mother for the sake of their own advantage which is inseparably bound up with the well-being of the people" (*The Protocols*). Sentences like this are more than just explanations of an imagined evil; they are propaganda for the moral and social framework that is implicitly the only bulwark against the Jews.

The bulk of the book describes the Elders' use of both capitalism and communism to destroy traditional institutions and consolidate power through money. Unsurprisingly, the Jews here are a stand-in for a modernity that the authors of the *Protocols* could see only as disastrous. The *Protocols* did not invent the idea of a secret society's responsibility for all the world's ills; a century of European panics over Freemasons deserves at least some of the credit. But, perhaps inadvertently, the *Protocols* add a key word to the lexicon of right-wing conspiracy, a word that in other contexts could seem, if not innocent, at least unthreatening: the goyim. The goyim (or GOYIM, as it is always written in the text) is a Hebrew term whose literal meaning is "the nations," but which functions simply as "gentiles," even if its deployment is something of a slur. But the goyim of the *Protocols* are not your embarrassing, xenophobic Jewish grandfather's goyim: they are the hapless dupes of the Jews who control the world.

Like the "new world order" discussed in the previous entry, "goyim" travels a circuitous memetic path. More often than not, its utterance by non-Jews (particularly on the Internet) marks the speaker as surely as a swastika tattoo marks a member of the Aryan Nations (a hate group whose name, ironically enough, could be freely translated back into Hebrew as "Aryan goyim"). The term appears frequently in Internet comment sections about the issues that animate conspiracists in America. To the uninitiated, the word seems strangely out of context. In actuality, the "goyim"

meme travels with its own portable context, placing the rest of the com-
menter's utterance within the framework of neofascist conspiracies.

Defining Conspiracy

Question: So what, then, is a conspiracy theory?
Answer: This is the wrong question.

Rather than develop yet another definition of conspiracy, we instead
have a broader understanding of the spectrum on which conspiratorial
thought lies. At one extreme we find Barkun's superconspiracy, predicated
on the epistemological obsession with connectivity. At the other extreme
is conspiracy not as a full-fledged theory or worldview but as a mode; here
conspiracy is a subject position that can be adopted and dropped at will
or unconsciously, invoking the individual memes of a coherent conspiracy theory without necessarily elaborating or committing to the theory
itself. We have also rehabilitated the concept of paranoia by divorcing it
from the person (as a diagnosis) and attributing it to a possibly temporary
stance (a paranoid subject position) that we all rehearse as consumers of
media. Most important, we have an approach to conspiracy and paranoia
that is not conspiratorial or paranoid.

Since this book is concerned primarily with narrative, there is always
the danger of privileging the elaborate, methodical conspiracy theories
that tend to get the most attention. But the Russia narratives I elaborated in the introduction, while largely conspiratorial, are not always
about a full-fledged conspiracy. To confine our inquiry to full-fledged
conspiracy would be misleading in two regards: first, it would overesti-
mate conspiracy by aligning it solely with the semiotic expansionism that
marks the biggest conspiracies, thereby playing into their incessant self-
aggrandizement. But second, it would underestimate conspiracy by
restricting it *only* to identifiable conspiratorial narratives, and thus ignore
the multiple ways in which the conspiratorial mode expresses itself in the
short-term adoption of a paranoid stance, as well as through the invocation of conspiratorial memes. Finally, we no longer need speculate about
the state of mind or intent of those who espouse conspiracy. This may be
an important question for politics, but it does not have to matter for the
discursive approach adopted for the purposes of this book.

The rest of this book shifts back and forth along the conspiratorial continuum. The next chapter, on conspiracy and melodrama, is more concerned with totalizing theories than with memes and modes, while others (such as the chapter on the imagined PC threat) are a bit harder to place. The chapter on "zombification" is about the moment when conspiracy becomes the snake eating its own tail: here paranoia becomes not just a discourse but a metadiscourse (with paranoid accusations of paranoia as part of mutual accusations of brainwashing). "Plots against Russia" is not a simple trip down the proverbial rabbit hole: there are multiple rabbits spread throughout numerous interconnected warrens. And just when it seems as though we have reached stable enough ground to sustain a metaphor, it turns out the rabbit has instead been pulled out of a hat.

2

Ruining Russia

Conspiracy, Apocalypse, and Melodrama

"By the way, why do you always connect what's happening to the Antichrist?"
"You mean you still don't understand that the Bible is encrypted sociology?"
—Sergei Norka, *The Inquisitor*, 279

Catastrophe of the Week

In the year 2000, New Line Cinema came out with a relatively novel schlock horror film about a group of teenagers who cheated Death and Death's relentless attempts to get back at them. It was called *Final Destination*, and it ended with the refreshing temerity of killing off its entire no-star cast (in increasingly baroque and bloody fashion). The title, the plot, and the body count turned out to be a challenge to sequel-happy Hollywood: try to make a series out of *that*. Three years later, the movie was followed by *Final Destination 2*, then, in 2006, *Final Destination 3*, then *The Final Destination 4* in 2009, and, in 2011, *Final Destination 5* (not to mention nine prose novels and a comic book miniseries). The word "final" turns out to be less the ordinal designation of a position in a sequence than simply a brand promising endless, iterative finality.

Now imagine the Soviet Union as a Hollywood blockbuster, complete with heroes, villains, and, of course, romance. The movie ends with the destruction of the entire country. Granted, it happens off-stage, as in a Greek drama (the final blow comes when the leaders of Russia, Ukraine, and Belarus meet in the middle of nowhere to sign documents declaring the Soviet Union defunct), but still, there is a finality to the story. If you're the director, what do you do for an encore?

As it happens, you do it again. And again. History repeats itself, first as tragedy, then as franchise. We're all familiar with stories about the end of the world: predictions of impending doom are an ironic constant of the last two millennia, while the American proliferation of doomsday cults, moral panics, and, of course, movies that lovingly blow up all our national monuments suggests that the United States is anything but immune. But Russia after the dismantling of the Soviet Union has the dubious honor of being one of the few countries in the world that are both pre- and postapocalyptic at the same time.

If we recognize conspiracy on both the small scale (the conspiratorial mode as expressed in individual utterances) and the large (global superconspiracies), then any conspiracy involving the apocalypse would clearly fit into the latter category. In Russia, conspiracy joins with apocalypse to create narratives of the destruction of the world in general (and Russia in particular) as the work of an evil, Russophobic cabal. Apocalyptic conspiracy is an existential threat, one that typically unfolds in a melodramatic mode (with binary oppositions between good and evil embodied as opposing actors in the plot). After 1991, such plots become self-confirming, closed loops: the destruction of the Soviet Union serves as proof of the ongoing threat to Russian statehood.

Waiting for the End of the World

Post-Soviet Russophone culture continually returns to the scene of this "crime," suggesting a trauma that can be processed only through repetition. We see this dynamic play out in a 1999 novel by the popular Ukrainian Russophone fantasy writers Marina and Sergei Diachenko. In an unnamed country that is most-likely post-Soviet Ukraine, citizens are taught from childhood to prepare themselves for the occasional apocalypse called *mryga*, usually predicted and announced through the media along the lines of an upcoming meteorological disaster. Each time, a precious few will survive by going through a set of mysterious gates, while others will perish. The novel's title is particularly evocative: *Armageddom*, an untranslatable pun that might best be rendered as "Sweet Home Armageddon." The apocalypse, though terrifying, is at once domestic and domesticated.[1]

The subheading for this chapter comes from a different source: the television program that ran on Russia's national TV6 channel from 1994 to 2002 under the name *Katastrofy nedeli* (Catastrophes of the Week). *Catastrophes* was one of many Yeltsin-era television programs devoted to bad news. Most of the others were daily updates about terrible, and occasionally comical, crimes committed in the capital and elsewhere, with all the loving detail of *CSI* but none of the special effects, and none of the comfort that comes from knowing that you're only watching fiction. *Catastrophes of the Week* widened the scope of post-Soviet bad news, covering all the juicy calamities to afflict the entire world over the previous seven days. As the capstone to the daily programs that seemed designed to make sure Russians knew that they were living in dangerous times, *Catastrophes of the Week* was in many ways the distillation of a post-Soviet apocalyptic sensibility: it is not enough that bad things happen, but they must also be transformed into discourse (narrative news and sensationalist video), and, most important, assimilated into the viewer's consciousness. Intentionally or not, the Russian media and culture industry after 1991 devoted a great deal of energy and airtime to "miserytainment," heightening the already pervasive sense of imminent collapse.

The years since the USSR ceased to exist show an evolving relationship to cataclysm: from roughly 1991 to 1998, apocalyptic narratives were primarily found in the realm of television news, print journalism, and opinion pieces. In Lacanian terms, these are narratives that purport to be about the Real, but whose drama plays out far more effectively in the Symbolic (if not the Imaginary). A slew of actual disasters (the 1998 financial collapse and several acts of spectacular terrorism), followed by an eventual economic upswing thanks to high oil prices, saw the apocalypse move back into the textual (and, by extension, audiovisual) realm that spawned it, temporarily returning to metaphysical rather than explicitly political questions. Soon, however, the specter of collapse (and, indeed, the specter of a time when all people could think about was collapse) would be invoked by Putin and his proxies as the raison d'être for his particular type of regime.

Post-Soviet Russia did not introduce apocalypticism to the Russian world.[2] It takes little expertise or erudition to note that eschatology (the preoccupation with the end of days) has deep roots in Russian culture. The country's conversion to Christianity in 988 brought with it a Christian teleology, framing profane history between the perfection of Eden at the beginning and the Second Coming of Christ at the end. Christianity brought the apocalypse to Russia, at least in the sense that "apocalypse" was originally understood. The word "apocalypse" literally means "revelation," but it has come to stand for the events described in Christianity's most famous Revelation: the last book of the New Testament. The Revelation of John sets a crucial pattern for much of the Christian world: the precondition to the establishment of the Kingdom of God and the salvation of believers is cataclysm. Only after the near-total triumph of the forces of evil will Christ return to redeem the world.

Medieval Russia would not be alone in seeing signs of impending apocalypse everywhere, but it would have the misfortune of suffering actual events that looked dangerously close to Armageddon. When the Mongols invaded Russia in the early thirteenth century, it seemed to many like the end of the world. By the same token, when the invasion proved to be merely history (that is, one terrible event among many), it colored Russian conceptions of what the Apocalypse would look like. With the benefit of hindsight, it becomes obvious to even the most eschatologically minded Russians that the Mongol invasion and the Tatar Yoke were not the Apocalypse, since both good and bad people lived to tell the tale, and the Second Coming did not follow. At best, it was a dress rehearsal for the Apocalypse (dress was casual, dismembering was optional). It also established a messianic pattern for Russia's role in the world, since it led to the national myth that Russia somehow stopped the Mongols from conquering Europe. Russia sacrificed itself, becoming the Christ of nations.

A purely Christian apocalypse has its villainy baked in: the enemies are Satan, the Antichrist, and our own sin. But once we move from that framework, we encounter that classic Russian conspiratorial question: who is to blame?

The marriage of apocalypse and conspiracy in Russia is largely a late and post-Soviet affair, though the two had been flirting for years. Since the last days of the Russian Empire, apocalyptic fervor has been a recurring phenomenon, one that, while sometimes invoking conspiracy, did not entirely rely on it. At the end of the nineteenth century, we find an increasingly decrepit Russian empire whose educated population was convinced that their way of life was coming to an end. Subsequently, Russia joined the rest of Europe in experiencing World War I as the death knell for the old world, but with a crucial ideological twist provided by the October Revolution of 1917. Leninist Russian revolutionaries inherited a Marxist teleology that looked surprising like that of Christianity: a golden age (primitive communism), profane history (feudalism and capitalism), eventually leading to socialism and the promised heaven on earth called communism.

Thus Soviet culture was teleological through-and-through, with any sacrifices and suffering in the present justified by the promised advent of the Radiant Future. This was, perhaps, conspiratorial, at least as a function of the all-encompassing planning that was the basis of the Soviet economy. One might imagine the Elders of Zion turning green with envy, if the common cause made by anticommunism and antisemitism hadn't already equated Bolshevism with the forces of International Jewry. But the communist teleology was too much of an open secret to be truly conspiratorial: everyone was supposed to be working for the end of the world as they knew it.

This incessantly optimistic teleology generally removed the apocalypse from the realm of threat (the works of the early Soviet writer Andrei Platonov being a noteworthy exception). The occasional dissident or émigré would dabble in the negative eschatology that is more familiar to the West (as Fridrich Gorenshtein did in *Psalm*, a 1975 novel whose rather sympathetic protagonist is the Antichrist), but official Soviet culture had little use for cataclysm. At least, for a *future* cataclysm; the films and novels about the Great Patriotic War after the defeat of Nazi Germany functioned as something of a safety valve, providing the one arena in which violence and brutality could be safely depicted (if only as part of a foundational myth).

Even Soviet science fiction flirted with disaster much less than did its Anglo-American counterparts; the main exception to this rule is Andrei Tarkovsky's 1979 art-house postapocalyptic *Stalker*, based on the Strugatsky Brothers' 1972 novel *Roadside Picnic*, and even this is an example of postapocalyptic disaster that takes on a distinctly local scale (only a few spots on earth have been turned into mysterious "zones" by aliens). It is fitting that we have to wait until just before the onset of perestroika, the period intended as an optimistic rebirth that ended up heralding an abrupt demise, for a Soviet end-of-the-world film: Konstantin Lopukhansky's 1986 *Pis'ma mertvogo cheloveka* (Letters of a Dead Man) was a rare Soviet glimpse into a worldwide postapocalyptic nuclear wasteland.

Perestroika inaugurated a new Soviet temporality, in which the previous two decades get characterized as stagnation: that is, time that functions as anti-time. Technically, time does pass, but it does not progress. By contrast, perestroika was part of a trinity of Gorbachev-era buzz words, including the famous *glasnost'* and the now-forgotten *uskorenie* (speeding up). Time was *supposed* to accelerate. Though perestroika ends up being as ideologically distant from Stalinism as possible, with the benefit of hindsight, its temporality looks rather like that of the 1930s: the fast-paced period between 1986 and 1991 is something of a Five-Year Lack of Plan.

The pace of change during those five years was staggering, especially by contrast to the previous twenty. And it was perestroika that intensified the latent strains of apocalypticism that already characterized Soviet culture: suddenly, the news went from all good (record-setting harvests, fabulously productive widget factories) to all bad (an earthquake in Armenia, nuclear disaster in Chernobyl, and rumors of coups and takeovers popping up at regular intervals). But it came to an end with a Keystone Cops coup attempt and the aforementioned December meeting that signed away the Soviet Union as if it were the unwanted issue of a no-fault divorce.

Yet, in one of the many great ironies of glasnost, this same five-year period was also the beginning of a golden age for conspiracy in Russia: now conspiracy could be openly discussed.

All Apocalypse Is Local

When Mikhail Gorbachev called for glasnost in 1986, he clearly had no idea what he was getting into. Unless we subscribe to the no-longer-entirely-marginal theory that he was an agent of the CIA whose job was to destroy the USSR—in that case, job well done. The distinction between these approaches says a great deal about conspiracy's appeal: five years of chaos and uncontrolled collapse become an evil agenda successfully implemented by traitors. Empirically, the result may be one and the same, but conspiracy at least provides an enemy as an almost life-affirming alternative to nihilism.

If Gorbachev's own words are to be believed, he saw glasnost as a means for mobilizing the masses toward positive change. His 1987 manifesto *Perestroika*, which became an international bestseller despite its soporific contents, indicated that glasnost would help people "to participate in the restructuring effort consciously" (75). What he got instead was one of the most prolonged outpourings of negativity ever seen. And conspiracy was a perfect fit.

One of the defining features of the cultural landscape under Gorbachev was the seemingly endless series of revelations about the falsification of history and the whitewashing of the regime's crimes. It's one thing to hear someone talk about a cover-up, which is a standard component of conspiratorial thinking (as with the alleged aliens in Roswell), but it's an entirely different matter for the government itself not only to validate the cover-up story but to be actively involved in exposing its predecessors' crimes. For all intents and purposes, perestroika proved that conspiracy was real.

For a conspiracy to be compelling, it must have a specific, presumably nefarious purpose. Surprise parties function like conspiracies (a cabal of friends are planning a party behind the guest of honor's back), but there's a good reason we don't put the two in the same category. Certainly a wide range of conspiratorial ideas gained an audience during and after glasnost, but the conspiratorial master trope was inevitably about the fate of the motherland. In the introduction, I talked about the "Russia narratives," the self-reflexive stories about Russia's nature and its role in the world; the late 1980s show us that the most compelling Russian conspiracy theories are about these narratives' end: plots against Russia. Decades after Stalin's death, glasnost built apocalypse, rather than socialism, in one country.

That conspiracy and apocalypse are connected is not at all surprising. As Stephen O'Leary puts it, "The discourses of conspiracy and apocalypse . . . are linked by a common function: each develops symbolic resources that enable societies to address and define the problem of evil" (6). But the localization of conspiracy and apocalypse in Russia is worth dwelling on. All apocalypse is local—even with the resources of modern communications networks, the end of the entire world can only be experienced by synecdoche. For someone dying in an explosion, there is presumably no way to differentiate between a localized bomb and total planetary destruction. Our knowledge that the rest of the world goes on without us could be emotionally significant (as Samuel Scheffler argues in *Death and the Afterlife*), but it is unknowable in the moment. American contemporary apocalyptic fiction certainly plays with this dilemma: the heroes of Justin Cronin's *Passage* trilogy and the protagonists of *The Walking Dead* have no idea whether the plagues visited on them are global or restricted to North America. For all intents and purposes, the rest of the world may as well be gone, since there is no longer any way to communicate with it. The Russian apocalypse, however, is different: it depends on the outside world's continued existence as the source of evil. The Russian apocalypse is the inversion of the postapocalyptic tales so popular now in North America: rather than effectively removing the rest of the world from the picture, the Russian apocalypse is the result of a global conspiracy to wipe the motherland from the map.

Much of the apocalypticism of the post-Soviet era can be traced to the dissolution of the Soviet Union as both apocalypse and anticlimax. The promise implied by an energetic Yeltsin gave way to a sclerotic, latter-day Brezhnev redux, albeit with much better special effects—Yeltsin's cringe-worthy twist couldn't have come about without the help of the best American cardiologists money could buy, and when Victor Pelevin closed out the Yeltsin era in his novel *Homo Zapiens* with the casual revelation that the entire Kremlin leadership was generated by CGI, readers could be forgiven for idly wishing that their next president could be produced by Pixar (as it turns out, if one believes the Duma's outrage about Putin and Dobby the House Elf, he was produced by Warner Brothers). With the Soviet Union gone, the culture seemed to be searching for the next candidate for a threat to its successor state's very existence. The media, already sensationalistic, become sensation-seeking, and the better part of the 1990s is devoted to this quest for catastrophe. Much has been made of the trauma of the Soviet collapse, but the early post-Soviet preoccupation with the next big disaster suggests not just a post-traumatic repetition compulsion, but perhaps even the possibility that the dismemberment of the Soviet Union was not traumatic enough.

The country moved from panic to panic: the coalition of Yeltsin opponents holed up in Russia's parliament building in 1993 was easily dispatched, never rising to the threat of civil war so often invoked by leaders and pundits. That same year, and partly inspired by the horrific end to the Waco standoff with the Branch Davidians in Texas, the Russian media and the Russian Orthodox Church discovered the danger of a so-called totalitarian sect: the Great White Brotherhood of Maria Devi Khristos. For two years, white-robed followers of the self-proclaimed female hypostasis of God and reincarnation of Jesus plastered her photo on walls and subway cars throughout the former Slavic republics of the USSR, and hawked their rather turgid literature on streetcorners and public markets. On two occasions I even saw the same Great White Sister harangue the audience at the Bolshoi Theater before she was pulled off-stage.

I have written extensively about Maria Devi before (and two decades later, probably remain her biggest fan), but I do want to highlight the aspects of this particular farce that speak to this chapter's topic.[3] A typically millenarian religious movement, the Great White Brotherhood published numerous pamphlets talking about the end of the world (which it had scheduled for November 24, 1993) and made references to the 144,000 who would be saved from death by fire. The various successor agencies to the KGB may have been competent in many areas (their ability to produce a false confession is still the envy of Guantanamo Bay), but they proved to be religiously illiterate. As a result, parents around Russia and its neighboring nations were told to watch out for the White Brothers, who would kidnap their children in preparation for the coming apocalypse. Moreover, they mistook the figure 144,000, which comes straight from Revelation, for a realistic census of the brotherhood's membership, rather than a wildly optimistic enrollment target. Add in the talk of fiery death, and the security agencies came to the conclusion that Maria Devi and her followers intended to set themselves on fire in downtown Kiev. The brotherhood was forced to reschedule the end of the world for two weeks earlier, and all their leaders were swiftly arrested, saving three countries from a nonexistent threat.

The story of Maria Devi Khristos is less her story, which was never properly understood, than it is the story of the media panic about her story. The Great White Brotherhood fiasco was not merely apocalyptic, but meta-apocalyptic. It turned the end-of-days scenario cobbled together by the group's leaders—Marina Tsvigun, a former Communist Youth League organizer, and Yuri Krivonogov, a washed-out computer scientist—into the threat of apocalypticism itself, not to mention a nefarious conspiracy to brainwash wayward youth. Russia was on the verge of calamity precisely because of a group that was obsessed with the end of days, and yet the brotherhood was only translating the free-floating anxieties about imminent catastrophe back into a garbled form of the religious discourse that spawned them. Moreover, the brotherhood's insistent focus on the Slavic successors to the Soviet Union (Russia, Ukraine, and Belarus) pointed back to the primal scene of post-Soviet apocalypticism: the dismantling of the USSR by those three countries. The brotherhood, and, even more, the media covering the brotherhood, promised to follow up on this 1991 anticlimactic Armageddon with an apocalypse truly worthy of the name. But in fact, the story of Maria Devi closes the circle by fizzling out as undramatically as the USSR itself.

Just one year after Maria Devi's end-of-the-world roadshow was canceled by the authorities, 1994 saw an equally emblematic failed apocalypse: the culmination of a nationwide media blitz that resulted in millions of Russian citizens investing in the country's largest pyramid scheme to date, Sergei Mavrodi's MMM (Borenstein, "Public Offerings"). Through soap-opera-style, serialized commercials about ordinary people investing their hard-earned rubles in this magical company—the former excavator operator Lenya Golubkov; the lonely, middle-aged Marina Sergeevna, "who trusts no one"; the elderly pensioners with only the dregs of a life savings—MMM was making its initial investors (or "partners," as they were called) very rich but threatened to bankrupt the gullible stakeholders who arrived late in the game. Like tragedies, pyramid schemes have a foregone conclusion: they are the chronicle of a swindling foretold. For the gullible and desperate "partners," however, the pyramid was to be a positive, joyful apocalypse: some of them would be among the elect, the "saved," who would become rich on other people's savings. The government and the media saw things differently: the crash of the MMM pyramid would have consequences even worse than the further impoverishment of Russian citizens. They warned that it would lead to a total collapse of the Russian banking system, although in reality, that would take another three years to happen. Special forces troops were sent in to arrest Mavrodi, the rather unimpressive little mummy entombed in the pyramid's base. The government would claim success in averting catastrophe, while Mavrodi's followers claimed to be the victims not of MMM but of the government itself, for plotting against the one man who could threaten the powers that be.

MMM has had a long and twisted sequel, but for my purposes, it is yet another example of a phenomenon that characterized media and culture in the 1990s, and that fueled growing apocalypticism. One of the great dangers bandied about in the early 1990s, for good reason, was the possibility of hyperinflation—an economic catastrophe in which money is worth less than the paper it's printed on. Russia dodged this particular bullet but indulged in endless rhetoric *about* hyperinflation. This rhetoric of hyperinflation was, like Maria Devi's apocalyptic screeds and Mavrodi's enthusiasm for his monetary scam, infectious: the discussion of the phenomenon starts to look just like the phenomenon discussed. The rhetoric of hyperinflation becomes the hyperinflation of rhetoric.

Like formerly valuable rubles on the verge of worthlessness, truth claims about catastrophe could escalate only if their authors wanted them noticed and considered. Catastrophe in the 1990s reproduced itself memetically, as both bits of information (the message) and a style of packaging the information (the metamessage). Thus it makes sense that each of these two apocalyptic events has had a sequel, and that, like most sequels, they are far less momentous. Mavrodi revived his MMM campaign as MMM-2011, to much less fanfare, while Maria Devi has changed her name to Julia Preobrazhenskaya and found a comfortable home as an Internet phenomenon: we have seen the second coming, and it is the messiah as LOLcats. In the current Russian media environment, with strict controls on television and fewer restrictions on the net, the end of the world will not be televised, but it will be hosted and mirrored on secure servers.

Though MMM and Maria Devi were the two most mediagenic pseudocatastrophes of the 1990s, they were not the only ones. But the others never coalesced into a single, discrete story: anxieties about loose nukes and the post-Soviet brain drain played themselves out in news reports and op-ed pieces about the black market trade in "red mercury," a secret Soviet nuclear compound that never actually existed. This did not stop security forces from arresting people for trading in it or, for that matter, criminals from selling something purported to be red mercury. But, as is appropriate for a fictitious weapon, the drama of red mercury played itself out mostly in fiction. Russia and Ukraine produced a forgettable 1995 film called *Caution: Red Mercury* about a black-market nuclear trade that reached all the way to the government, while, in the West, an equally obscure thriller by the same name appeared in 1997. Red mercury's most enduring afterlife (or, perhaps, half-life) is as a 2004 video game available on Windows, XBox, and Steam. Though it never quite caught on as a cause for mass panic, it did serve as a convenient repository of post-Cold War nuclear fears: now atomic weaponry would not bring about a global apocalypse. Instead it had become something closer to a viral contagion, in which the anxieties are as much about boundary crossings and purity as they are about survival. Meanwhile, the actual Soviet nuclear catastrophe that heightened the sense of post-Soviet nuclear danger has become part of one of the most popular series of video games ever to come out of the former Soviet space: the *S.T.A.L.K.E.R.* series, an immersive combination of first-person shooter and scavenger hunt that conflates the mysterious "zone" of Tarkovsky's film with the radioactive zone of exclusion surrounding Chernobyl.[4]

What is important here is that these pseudocatastrophes unfolded as a media phenomenon. Indeed, it is particularly telling that the culture scales down its production of narrativized apocalyptic threats once it finally starts experiencing the serious catastrophes that had been expected since the late Gorbachev years. There was no need for a story about fiscal collapse after the 1998 financial crisis: the failure of banks and businesses rendered these anxieties real, and thus obviated the need for them to be so thoroughly discursive. Meanwhile, talk of out-and-out civil war in the Russian Federation was replaced with real war in Chechnya, the huge death toll and destruction of anything like ordinary life in the breakaway republic, and the appalling acts of terrorism on the civilian population in Moscow, Petersburg, and Dagestan.

If "real" catastrophes "cured" the mediated desire to produce discursive catastrophes, this may well have something to do with the way in which catastrophes are framed and experienced. The topic simply begs for a comparative perspective, particularly from the profound insights of Marita Sturken in her 2007 monograph, *Tourists of History: Memory, Kitsch, and Consumerism from Oklahoma City to Ground Zero*. Sturken identifies a striking pattern in the American narrative of catastrophe and recovery, one that seems predicated on a kind of selective amnesia. After each and every catastrophic event, we are told that America has lost its "innocence" (15–18). The term "innocence,' of course, is suggestive of at least two qualities: first, the lack of guilt; and second, the lack of (usually sexual) knowledge. Clearly, it is the second aspect that is at stake here (since no discussion of American guilt is entertained in the immediate aftermath); America, then, undergoes a serial loss of innocence that defies logic but reinforces a particular American subject position that this narrative wants to maintain: an America that, after engaging with the world, can retreat to a blissful state of knowing no evil. It is a return to Eden made possible by a discursive bulimia: we eat the fruit of the tree of knowledge, and then purge it before it can be digested.

Sturken's approach to the American narrative of catastrophe and recovery is important for us precisely because of how irrelevant it is to the Russian context. The subject position posited by and for Russia is never one of innocence; quite the contrary, it assumes a resigned and melancholy experience, a kind of end-of-the-world-weariness. Catastrophe is lamentable but familiar, and, indeed, to be expected. Svetlana Alexievich even calls the first section of *Second-Hand Time* "The Consolation of Apocalypse" (15). Here we have one of the discursive keys to the Putin regime: Putinist rhetoric has never been about preventing the smaller, localized catastrophes that beset the country; instead, it is about fending off the greater cataclysm of total apocalypse.

Indeed, if critics from the far right such as Alexander Prokhanov and the remaining liberal intellectuals—Masha Gessen, for example—are to be believed, Putin came to power on the crest of a catastrophe that was both real and manufactured: the series of apartment bombings in Moscow that served as a pretext to both a renewed war in Chechnya and the recreation of the security state.[5] The government blamed Chechen terrorists, but Russian journalists quickly found several holes in the story, leaving the Russian public two stark options: believe the state, and therefore support renewed action in Chechnya, or blame the state and accept the idea that the lives of average Russian citizens mean absolutely nothing to the men in power (Anderson). If the bombings were a government plot, then it was a cynical bet on the end of cynicism, an assumption that the majority of the population would choose to believe that their strong and decisive leaders were fighting internal enemies. Either way, the bombings were a preview of the problem of belief and debunking that would plague the news media across the world over a decade later: in the absence of an irrefutable factual framework that could convince citizens across the political spectrum, Russians were put in a position of choosing the facts that best supported their belief system (in a state media environment that pushed one narrative far more than another).

Death of a Nation

The two signal apocalyptic moments of the 1990s—panic over "cults" and the anxiety over financial machinations that could destroy the economy— were outliers in the developing conspiratorial discourse of post-Soviet Russia, in that they were perceived as primarily internal phenomena. The fringe political writings of the 1990s, however, pointed in the direction of conspiracy's greatest potential for growth, a potential that would be fulfilled in the following decade: the apocalyptic threat by enemies from without.

Conspiracy and apocalypse meet at a point that might uncharitably and unscientifically be considered national paranoia: the conviction that most of the world wants to destroy Russia, exacerbated by the nagging sense of the country's vulnerability. But even if we momentarily accept the "paranoid" label, we must immediately add the qualifier "justifiably." In the twentieth century alone, the Western Allies sent a military expedition to intervene in the Russian Civil War (1918) and the Soviet Union was invaded by the Nazis, whose defeat was followed by the formation of a coalition of powerful countries dedicated to, at the very least, containing the "Soviet threat." The same century also saw the collapse of statehood on two separate occasions (1917 and 1991). Hence the popular appeal of Putin's rhetoric of state sovereignty: failed statehood is not just conceivable; it is part of the lived experience of the majority of the adult population.

The very plausibility of the idea that Russia is under siege means that the existential threat to Russia is an available and frequent trope in the Russia narrative. The trope's ubiquity is a function not just of the acceleration of historical time experienced in perestroika and its aftermath, but also the ways in which novelty, anxiety, and uncertainty constantly upped the ante.

Conspiracy adds a particular valence to catastrophe, in that calamities are part of a plan—rather than simply a sequence of unrelated events, disasters are *emplotted*. Conspiracies to destroy Russia harness the teleology of apocalypse to the structure of narrative; the result is a hybrid genre whose rules and tropes become legible and even predictable, once the constituent components of the drama are identified. In the case of "plots against Russia," the generic conventions at work are those associated with melodrama.

Melodrama

Full-fledged conspiracy theories seem to thrive according to a law of increasing complexity: the longer a conspiracy theory lasts, the more likely it is that the underlying storyline has been growing ever more convoluted. Here conspiracy theory resembles serial narrative: for the plot to continue, it must be able to add and recombine new elements. Yet underlying both the paranoid worldview of conspiracy and the melodramatic underpinnings of most serial entertainment is an easily graspable simplicity rather than complexity, in that both serial melodrama and conspiracy are based on a binary, Manichaean model. Quite simply, there are good guys and bad guys, the embattled forces of virtue (the counterconspirators) and the hidden manipulators hell-bent on ruining the nation or dominating the world (the conspirators).

Conspiracy can account for complexity rather than simply rejecting it, but the complexity becomes immediately comprehensible as a superstructure built on binary simplicity. The world is much more complicated than it might initially appear, but it is not chaotic; indeed, it is the antithesis of chaos, since conspiracy emplots what might otherwise be senseless and random, transforming it into story. And the resulting story is inevitably a melodrama.

Melodrama is the default narrative form that conspiracy takes when it leaps from the rarified world of pseudoscholarly tracts to fiction (even if the fiction itself is often a thinly disguised tract). Though popular melodramas are usually concerned primarily with personal dilemmas, they nonetheless share an essential dualistic and even paranoid worldview with conspiracy theory. As Peter Brooks argues in *The Melodramatic Imagination*, "the center of interest and the scene of the underlying drama reside within . . . the 'moral occult,' the domain of operative spiritual values which is both indicated within and masked by the surface of reality" (5).

Characterization in melodrama can seem highly schematic, especially given the tendencies of the protagonists of classic melodramas to verbalize their motives and identify their values, but this insistence on rendering everything explicit serves the larger philosophical purposes of revelation: "The melodramatic mode in large measure exists to locate and to articulate the moral occult" (Brooks, 5). Such an emphasis on revelation is a perfect vehicle for the agenda of conspiratorial narrative, whose dramatic impetus depends on a similar tension between secrecy and disclosure. To be compelling, conspiracy must first convince or remind the audience that the real truths about our world are being hidden, whereupon much of the rest of the narrative is concerned with exposing the secret truth.

Conspiracy and melodrama share more than just the structural principle of secrecy and revelation; despite the different scales on which they operate (the global vs. the personal), they distribute truth and secrecy among a common cast of characters reflecting a single, shared worldview. Melodrama depends on the deployment of the moral occult as an "intense emotional and ethical drama based on the Manichaean struggle of good and evil" (Brooks, 12). The melodramatic world is one in which "what one lives for and by is seen in terms of, and as determined by, the most fundamental psychic relations and cosmic ethical forces. The polarization of good and evil works toward revealing their presence and operation as real forces in the world. Their conflict suggests the need to recognize and confront evil, to combat and expel it, to purge the social order" (Brooks, 13). Thus melodrama requires two consecutive actions from its heroes in relation to evil: recognition or revelation, and confrontation. This two-step path is also followed by the heroes of conspiracy fiction, who must have their eyes opened to the true causes of the evil around them (essentially a conversion experience) and then dedicate themselves to the just cause of the opposition.

Neither conspiracy nor melodrama recognizes any middle ground. Melodrama is governed by the law of the excluded middle, a denial of any path other than total commitment to good or evil (Brooks, 15). Brooks sees a strong connection between the Manichaeism of melodrama and revolutionary politics: "Like the oratory of the Revolution, melodrama from its inception takes as its concern and *raison d'être* the location, expression, and imposition of basic ethical and psychic truths. It says them over and over in clear language, it rehearses their conflicts and combats, it reenacts the menace of evil and the eventual triumph of morality made operative and evident" (Brooks, 15). Such revolutionary oratory presupposes that the truth is already being rendered public, yet the same insistence on simplicity holds true when the political opposition remains underground, operating along conspiratorial models. In the world posited by conspiracy, the convoluted web of secret organizations, mysterious weaponry, and insidious propaganda is ultimately the superstructure resting on a binary base.

The Protocols of the Elders of Tartu

Why does melodrama, with its Manichaean world view, fit so easily with Russian conspiratorial thought? One obvious, if partial, explanation is the binarism that has long been thought to be central to Russian culture itself.[6] As Yuri Lotman and Boris Uspensky argue, one of the defining characteristics distinguishing Russian culture from that of Western Europe is "its essential polarity, a polarity expressed in the binary nature of its structure" (31). Unlike Western Catholicism, whose definition of the afterlife included the possibility of Purgatory, Russian Orthodoxy saw no middle ground between salvation and damnation. These divergent views of life after death have serious ramifications for the two religions' notions of behavior: the Catholic and, subsequently, Protestant world posited a neutral behavior zone, neither holy nor unholy, where the Russian medieval system saw only the sacred and the profane (Lotman and Uspenskii, 31–32).

In Brooks's terms, the Orthodox worldview operated according to melodrama's law of the excluded middle.

As a result, Russian culture of the medieval period and later viewed the world in terms of stark contrasts, such as Russia vs. the West, or Christianity vs. paganism. One can also argue that for more than two centuries, Russian culture has searched for ways to overcome binarism (the tripartite Hegelian synthesis, the perennial talk about a "Third Way"), but otherwise Russian culture is binary by default. As Boris Gasparov points out in his introduction to an English-language collection of Tartu School essays on semiotics, it is easy to find counterexamples to Lotman and Uspensky's arguments (Gasparov, 27), but the binary model is compelling, at least as a place to start. Even if their model does not explain all of Russian culture—and Lotman and Uspensky claim validity only through the eighteenth century—it clearly applies to an important part of it, or at least to the way Russian cultural discourse has traditionally been constituted.[7]

As one might expect, this emphasis on binarism cuts both ways: Lotman and Uspensky's text is both a model of Russian binary thought and an example of it, given that the argument is predicated on the very binary oppositions that are the object of analysis—in particular, Russia vs. the West.[8] One can take this connection further: the semiotic discipline that produces this binary model is itself so thoroughly indebted to binarism that it is predisposed to see dichotomies. Derrida's critique of structuralism identifies this insistence on duality as a defining feature of Western thought, and here the term "Western" would presumably include rather than exclude Russia. But if one historicizes Soviet semiotics, looking at it as not simply the product of "Western" thought writ large, but as a theory with strong roots in its more immediate political and cultural environment, then semiotics can become the object of cultural analysis rather than exclusively its subject. Semiotics, for all its richness and heuristic productivity, proves to be a key example of a long-standing Russian cultural predilection for systems theories and modeling, including not just formalism and structuralism but the metaphysical systems constructed by Silver Age philosophers and poets, Alexander Bogdanov's tectology, Vladimir Vernadsky's noosphere, and Lev Gumilev's ethnogenesis.

This emphasis on systems fits in with one of the other major intellectual trends of the post-Stalin era: the ITR discourse as analyzed by Mark Lipovetsky. Though ITR stands for *inzhenerno-tekhnicheskii rabotnik*, meaning engineer/technical employee, the term's scope is far broader, applying to the discourse of the technical intelligentsia as a whole. Lipovetsky uncovers the essentialism at the ITR's core, an essentialism he attributes not just to the "scientific mind" but to an inverted version of Soviet ideology's preoccupation with "the progress of mankind" and "the Soviet people" (116). If semiotics was of interest only to a relatively small group of specialists, ITR discourse spread throughout the entire intelligentsia, as well as shaping and being shaped by important segments of mass culture, in particular the science fiction of the Strugatsky Brothers.

This predilection for theorizing, whether rooted in ITR discourse or semiotic notions of binaries, leads not only to explanatory models of the world but to the modeling of such models in Russian fiction, largely by featuring characters who are themselves obsessive theorizers. The obvious example here is Dostoevsky, who, if he did not invent this particular motif, developed it more than anyone before him (cf. Raskolnikov, Ippolit, Ivan Karamazov). Since Dostoevsky, Russian authors have populated their novels with theorists of all stripes, from Olesha's Ivan Babichev to the home-grown philosophers parodied by Pelevin in *The Buddha's Little Finger*. Contemporary popular fiction also reflects a theorizing tendency, from the prolonged explanations of human nature in Viktor Dotsenko's *Mad Dog* series of action/adventure potboilers to offhand comments about personality types in the first volume of Vasily Zvyagintsev's *Odysseus Leaves Ithaca* (Odissei pokidaet Itaku). When viewed in this context, semiotics both exemplifies Russian cultural binarism (to extend Gasparov's argument beyond the Lotman and Uspensky essay) and serves as an example and metasystem for a cultural tendency toward the construction of, and search for, systems.

If one can generalize about the tendency of human mental processes to look for patterns where they may not exist (pattern recognition), Russian culture backs up this tendency with the weight of literary, philosophical, and scientific authority. Granted, there is a circularity to this argument that either renders it spurious or makes it into the kind of closed system that conspiracists find so appealing: semiotics, the system of systems, functions as the ur-conspiracy that is usually behind multiple layers of plots in paranoid fictions—in this case, a cabal of old men in Tartu, many with suspiciously Jewish surnames. By no means do I intend to make any argument about anything as dubious as "national character," nor do I wish to argue that Russian culture is somehow inherently paranoid; rather, the point is that Russian culture can and has provided a comfortable backdrop for conspiratorial thought.

The Truth Shall Not Set You Free

There are obvious political realities that made twentieth-century Russia a breeding ground for conspiracy. The Soviet regime operated according to a conspiratorial epistemology: information was a rare commodity to be hoarded and rationed at the top. The paucity of reliable information, and the nakedly partisan nature in which information was presented, not only facilitated skepticism about official pronouncements, but also left a knowledge vacuum easily filled by speculation and rumor.

Here we must recall the dynamics of glasnost and chernukha (pessimism, naturalism, and muckraking): while the policies of glasnost purported to fill in the "blank pages" of history, these pages had never been truly blank (Borenstein, *Overkill*, 7–17). The facts had been known or suspected, or speculation had filled in the gaps. Glasnost functioned on the boundaries of revelation and confirmation, since what was brought to light was never entirely unknown. Rather, it is the fundamentally melodramatic ritual of exposure (*razoblachenie*) that endowed the disclosure with meaning and power. It is not that the truth could "set you free"; the truth *itself* was set free, released from the confines of conspiratorial epistemology.

Yet glasnost, rather than sounding conspiracy's death knell, gave it a new lease on life. The exposure of the hidden truth may have meant the end of specific secrets, but it ultimately confirmed the prevalence of secrecy and the validity of conspiratorial epistemology ("Who knows what else they're keeping from us?"). This is particularly understandable given the pendulum swings of Soviet-era reforms, dating back to Khrushchev: partial truths were doled out during the Thaw, only to be elaborated under Gorbachev, but the slow, multistep process of revelation was not conducive to the belief that the "whole truth" had been disclosed. Hence the rise of chernukha and the obsession with the repetition of no-longer-new secrets, the ritualistic airing of familiar dirty laundry: like pornography, both chernukha and conspiracy trade in the revelation of what we have already seen before but must not be exposed in polite company. Pornography requires endless variations on the familiar in order to keep customers' interest, but what is it that conspiracy sells? What keeps the consumers coming back for more? Conspiracy thrives in the world of entertainment, yet the available variations to the conspiratorial plot are only slightly greater in number than those than can be found in "men's magazines" and sex videos.

Clearly, something very important is being replicated and confirmed, and, at least in the post-Soviet case, the source of appeal seems to be the paranoid framework itself. As the examples discussed below show, conspiracy offers an easily comprehensible and productive alternative to the nightmare vision of *bespredel* (total chaos). Bespredel accentuates the pessimism and negativity featured in the chernukha of the perestroika era and strips away all hope that the world could ever make sense (Borenstein, *Overkill*, 197–200). Conspiracy and bespredel are two diametrically opposed worldviews based on largely the same data. Where bespredel presents a Hobbesian view of the world, deprived of any higher purpose and prey to unending chaos, conspiracy provides "teleological warmth" and the reassuring image of history's guiding hand. If no one is responsible for the terrible state of the world, then there is no one to blame and no one to fight. The presence of actual enemies—evil plotters dedicating their lives to ruining all that is good—represents a fundamentally optimistic vision, facilitating stories of heroism, rescue, and power; hence the affinity between conspiracy and the action story (*boevik*). Counterintuitive as it may seem, not only do the Elders of Zion, the Harvard Project, and the sinister Masons help make sense of the world, but they also leave room for hope.

Conspiracy theories prospered in the 1990s, and, given their global scope, it should be no surprise that their ubiquity was global. The rise of online communication was a boon for the conspiratorially minded; indeed, the Internet now looks like conspiracy's natural habitat. But even by the late 1990s, the Internet had only begun its path to global media conquest, and in Russia, it would become a truly popular phenomenon only in the twenty-first century. In the first post-Soviet decade, conspiracy would have to content itself with the traditional media.

Even here, though, there were important differences between conspiracy's spread in Russia and the West. To a far greater extent than in the United States or Europe, conspiracy in Russia thrived on the cool medium of print, rather than relying on the visceral appeal of film and television. Michael Barkun argues that Americans had come to take conspiracy theories for granted, thanks to the continual migration of conspiratorial motifs from the world of esoteric pamphlets, zines, websites, and pseudo-scholarly tracts to blockbuster movies and hit TV series (179–84). Chris Carter's hit series *The X-Files* and its darker cousin, the less successful but more internally consistent *Millennium*, relied on a constantly growing accumulation of rival conspirators and outlandish plots to keep its viewers coming back every week.[9]

In post-Soviet Russia, conspiratorial explanations for current events sprang into life almost as though they were the product of some kind of instant intellectual parthenogenesis; recall the theory of Putin's responsibility for the Moscow apartment bombings. No sooner were residential buildings targeted by apparent terrorism than people started to speculate that the security services were actually behind the attacks. Yet conspiracy as entertainment was largely confined to novels.

At least one of the reasons was economic, following the same logic that explained the greater presence of the domestic boevik in prose than in film or television: print is quicker and cheaper. This explanation becomes all the more compelling when we factor in the close ties between the boevik genre and the conspiratorial mode; the Manichaean nature of the boevik adventure plot is particularly conducive to the struggle against shadowy secret societies.

This is not to suggest that Russian audiences did not welcome conspiracy-oriented entertainment in other media. *The X-Files* was a big hit in the Russian Federation, under the name *Secret Materials* (Sekretnye materialy). But the local *X-Files* knockoffs that one might expect in a market-oriented entertainment culture could be found on the bookshelves, not the airwaves: in 1999, Konstantin Maksimov began a new series of hardcover novels under the rubric The Seven Seals of Mystery (Sem' pechatei tainy), which relate the adventures of various Russian secret service agencies in their fight against vampires, witches, and other occult threats. The cover of each volume contains the phrase "secret materials," which is arguably generic enough not to be considered a direct trademark infringement, but the interior advertising copy leaves little room for doubt: "Konstantin Maksimov presents his new cycle *The Seven Seals of Mystery*—a domestic [*otechestvennaia*] version of the American *Secret Materials*" (Maksimov,

Vidiashchii smert', 286). Sergei Lukianenko's *Night Watch* series fills a similar niche (in this case, supernatural creatures are responsible for policing themselves and investigating paranormal crimes), but the first installment would be adapted as a big-budget movie only in 2004, after the Russian film industry had begun its recovery.

Die, America, Die!

The sole exception of which I am aware was a short-lived pseudodocumentary series on ORT by the journalist Alexander Gordon, titled *A Collection of Fallacies* (Sobranie zabluzhdenii). If you can imagine *The X-Files* as a cross between a poorly dubbed 1950s Japanese monster movie and *La jétee*, starring emotionless mannequins with all the sexual chemistry of a middle-aged Ken and Barbie as they discuss the latest email blast from your racist uncle, then there is no need to bother watching *A Collection of Fallacies*. Gordon, who began his broadcasting career in the United States, returned to Russia in the 1990s and attracted attention with a program claiming that the US moon landings were all an elaborate hoax, a familiar trope among American conspiracy circles (Golovanov).

In *Collection of Fallacies*, Gordon followed up with a fictional space program of his own: Gordon played the part of the "Keeper of Eternity," who watches over the history of Earth and studies it with the help of a female fellow agent. Gordon combines a familiar perestroika-era preoccupation with the "blank spots" of history and a science fictional premise that actually allows the characters to realize the metaphor of perestroika's "return of history": they travel through time. Gordon's interest in the science-fictional aspects appears to be minimal—certainly, whoever was watching *Collection of Fallacies* was not tuning in for the special effects or the suspense. The male and female aliens were given virtually no defining personal characteristics, thereby making them difficult to "ship" (the fan-fiction practice of imagining sexual relationships between uninvolved characters). What is more, the director's insistence on having them communicate with each other telepathically resulted in repeated, drawn-out scenes of the two of them simply looking at each other and walking while their dialogue is conducted exclusively in voiceovers. It was television, but just barely.[10]

Though one could imagine a historical/science fiction docudrama that is not necessarily based on conspiracy, hidden plots and secret agendas often provided the motivation for such time-traveling adventures. Vasily Zvyagintsev's science fiction epic *Odysseus Leaves Ithaca* (twenty-one volumes by the time of the author's death) is held together by the machinations of two alien "superintelligences" that have been manipulating human history—a truth that was allegorically reflected in, of all things, Daniil Andreev's mid-twentieth-century religious/philosophical tract about the inherently melodramatic struggle between light and darkness, *The Rose of the World* (232); it is up to the human protagonists to help them when warranted and foil them when necessary.

Unlike Zvyagintsev's characters, Gordon's agents are tourists rather than action heroes, observing the tragedies of the past century without getting involved. When conspiracy appears, it is not part of the aliens' own agenda, but rather it is the object of their research and revelations. The Spengleresque fifth episode, "The Decline of America" (Zakat Ameriki), which aired on May 25, 1999, follows a typical pattern of sophisticated conspiratorial discourse in that it purports to expose both the "real" conspiracies that govern the world and to warn about the proponents of specious conspiracy theories who threaten world peace. As the agents traverse US geography and history, they become increasingly convinced that the United States is on the verge of civil war. Right-wing militia groups and white supremacists (the film cites *The Turner Diaries*) are preparing for armed combat, while Hasidic bankers have a stranglehold on the US financial markets. The antisemitic calumny is all too common in conspiracy circles, though it is a bit surprising here in a show by a Jewish director. In any case, Gordon's narrative is both familiar (in that it touches on standard Russian conspiratorial tropes) and bracing for national pride (the Soviet Union may have collapsed, but the United States is about to have it worse).

This projection of national collapse onto the surviving superpower was quite common in Russian entertainment (recall Danila's declaration to the French partygoer in *Brother*: "Skoro vsei vashei Amerike—kirdyk" [All that America of yours is gonna get it]), even before the 1999 US-led NATO bombing of Yugoslavia unleashed years of seething anti-American resentment. In conspiratorial narratives, the United States was, more often than not, the source of the motherland's woes, but only because it feared that Russia's untapped potential and superior spiritual and intellectual resources could threaten American hegemony. Positing America's collapse could be a source of deep satisfaction in the face of the country's unilateralism and self-congratulatory framing of the end of the Cold War as an American victory. In addition, the portrayal of the United States as a powder keg served the self-replicating interests of conspiratorial discourse itself. It facilitated the recombinations of Russian and American paranoid tropes into new, more intricate storylines, threatening to turn conspiracy into an abject double of the globalization it so often condemned: the United States gets *The Protocols of the Elders of Zion* in exchange for *The Turner Diaries*, while both have Germany to thank for exporting *Mein Kampf*. Moreover, national collapse becomes a phenomenon of almost infinite regression, facilitating the mixture of apocalyptic and postapocalyptic temporalities that characterized Russia in the wake of the USSR's dissolution. Perversely, the globalization of conspiracy makes the end of the world a repeatable phenomenon of local proportions: it *can* happen here, because it is happening everywhere.

Conspiracy theories are complicated systems, and maintaining them could require a great deal of work. Fortunately, the conspiratorial ecosystem is built on a conservationist ethic: nothing goes to waste. Ideologues show no hesitation about recycling earlier theories in the service of new, more timely conspiracies. In the US context, Michael Barkun has demonstrated the facility with which UFOlogists adapt both the structure and the details of foundational paranoid texts such as *The Protocols of the Elders of Zion* along with material from proto-New Age sources such as Madame Blavatsky's *Secret Doctrine* and turn-of-the-century pulp science fiction—stories of evil, subterranean lizard people by Edward Bulwer-Lytton and Robert E. Howard (31–33). The repeated invocations of the same source material add weight to the conspiracists' claims, buttressing their works with a pseudoscholarly authority.

Post-Soviet Russia had several lines of conspiratorial thought that at times functioned in parallel, and at other times came together, often in extremist newspapers such as Alexander Prokhanov's *Zavtra* (formerly *Den'*). Before we can leave the 1990s, we must take a look at the conspiracy theories that post-Soviet Russia inherited and refined. We begin with the one that fits best with the Russian and European conspiratorial classics, particularly *The Protocols*: Grigory Klimov's dark vision of the Harvard Project (*garvardskii proekt*).

The Union of Concerned Mad Scientists

The Harvard Project gives the antisemitism of the *Protocols* a pseudoscientific veneer, updating them with the preoccupations of the Cold War (mind control, the US threat) and contemporary sexual panic (predatory homosexuals and militant lesbians), and reinforcing the religious dimension by approaching biblical texts and confessional differences in terms of genetics and evolution. For the post-Soviet era, the Harvard Project takes on yet another sinister dimension, as it is easily conflated with the economic "shock therapy" programs advocated by Harvard economists such as Jeffrey Sachs.

Grigory Klimov developed an all-purpose demonology that gives the appearance of rigor while actually being extremely flexible. The result has all the hallmarks of the most baroque conspiracy theories to attract attention in the West, such as Lyndon LaRouche's assertion that the queen of England is an international drug kingpin working with the Rothschilds, or that the US government is under the extraterrestrial heel of spacemen with a baffling penchant for anal probes and cattle mutilation. Klimov finds his enemies slightly closer to home: for decades, Russia has been under siege by a cabal of genetically defective Jews and homosexuals (virtually synonymous in Klimov's lexicon), plotting the country's downfall from behind the ivy-covered walls of Harvard University.

Though Klimov is far from a household name in Russia, let alone in the West, his paranoid vision has serious ramification for post-Soviet conspiracism, even if his influence is not always direct. Klimov's paradoxical combination of antisemitism, anticommunism, and Russian nationalism with a strong respect for the Soviet incarnation of Russian statehood that his antirevolutionary diatribes would seem to attack, proved remarkably prophetic. Years before the dissident Igor Shafarevich would denounce both communism and Judaism as inherently hostile to life itself, and decades before the Soviet Union ceased to exist, Klimov articulated the worldview that would come to be associated with the Red/Brown opposition.[11]

Klimov's vision of an anti-Russian conspiracy itself resembles the monstrous progeny of Cold War mad science that was such efficient fodder for the pop cultural mill throughout the world. Like Godzilla and the plethora of giant, radioactive vermin that attacked the major metropolitan centers of the United States and Japan on the movie screens of the 1950s or the dangerous biological, nuclear, and psychotropic weapons let loose from ex-KGB laboratories in post-Soviet Russian thrillers, Klimov's Harvard Project is a freakish offshoot of Cold War propaganda battles that has far exceeded the intentions, not to mention the lifespans, of the researchers who inspired it.

According to his now defunct official website, http://klimov.brave host.com/, which had been maintained by the Gregory Klimov Online Fan Club Moscow, Grigory Petrovich Klimov was born Igor Borisovich Kalmykov, not far from Rostov-on-Don in 1918. In 1945, he was employed as an engineer in Soviet-occupied Berlin, defecting to the Allies' zone in 1947. From 1949 to 1950, he claims to have worked for the CIA on a secret plan to destroy the Soviet Union, codenamed the "Harvard Project," which was followed by the "Cornell Project" for psychological warfare in 1958–1959. As his website puts it, his participation in the Harvard Project "affected his entire life and work," but "since psychological warfare was literally a war of psychos, Grigory Petrovich, being a normal person, could not continue to participate in a performance whose script was written by sick people."

Instead, he produced a cycle of novels and essays that purport to expose the evil machinations of the Harvard Project's masterminds: *The Prince of This World* (Kniaz' mira sego, 1970), *My Name Is Legion* (Imia moe—legion, 1975), *The Protocols of the Soviet Elders* (Protokoly sovetskikh mudretsov, 1981), and *Red Kabbalah* (Krasnaia kabbala, 1987). Initially distributed among Soviet émigrés, copies of these books made their way into the Soviet Union before perestroika, after which they were eventually reprinted by right-wing Russian publishing houses—particularly, but not exclusively, Sovetskaia Kuban' in Krasnodar. In interviews (Mogutin) and elsewhere on his site, Klimov claimed that the total print run of all his books is "more than 1,100,000 copies," an assertion that is impossible to verify.[12] Moreover, Klimov repeatedly declared his willingness to have his books printed by anyone anywhere, forgoing copyright and royalties, and has made his texts freely available on the Internet.[13] For Klimov, the most important thing was to get his message out; thus in 1997, he not only granted an interview to the gay journalist Yaroslav Mogutin for *Pechatnyi organ* but even agreed to have the text of the interview reprinted on his own website, despite Mogutin's thinly veiled contempt for his subject and his insistence on faithfully transcribing all of Klimov's grammatical mistakes and misplaced accents.[14]

Klimov's depiction of the Harvard Project does have a basis in the culture of military/industrial think tanks funded by the US government in the 1950s, but from a vantage point that distorts the results of this research while highlighting the improbable oddities that actually characterized US anticommunist psychological warfare. When discussing the Harvard Project, Klimov often invokes the name of Nathan Leitis, a University of Chicago graduate who joined the Rand Corporation in 1949 after working as an adviser to the US government during World War II. Leitis first made his mark at Rand with the 1951 publication of *The Operational Code of the Politburo*, which Ron Robin describes as "the most conspicuous attempt to fuse psychoculture and elite studies during the early Cold War years" (131). Leitis treated communism as a "secular religion" (xiv) and assumed that its leaders and adherents followed Marxist-Leninist Holy Writ without fail. His "operational code" (a quasi-semiotic elaboration of the rules and motivations that guided Bolshevik leaders) was a marvel of exegesis, teasing out decision-making patterns from numerous volumes of communist theory and official pronouncements.

In accepting a total identification between the official pronouncements of Soviet leaders and their actual behavior and motivations, however, Leitis assumed a transparent consistency that reduced the Politburo to a largely one-dimensional body that always followed through on its own logic, however tortured. He treated the Politburo as an essentially conspiratorial organization that plotted endlessly, with the result that the Soviet leaders resemble none other than the proverbial Elders of Zion, whose purported protocols strained credibility most when the gathered conspirators elaborated their plans and evil motivations so baldly.

As his work evolved, however, Leitis began to posit a Bolshevik inner life, complete with subconscious motivations that could explain what he saw as the Soviet leaders' uncompromising fanaticism. In 1955, Leitis threw Freud into the mix, suggesting that the "Bolshevik belief that they were surrounded by enemies with 'annihilatory designs' was a classical paranoid defense against latent homosexuality" (Leitis; Robin, 133).

Finally, we should recall Leitis's contribution to the discourse of "brainwashing." The term was introduced to the general public in 1956 by the journalist Edward Hunter, in an exposé of Chinese "thought reform techniques" used as ideological coercion on prisoners of war (*Brainwashing*).[15] However, it was Leitis who had provided the "scientific underpinnings for the brainwashing theory" two years before in a Rand Corporation study, *Ritual of Liquidation* (1954) (Robin, 167). In his examination of the self-incriminating confessions made by defendants during the Stalinist show trials, Leitis "implied that the act of embracing communism was in itself abnormal, most probably the result of a powerful strategy to overcome the mental defense mechanisms of normal human beings" (Robin, 168). Communism itself was a form of mind control.

Attack of the Degenerate Gay Jews

Klimov's Harvard Project combines the three key strands of Leitis's work—"secret" codes, latent homosexuality, and mind control—and adds a fourth, metatextual layer connected to the ethnic background of notable figures in the Rand Corporation and Russian Bolshevism: both the anti-Soviet Harvard Project and the Soviet government itself are the product of an international Jewish conspiracy.

The fundamentals of Klimov's theory are laid out in *The Prince of This World,* only to be elaborated ad nauseam in the rest of his books, articles, and interviews. Maxim Rudnev, one of the two brothers who are the protagonists of *The Prince of This World* and its sequel, *My Name Is Legion,* rises through the ranks of the Russian secret services thanks to far-ranging research combining the history of the occult, the secrets of the Jews, existentialism, Russian literature and religious philosophy, Cesare Lombroso's criminology, Max Nordau's theories of degeneration, contemporary genetics, and Alfred Kinsey's reports on male and female sexuality. The resulting "science," called both "higher sociology" and "dialectical Christianity," proves that the New Testament in general, and Revelation in particular, is more than a spiritual testimony: it is the encoding of biological and psychological fact in the language of mysticism.

Rudnev discovers that a large portion of humankind is inherently defective, bearing the "mark of the beast" in its genetic makeup. This group is constantly on the rise, thanks to the increasing degeneration of the populace caused by mixed marriages to homosexuals and Jews. For it is the Jews who are the most significant and organized contingent of "Legionnaires," as Klimov calls them, and it is the Jews who are also more prone to "latent homosexuality" and lesbianism. Klimov at once attempts to ground his demonology in the body (through spurious genetics) and to free his pet pathologies from their literal meanings: virtually every famous person identified in Klimov's work—including Lenin, Stalin, and Hitler—is at the very least a "quasi-faggot" (*polupederast*) and "part kike" (*s prozhid'iu*), even if they have never actually engaged in homosexual activities or have any known Jewish background.[16]

Thanks to his esoteric knowledge and iron will, Maxim Rudnev quickly climbs through the ranks of the People's Commissariat of Internal Affairs (NKVD) to become Stalin's "Red Cardinal" and mastermind the purges. In describing both Rudnev's philosophy and the evolution of Soviet history, Klimov follows the familiar conspiratorial pattern of using analogy and metaphor as proof, but he goes a step further: analogy and metaphor collapse in on themselves into total identity between the objects that are compared. Rather than simply compare Stalin's Terror with the Spanish Inquisition, the Terror and the Inquisition become one. It is not just that Rudnev has learned the lessons of inquisitors and witch hunters by reading *Malleus Maleficarum* in order to employ medieval methods against modern enemies: instead, the enemies of the Inquisition and the enemies of Stalin are one and the same. In each case, the forces of order are hunting down and exterminating a category of people whom Rudnev insists on calling "Satanists" (*satanisty*), "witches" (*ved'my*) and wizards (*kolduny*), for the "enemies of the people" have always been the "Legionnaires," whose chromosomal deficiencies turn them into power-mad, homosexual revolutionaries.

Naturally, the Legionnaires are primarily Jewish, which further strengthens the unity (rather than the parallels) between the Inquisition and the Terror: Maxim's skeptical younger brother, whose path toward enlightenment serves as the excuse for long disquisitions of Klimov's theories, is shocked to discover that nearly all the members of Stalin's discredited inner circle had Jewish wives, "as if some special marriage bureau's job was finding Jewish wives for the Kremlin's leaders" (chapter 6). Thus weeding out the hidden Jews is just as important for the NKVD as it was for the Inquisition. Moreover, the biological drives of the Legionnaires explain why revolutions must always "eat their young": all revolutionaries are "permanent revolutionaries," by their very nature; they will subvert any society in which they live, even if it is the society they themselves founded. Klimov and his characters can fight against their perceived

Jewish conspiracy in defense of a social order they claim was created by Jews (the Soviet system) and using theories developed by Jews (in *My Name Is Legion*, the narrator describes the Harvard Project as "Nathan Leitis and a whole host of elders of Zion with long, Marxist beards and limping on their left leg" (359).

Though the conservative Russian Writers' Union accepted Klimov as a member, his conspiratorial synthesis is too baroque to be adopted wholeheartedly by a mass movement or become thoroughly mainstream; *Zavtra* usually cites Klimov with approval and congratulated him on his eightieth birthday (Bondarenko). But Klimov, who spent all of the 1990s in his apartment in Queens, was not in a position to bring his ideas wider exposure. Instead, his books and articles were mined for useful ideas and motifs by a much savvier set of writers: the Norka analytical group, established in 1995 around the figure of Sergei Norka.[17]

Nobody Expects the Russian Inquisition

Several months before the fanfare that greeted the 2004 publication of Philip Roth's foray into counterfactual history, Russian readers were treated to the third installment in a series of novels by Sergei Norka: *The Plot against Russia* (Zagovor protiv Rossii). One does not have to share the paranoid and persecuted worldview of either novel's characters to find the similar titles remarkable, though not, in and of themselves, suspicious. At most, such synchronicity (another essentially paranoid concept, substituting a sense of cosmic balance for the evildoer's guiding hand) suggests that, by the early years of the twenty-first century, both Russia and the United States had conspiracy on the brain.

Yet beyond the near-identical titles, the two books have little in common: while some reviewers noted the timeliness of Roth's releasing a book about a fascist 1940s America in the age of the repressive Patriot Act, *The Plot against America*, with its antisemitic pogroms fostered by a pro-Nazi Lindbergh administration, partakes of a very familiar American fictional tradition.[18] Though comparisons have been made to the anti-authoritarian cautionary tale, à la Sinclair Lewis's *It Can't Happen Here*, *The Plot against America* looks backward rather than forward, essentially mainstreaming the alternate history genre. Roth's plot is thus safely confined to the past rather than looming over our present: it *can* happen here, but it didn't. Fifth-column plots against the United States are a staple of Christian identity and militia fiction, but they are largely alien to the mainstream book market—although Anne Coulter's accusation that all liberals are guilty of treason does come close. Conspiracy-minded television shows such as *24* bend over backward in the attempt to attribute terrorist threats to anyone but the usual suspects, engaging in a game of infinite regression that manages to deflect the show's animus from the standard demonology it initially invokes.[19] In Russia, conspiratorial story-telling is both more old-fashioned and more mainstream.

Norka's *The Plot against Russia* stays on familiar territory. The book's cover, featuring a rather predatory-looking eagle against the backdrop of the Kremlin and the US flag, is a handy condensation of current Russian conspiratorial mythologies: all it lacks is a Star of David and/or an Islamic terrorist to turn this increasingly familiar picture into a comprehensive panorama of Russian chauvinist demonology. The novel's blurb makes its political agenda clear.

> The CIA has developed a secret project for the collapse of the USSR, suck-ing Russia into a spiral of debt and instituting external control of the coun-try. The essence of the project becomes known to a small group within the Soviet leadership. This secret organization tries to outfox the Americans, but the situation gets out of control. The only ones who can save Russia, which has now turned into a criminal state, is the Russian Underground Resistance . . .

If the plot summary, combining the chaos of post-Soviet Russia with the intrigues of Cold War spy novels, sounds a shade retro, it is because Norka has proven particularly adept at seizing on contemporary trends in nostalgia and anti-Americanism while weaving them seamlessly into a century-old tradition of Russian national-chauvinist parables, a lineage that dates back to Sergei Nilus's forged *Protocols of the Elders of Zion* and is reinforced by Klimov's xenophobic novels.

Though the book was completed four years into the twenty-first cen-tury, it can nonetheless serve as a compendium of 1990s conspiratorial thinking, which has survived the turn of the century largely intact. In the last years of the 1990s, the Norka group began publishing op-ed pieces in the Russian press, eventually establishing a website to host its recent work. But its largest project has been the series of short novels that culminated in the omnibus edition *The Plot against Russia.*

The Plot contains the Norka group's previous two books—*The Inquisitor* and its prequel, *Wretched Rus,* here republished as "The Harvard Project"—in chronological order, followed by a new, third part titled *The Law of Vengeance* (Zakon vozdaniia). In a book touted as new, made up mostly of reprints, *The Plot against Russia* provides the shock of the old. Even in the trilogy's final form, *The Inquisitor* remains the heart of the story; the events it recounts are largely retold from a different point of view in the final segment, while *Wretched Rus/*"The Harvard Project" merely projects the plot back into earlier Soviet history. *The Inquisitor* is about the rise of the Dark Horse (*Temnaia loshchadka*), a man who appears virtually out of nowhere and is elected president of Russia, whereupon he wins a referendum granting him dictatorial powers in order to halt the waves of crime and corruption that have crippled the country.

The Dark Horse is only the public face of a larger conspiratorial organization that is dedicated to freeing Russia from the chaos caused by the West, its puppets, and evil forces within the former Soviet Union itself. Eventually, this group, led by a man nicknamed the Cardinal, establishes the Holy Russian Inquisition, which kidnaps criminals, steals their money, and surgically removes their eyes as an object lesson to others who would ruin the motherland.

The Inquisitor makes Norka's debt to Klimov absolutely clear. Halfway through the novel, the Cardinal explains to the narrator, a skeptical journalist who is slowly coming around to the Dark Horse's side, the theories behind his work. First he takes out a photograph, telling the narrator: "This is our spiritual father, as it were. Grigory Petrovich Klimov" (*Inkvizitor,* 222). The Cardinal briefly summaries Klimov's biography (including the Harvard Project), recapitulating Klimov's discussions of Legionnaires, revolutions, and mind control while going into more detail about the genetics that "prove" Klimov correct (222–28).

Norka performs two extremely important transformations when he brings Klimov into his fictional world. First, he makes much tighter connections among the Harvard Project, the Legionnaires, and Soviet history. Where Klimov insisted on the virtual identity of the Spanish Inquisition and the Great Terror, Norka prefers to emphasize cyclicity in the historical parallels he draws between the Terror and the new Holy Inquisition of the

1990s. For Norka, both campaigns are the struggle of the forces of order against evil businessmen who are facilitating the flight of capital abroad: the Terror was actually Stalin's way of stopping the NEPmen (the small-scale entrepreneurs who thrived in the liberal 1920s) from impoverishing the Soviet Union, while the Holy Inquisition is stopping the organized criminals who are continuing a process of capital flight begun with the late Soviet bureaucrats' funneling of the proverbial "Party's gold" to offshore bank accounts.

Historically, this parallel is spurious, but it reflects the even more significant alteration that the Norka group has made to Klimov's "higher sociology." Klimov's definition of the Terror as the latter-day Inquisition depends on his identification of the Jews as history's archvillains, but in the constituent parts of *The Plot against Russia*, the Jews are almost absent as a category.[20] Nor are homosexuals to blame for the collapse of any of the various incarnations of Russian statehood. As radical as Norka's vision of a well-intentioned but murderous anticriminal dictatorship may be, the regime of the Dark Horse shares little of the intense racism and sexual obsessions of its "spiritual father," Grigory Klimov. Yes, the Legionnaires must be exterminated, or at least subdued, and no methods are too harsh in combating their evil influence on a benighted Russia, but the Legionnaires are no longer identified with any particular racial or sexual minority.

The assertion of a genetic predisposition to evil reeks of fascism, but it is a fascism that has become thoroughly deracinated. The Legionnaires are predisposed to evil because of who they are, but most of them only commit evil deeds when social conditions allow it, or when foreign and domestic mind control campaigns bring out their terrible nature. Norka's soft-pedaled Klimovism manages to have it both ways. On one hand, there is an entire class of people whose genes render them a threat, but on the other hand, such people only become enemies of the people when they actually start committing inhuman acts: evil is as evil does. The villains are not the Jews per se, but they fulfill many of the functions that Jews do in conspiratorial demonologies.

And what is the nature of the Legionnaires' evil acts? Crime, corruption, and random, senseless violence. In other words, bespredel. Now bespredel has an explanation, however far-fetched. It is the result of genetic degeneration, combined with cynical mind control orchestrated first by the Harvard Project, then by forces within the Kremlin who seized Harvard technology and used it for their own ends. All three parts of *The Plot against Russia* are interspersed with quotations that are purportedly drawn from the Russian press: reports of terrible violence, economic scandal, and overall decline. These excerpts ground Norka's fiction in the world of bespredel, with which the reader cannot help but be familiar, and pave the way for the protagonists' eventual acceptance of dictatorship and terror as the only remedy. As in so many ideological and utopian novels, the protagonists themselves are stand-ins for the implied reader, modeling a conversion experience that can be shared by anyone who turns the page.

The Inquisitor and the rest of Norka's fictional project are the most systematic incarnation of a recurring fantasy from the 1990s: fighting criminal bespredel with state bespredel (Borenstein, *Overkill*, 198–99). The revenge fantasy of crime fiction is transfigured into an ideology of systematic purification, as enacted in *The Law of Vengeance*, the only part of *The Plot* that had not been published before the 2004 omnibus edition. Here the narrator is a successful businessman whose family is tortured and killed by thugs; the Inquisition not only facilitates his revenge on the men who wronged him but gives him a new purpose as part of its special subsection devoted to the extermination of other such chaos bringers. No longer will lone gunmen avenge individual atrocities; now they will be an army of the righteous, restoring order to a disorderly world.

When the Norka group assembled *The Plot against Russia* from its three component parts, it did more than merely change their order and alter some titles. In *The Inquisitor*, the excerpts from the press have specific dates: the first one is from the March 29, 1994, edition of *Izvestiia* (*Inkvizitor*, 3), but in *The Plot against Russia*, all specific dates are removed (now the citation is for "March 29, 199–" (*Plot*, 275). One reason for such changes presents itself immediately: *The Inquisitor* takes place in the 1990s immediately after Yeltsin's departure, but by 2004, the events described in the novel have not yet happened.

Another reason for the change is that the events actually *have* happened, but later and not exactly as described. The renewed interest in Norka in the early twenty-first century and the Norka group's increased activity on the Russian op-ed pages has come about because ten years later, *The Inquisitor* basks in the glow of fulfilled prophecy. In the afterword to *The Plot against Russia,* the authors write that, in the past four years, they have been constantly bombarded with a single question: "Is Vladimir Vladimirovich [Putin] the Dark Horse described in the novel?" (749). Their answer is a firm "no," and yet the contrast between Yeltsin and Putin, and the extent to which Putin himself seemed to come out of nowhere, lends *The Inquisitor* a retroactive piquancy that it once lacked. Putin's "dictatorship of the law," his clampdown on the media, the selective prosecution of oligarchs who have incurred his wrath, and even the war on Chechnya are mild in comparison with the Dark Horse's regime, but a novel describing an unknown bureaucrat's rise to power thanks to the machinations of a secret cabal certainly takes on new relevance in the post-Yeltsin era.

Harvard: The Mutant Menace

The Norka group's *Plot against Russia* is probably the most detailed extrapolation of the Harvard Project since Klimov, but it is far from the end of the story. To follow it further, we have to make the "species jump" I alluded to earlier, when conspiracy theory moves from text to multimedia at the dawn of the twenty-first century. What happens when the Harvard Project meets the Internet?

In the blogosphere and on YouTube, the Harvard Project has mutated. If the Harvard Project were a living organism, we would say that it mated with its better-known cousin, the Dulles Plan, and gave birth to the Houston Project, but not before picking up a nasty hereditary bug known as the Golden Billion. I will address Dulles, Houston, and the Golden Billion before circling back to Harvard. But before moving on, I'd like to consider the strange flexibility of the Harvard Project brand, a flexibility that becomes even more ironic when you consider the university's motto: *Veritas*, "Truth."

A Google or YouTube search for "Harvard Project" in Russian yields no shortage of rabbit holes to go down. What becomes clear, however, is that the Harvard Project discussed in the videos contains only a few traces of Klimov's original vision. This is partly because, as current conspiracists often point out, the Harvard Project was a plot to destroy the Soviet Union. Now that Harvard can comfortably fly a "mission accomplished" banner, it would seem that believers should consider it a matter of simple historical record.

The subsequent iterations of the Harvard and Houston Projects will have a built-in confirmation bias: Harvard will be adapted to fit what already happened to the Soviet Union and Russia in the 1990s—or at least, what happened from a quasi-fascist point of view—thereby presenting itself not just as prophecy (Klimov's version) but as prophecy fulfilled. In turn, this means that the parts of the conspiracy dealing with the future (mostly the Houston Project) will appear credible—after all, they're presented along with the Harvard Project, and the Harvard Project turned out to be true!

Once it has left Klimov's hands, the Harvard Project proves to be aptly named: it is an open-ended fantasy of impossible achievement, subject to the same circular logic that reinforces American parents' desperation to get their children into an Ivy League school. Ideally, the Harvard/Houston conspiracy would come with a familiar disclaimer, "Past performance is no guarantee of future results," but that would be contrary to the conspiracist worldview.

If, by the twenty-first century, the Harvard Project had become something of an empty signifier (Klimov didn't age well, even when he was still alive), its content would soon be filled by its far better-known counterpart, the Dulles Plan.

The Dulles Plan: American Information Warfare

That the Dulles Plan would effectively supplant the Harvard Project in the Internet Age is understandable: the Dulles Plan was made for the Internet, even if its makers lived under a regime that registered typewriters as potential threats to public order. The Dulles Plan was a predigital Internet meme, from back in the days when memes had to walk twenty miles in the freezing cold before finding a gullible host to infect. As in the United States, some of these hosts are famous and influential, including the Oscar-winning film director Nikita Mikhalkov.[21] The Dulles Plan owes a clear debt to *The Protocols of the Elders of Zion*, as much for its origin story and its formal qualities as for its content. Like the *Protocols*, the Dulles Plan takes a primitive view of human psychology and assumes a downright slipshod approach to secrecy: evil people know that they are evil, and delight in revealing their evil plans and motivations. And their minutes, bylaws, and vision statements are constantly falling into the wrong hands.

Moreover, the Dulles Plan is the result of a plagiarism even clumsier than that of the *Protocols*. The *Protocols* forgers at least had the decency to steal a source written in a foreign language, but whoever first came up with the Dulles Plan lifted it from one of the most popular novels and films of the Brezhnev era: Anatoly Ivanov's *The Eternal Call* (1971–1976; 1981; adapted for television from 1973 to 1983). One of the villains delivers a speech that, word for word, ends up attributed to former CIA Director Allen Dulles (Ivanov, 513)

Why Allen Dulles? Probably for the same reason that Klimov chose the Harvard Project as his conspiracy's name. Just as Harvard Project proponents often link to the website of the actual study of Soviet life performed by Harvard researchers in the 1950s—an English-language study they can be fairly confident none of their audience will bother to read—Dulles was a notorious cold warrior, coining the term "massive retaliation" in a speech in 1954 and responsible for overseeing US anti-Soviet espionage activities.[22]

The Dulles Plan is relatively short, although it may not feel that way after a paragraph or two, so I offer my own translation into English:

> A tragedy will play out on a grand scale, step by step: the downfall of the most obstreperous nation on earth, the final and irreversible loss of its identity. For example, we will slowly weed out all social significance from its art and literature; we will retrain the artists and writers, drive out the desire to portray and study the processes that take place in the hearts of the popular masses. Literature, theater, and film shall all depict and praise the basest of human feelings.
>
> We will support and promote those so-called artists who will impose and imprint onto human consciousness the cult of sex, violence, sadism, treachery—in a word, IMMORALITY. We will cause chaos and confusion in the state government.
>
> We will quietly, but actively and constantly facilitate bureaucratic despotism and the flourishing of bribery and lack of principle. Bureaucracy and red tape will be held up as a virtue. Honesty and propriety will be mocked, needed by no one, a simple remainder of the past. Impertinence and impudence, lies and deception, drunkenness and drug addiction, animal fear of others and shamelessness, treachery, nationalism, and ethnic animosity—most of all animosity and hatred toward the Russian nation, we will skillfully and quietly cultivate it all, it will all blossom.

And only a few, only a few will guess and even understand what is happening. But we will put these people in a position of helplessness, make a mockery of them, find a way to slander them and declare them the scum of the earth. We will tear up the spiritual roots, vulgarize and destroy the bases of national morality.

Thus we will undermine generation after generation. We will get the people when they are children, youths, and we will bet on YOUTH—we will corrupt, prevent, and degrade it. We will make them cynics, vulgarians, and cosmopolitans.

That is how we'll do it! (Ob"edinenie)

One of the most striking things about the text of the Dulles Plan is its obsession with popular culture. The Dulles Plan is as much media theory as conspiracy theory, a perhaps unintentional example of an outdated model that assumes propaganda works as intended, and that audiences are helpless to resist, a point I explore in more detail in chapter 5). Consistent with Soviet policies that carefully restricted access to media, culture, and information, the Dulles Plan can only make sense if culture is understood in narrow, quasi-biological terms. The Dulles Plan is based on an implicit definition of media and consumer, emphasizing media's nutritional content. While some forms of cultural production are, quite simply, good for you (the classics, for instance), there are others that are not merely innately harmful, but whose entire purpose is moral or ideological harm. The audience, meanwhile, is totally passive.

Compare this with the conspiratorial mania that characterized the Stalin years: certainly, censorship was strict and propaganda was unrelenting, but the crimes of which alleged conspirators were accused were not restricted merely to anti-Soviet agitation.[23] "Wreckers" were sabotaging industrial projects, and spies and internal enemies were engaged in assassinations and attempted murder. The Dulles Plan turns out to be perfect for both the Cold War and its aftermath; violence and subversion are now entirely discursive.

Equally important is the Dulles Plan's focus on youth. By positing nearly all forms of popular youth culture as dangerous—something the plan shares with moral panics throughout the modern world—the Dulles Plan weaponizes the generation gap. Young people are not merely strange and perhaps impertinent, the perennial complaint about "kids today";

they are the victims and perpetuators of warfare against everything the country stands for.

It is the combined focus on media and youth that ensures the Dulles Plan's longevity. The structure of cross-generational misunderstanding can endure even as the content of youth culture changes (as Americans with long enough memories will recall, the evolution of popular music is also the story of successive moral panics, from jazz to rock to hip hop). The generation vilified by the Dulles Plan in its early days is now the generation that could find itself appalled by its own children's culture.

If we borrow the language of Putin's third term, the Dulles Plan is all about values.[24] Thanks to the plan, conspiracy is a culture war. Or, to once again borrow from today's terminology, information war.

Chronicle of a Death Foretold

After the Soviet collapse, the Harvard Project, once its own independent force for xenophobic paranoia, was superseded by the Houston Project. Or, to be more precise, it has been subsumed: annexed, like a disputed discursive peninsula, by a larger, neighboring narrative with quasi-imperial ambitions. For Americans, this produces a peculiar imaginary geography, where Harvard and Houston, two names rarely uttered in the same breath, coexist on opposite sides of a shared border. For the early Putin era, though, this game of topographical Boggle is actually prophetic: ideas (Harvard) are trumped by oil (Houston). Not to mention the fact that Putin's first terms in office coincided with the presidency of a former Texas governor. An imaginary, evil Texas is the perfect straw man to petrify a petrostate.

The Houston Project, while as much a flight of fancy as the *Protocols* or the Dulles Plan, appears to share one of the few saving graces of the Harvard Project: it is not the result of plagiarism. In fact, it seems to be entirely unsourced. Appropriately enough for a digital phenomenon, it may not even have a clearly defined original. The earliest discussions that I've found are based on the reinterpretation of the Harvard Project by General Konstantin Pavlovich Petrov (1945–2009).

After a long career in the military hierarchy, Petrov turned to politics in 1991, when he developed the "Concept for Social Security" (Kontseptsiia obshchestvennoi bezopasnosti), a name whose appeal partly lay in its abbreviation (KOB is reminiscent of Stalin's nickname, Koba). Kicked out of the military in 1995, Petrov turned to neopaganism, assuming the spiritual name "Magus Meragor," though he stuck with the more conventional "Petrov" in his public life.

He took up politics in earnest and, in 2000, founded the "Union" Conceptual Party (Kontseptual'naia partiia "Edinenie" [KPE]), which lasted for seven years. The Union Party's general line consists of familiar Red/Brown paradoxes, particularly the fusion of Stalinism with Russian Orthodox piety (the Russian abbreviation for the Soviet Union, CCCP, is said to stand for "Sviataia sobornaia spravedlivaia Rossiia" (Holy Synodical Just Russia). The party in general and Petrov in particular were fond of a large variety of conspiracy theories and did not hesitate to bring the "truth" to anyone who would listen.

Petrov's death in 2009 at the age of sixty-four gave rise to a whole new set of conspiracy theories about his "murder" (with the CIA naturally being the most likely assassin) (Tal'kovskii). But for our purposes, it is his 2004 audio lectures and their subsequent publication in book form (in 2008) that are of primary importance. In these books and lectures, he establishes his version of the Harvard Project, which quickly gets reinterpreted by conspiracists as the precursor of the Houston Project. Petrov himself refers to Yuri Begunov's 1996 book *Mysterious Forces in Russian History* (Tainye sily v istorii Rossii), but my edition contains only three mentions of Harvard, all of them relatively benign.

Instead, Petrov simply informs us that Soviet Intelligence in the early 1980s managed to get its hands on the so-called Harvard Project, which consists of three volumes: *Perestroika*, *Reform*, and *Culmination*.[25] *Perestroika* is more or less what one might expect: a reinterpretation of Gorbachev's reign as the fulfillment of the CIA's evil plans for the Soviet Union's downfall. *Reform* conveniently assumes that a new leader takes power; this man's job is to liquidate the Soviet Union, the Communist Party, the Red Army, the global socialist system, and, of course, socialist consciousness. *Culmination* is a bit more novel: it involves the genocide of the Russian people in order to free up the country's resources and make room for the rest of the world's population.

It is this last part that gets rebranded as the Houston Project. Searching for the "Houston Project" reminds us of the beauty and complexity of conspiracy as a viral Internet phenomenon: no one really owns it. As a result, its manifestations and elaborations vary wildly. For sheer entertainment value the best source is also one of the most idiosyncratic: a two-part documentary titled *Intervention: The Harvard-Houston Project* (Interventsiia. Garvardsko-khiustonskii proekt) Though it was produced by "Svyatyna Works with the participation of the United Slavic Front" (Ob"edinennyi slavianskii front), a closer examination of the Internet sources suggest that the "Front" consists primarily of Ukrainian-based Andrei Svyatyna, whose personal website offers legal services at reasonable rates and virulent antisemitism for free.

Part of the beauty of *Intervention* is that of the Grand Conspiracy at its purest, throwing in everything but the kitchen sink. Over the course of three hours, we hear about US funding for the Orange Revolution, the CIA's assassination of General Petrov, the State Department's appropriation of Gene Sharp's writings about popular resistance in order to foment color revolutions, the Rockefellers, microchips, Hitler's rise to power as part of Jewish capital's plot for Slavic genocide and the creation of the state of Israel, and the current situation in Ukraine.

But reducing *Intervention* to its content would be a shame, since the other part of the film's appeal is that, aesthetically, it embraces randomness to the point of insanity. *Intervention* is available on YouTube, but I have provided a different link because YouTube shows the film without sound due to copyright violation. It is difficult to tell exactly which media company complained to YouTube, because stolen audio material is the film's dominant artistic principle. After several minutes of apparently irrelevant martial arts footage and a long discourse on Japan, *Intervention* spends a significant chunk of time showing a nearly black screen with two audio soundtracks, one in English, one in Russian, and both taken from the film *Avatar*. Later the producers employ the *X-Files* theme song, followed by a clip from *The Matrix*. Perhaps the best moment of theft comes in the second part, when we hear a man's voice reading aloud a segment of the Houston Project about the use of rock music and the "propaganda" of sex to corrupt young people and destroy all national pride. He is accompanied by an instrumental version of "Feelings."

Certainly, the creative choices made by Svyatyna Works are specific to *Intervention*, but the eclecticism motivating them is not. This is why discussing the various grand conspiracies to destroy Russia (Harvard, Dulles, and Houston being just the most noteworthy) in isolation is pointless. Each individual conspiratorial tract is an attempt at a grand, systemic edifice, but internal coherence and distinction from possibly competing theories is not the point. Quite the contrary: within a broad discursive framework, such as plots to destroy Russia, there is no such thing as a competing theory. It is all true.

And now we can move on to Houston.

Selling Russia: Retail, or Wholesale?

Compared to the Houston Project, both Harvard and Dulles look like underachievers. It is with the Houston Project, as elaborated by General Petrov and his many imitators, that conspiracists really start thinking big. Harvard and Dulles confirm my earlier point about the apocalypse as local event: the end of Russia may as well be the end of the world, if you live in Russia. The Houston Plan loops around to global annihilation while never losing sight of the centrality of Russia.

The Houston Plan goes back to the conspiratorial well (no, not anti-semitism; that particular poisoned well was already tapped out by the Harvard Project): the cabal of multinational schemers who *really* run the world. The renewed emphasis on the cabal is the result of a Western import. By the beginning of the twenty-first century, many of the more popular English-language conspiratorial tracts have been translated and published in Russia. John Coleman's *Conspirator's Hierarchy: The Committee of 300* is repeatedly referenced in Houston and Houston-adjacent conspiratorial writings; as the title suggests, it describes the machinations of our true overlords. Many of Coleman's tropes were then picked up by RT/Russia Today, the Russian English-language television channel that has provided a home for the lunatic fringe.

Thus Russian conspirators and Western conspirators end up speaking the same language, constantly referring to the Trilateral Commission, the Council on Foreign Relations, and the Bilderberg Group. The Bilderberg Group is an elite club whose secrecy has sparked a predictable set of claims as to their true activity, and whose leaders (the "Olympians") are conspiring to corrupt the world's youth along the lines laid out in both the *Protocols* and the Dulles Plan.

The Houston Project is predicated on one of the obsessions of post-Soviet political culture: the fate of Russia's natural riches. The project's plan to destroy Russia as a state by dismembering it into dozens of tiny statelets is, at first glance, nothing more than a resource grab, supported by numerous fictitious quotations by Western leaders. Since 2006, the Russian media and blogosphere have been claiming that former Secretary of State Madeleine Albright lamented the injustice of Russia's share of the world's oil and mineral wealth (Siberia should therefore be under international control).

Albright herself has denied saying any such thing, while Putin has managed to have it both ways: "I'm not familiar with this quote by Madame Albright, but I know that such thoughts wander through the minds of certain politicians" (as quoted in Smolchenko). This fake quotation is part of a perfect feedback loop, reinforcing both the rapaciousness of Americans—particularly the Clinton administration, responsible for the bombings in Serbia—and the greatness of Russia itself. And its way was paved by the Houston Project.

For the Houston Project, the expropriation of Russian resources is only the beginning. The real goal of Western conspirators is far more evil, as well as a much more primal threat to blood-and-soil notions of Russian identity. The Houston Project makes literal one of the primary metaphors of national betrayal: that Russia is being bought and sold. Now the truth comes out: the West is plotting to take the Russian land itself. Why?

The Last Resort Property

It seems the West wants to move to Russia. It turns out that Moscow isn't just the Fourth Rome; soon, all of Russia will become the next Mt. Ararat (even though the first one is practically a neighbor). When the rest of the world succumbs to ecological catastrophe, only Russia will remain habitable. This scenario is the result of yet another mutation in Russian conspiracy theory. Just as the Houston Project is packaged as the next, more detailed iteration of the Harvard Project, its detail is drawn from yet another set of sources. Much of the content of the Houston Project is filled by the growing lore accruing to a powerful local, Russian conspiracy called the Golden Billion (*Zolotoi milliard*).

First put forth by A. Kuzmich (the pen name of Anatolii Kuz'mich Tsi-kunov) in a book called *The World Government Conspiracy: Russia and the Golden Billion* (Zagovor mirovogo pravitel'stva: Rossiia i "zolotoi milliard," 1994), the Golden Billion was quickly popularized by the pro-lific Sergei Kara-Murza and has become a staple of contemporary Russian conspiratorial thought (Kara-Murza, chapter 18). The Golden Billion rep-resents a real change in the Dulles/Harvard rhetoric of conspiracy, in that it is based less on (bad) social science than it is on (bad) natural science.

In a refreshing change from what is familiar to followers of American conspiracy and right-wing discourse, the Golden Billion takes the prospect of ecological change seriously. So seriously, in fact, that most of the plans of the "world government" are predicated on looming global disaster. The coming cataclysm is not just a matter of climate change or even the depletion of fossil fuels; the Golden Billion is a nightmare vision of over-population. The Golden Billion weaponizes Malthusianism. The "billion" in "Golden Billion" refers to an imagined, ideal population for a sustain-able planet; the "Golden" part describe the class dynamics on which the conspiracy is built. The developed world is maneuvering to a point where one billion people, the wealthier people from the wealthiest part of the globe, populate the planet. It is not the meek but the rich who shall inherit the earth—which makes some sense, since they have the most experience with inheritance.

The Golden Billion also confirms the Russocentrism I posited in the previous chapter. If the only inhabitable territory left on the globe were in, say, Africa or Australia, the theory would be far less compelling. Rus-sia would be destroyed, but only as part of a larger story of calamity. The Golden Billion tells the opposite story: it is the God-given right of Russia to survive the apocalypse, but the West is conspiring to steal Russia's very destiny. Here the power and desirability of the Russian land are reinforced precisely by the covetousness of the enemy, and the struggle against this plot can be yet another heroic tale of the defense of Russia from invasion.

The Golden Billion gathers together many of the most important tropes of benighted, post-Soviet Russia—the need to defend the country's natu-ral resources from a rapacious West, the West's demoralization of Rus-sia's youth, destruction of Russia's economy, and destruction of public health—into one compelling narrative, a story combining historical touch-stones such as the Great Patriotic War with science and pseudoscience.

It also builds on and sustains the hostility toward population control encountered throughout the Russian media in the Putin era, in which the distribution of condoms is a clever Western plot to bring down Russian birth rates. This idea is often reinforced by an unsourced but frequently repeated quote from Margaret Thatcher that "Russians should be reduced to fifteen million" (from a population ten times that size). All of this can be summed up in a phrase that is common to Russian extremist discourse and made more mainstream by the conflict in Ukraine: "The genocide of the Russian people."[26]

It is also time to state the obvious: the Harvard Project, the Dulles Plan, the Houston Project, and the Golden Billion make sense only if you assume a widespread, deep-rooted hatred for Russia and the Russian people that goes beyond the vagaries of contemporary politics. We must reckon with the specter that, if it is not haunting Europe, certainly haunts Russia: the specter of Russophobia.

3

Lost Horizons

Russophobia, Sovereignty, and the Politics of Identity

> Bards of the Nations, say, what set you seething,
> Threats of Anathema at Russia breathing?
> — Alexander Pushkin, "To the Slanderers of Russia"

From Russophobia, with Love

Who are the enemies of Russia? Who is it that hates Russia so much, and why? This is not an idle question; in August 2016, the Russian Ministry of Culture allocated 1.75 million rubles for a study of "technologies of cultural Russophobia and state-administrational responses to this challenge" ("Russian Government"). Moreover, any news story alleging misdeeds on the part of the Russian government is sure to be followed by its dismissal as "Russophobia." Russophobia may or may not be on the rise, but the fight against it is definitely picking up speed.

In positing a set of external and internal forces that are inherently hostile to Russia by default, Russophobia, which will be defined and discussed at length below, as a concept has become key to the discourse of Russian statehood and identity. To invoke Russophobia is to rally the population against an implacable enemy while reminding that same population of its collective identity. One might even be tempted to call it a variation on identity politics, were the term not so fraught as to make "Russophobia" appear simple and neutral. Moreover, "identity politics" would imply a stronger ethnic component than is actually warranted, for Russophobia deftly balances nationalist impulses (i.e., the concerns of ethnic Russians) with the multiethnic (possibly, but by no means necessarily, imperial) reality of the Russian Federation. Russophobia becomes important as part of the national renegotiation of the country's selfhood in the wake of the Soviet Union's destruction, part of the forces that threaten the fetishized sovereignty of the Putin era.

The concept would seem to be straightforward: those who argue that Russia's critics are guilty of Russophobia insist that a fundamental, irrational hatred toward Russia itself is the prime motivator. But accusations of Russophobia do not exist in a vacuum: they express at least as much about the accuser as the accused. Russophobia presupposes Russia as a victim of hostile forces, often conspiring against the motherland out of a desire for domination, destruction, or destabilization. These narratives of Russian victimhood play out within the Manichaean, melodramatic framework of the large-scale conspiracy theories discussed in the previous chapter. Besides the obvious political utility of reflexively deflecting blame for anything with which the Russian state or government might be faulted, the narratives also do important ontological work, establishing a relationship between self and other that starts to look suspiciously like a kind of mirroring. Consider Channel One's response to the news that the Russian double agent Sergei Skripal may have been poisoned by Russian agents in England. The channel's director, Dmitry Kiselyov, labeled London a "death trap for Russians" and speculated: "If you think hard about it, only Britain stands to benefit from the poisoning of the GRU colonel. Simply to nourish its Russophobia" ("Britain Poisoned"). The discourse of Russophobia locks Russia into a dyad with the perceived enemy, displacing actions and attributed initially to one party as a shared characteristic of both. This sharing is not simultaneous but rather a time-share: the accusation is passed back and forth like a football.

In structure, the discourse of Russophobia resembles a narcissistic self-regard, manifesting a preoccupation with how Russia "looks" from an imagined external view. The presumption of hostility, rather than tearing down a sense of Russian greatness, reinforces it, using external animosity as a gauge of importance. In the last chapter, we saw how so many of the large-scale Russian conspiracy theories presumed the country's central place in world history, thereby justifying the need for so many plots against it. As we look closer at the resurgence of the Russophobia discourse in the wake of the Soviet collapse, we see how closely tied it is to a sense of Russia's existential precarity. In part as a response to the chaos of the 1990s, the culture of the Putin era is preoccupied with rectifying the problem of Russia's "object impermanence": years of entertaining the possibility of Russia's total destruction have been remedied by the continued reassertion of Russia's existence and its centrality on the world stage. And here the discourse of Russophobia has been crucial.

What Isn't Russophobia?

Like so many marginalized ideas, Russophobia has moved from the fringes to the mainstream since Putin came to power. Though the term has a long history (dating back at least to a letter by the Russian poet Fyodor Tyutchev in 1867), it began to gain currency only in the 1980s, thanks to the work of Igor Shafarevich (Mettan, 39). This is not to say that the phenomenon Russophobia purports to describe did not exist before the term was coined; quite to the contrary, Russophobia follows a path parallel to homophobia, or at least to homosexuality. Just as homosexual acts clearly occurred before the invention of the modern homosexual at the turn of the last century, the idea of anti-Russian sentiment gains discursive power only when the term becomes available. The word "Russophobia" inevitably forms and deforms the contours of the debate about hostility to Russia. Accusing someone of hating Russia and charging them with Russophobia appear to be the same thing but function quite differently.

The slipperiness of the word is a function of the vagueness of its referent: just what, exactly, is the object of the "phobia"? Is it Russia, or ethnic Russians? If it's Russia, then the term belongs more to geopolitics; if it's ethnic Russians, then we are dealing with xenophobia or racism. The confusion is part of the larger question of Russian-related nomenclature in the Russian language: Russian provides two terms for "Russian," one derived from ancient Rus' (*russkii*), the other from modern Rossiia (*rossiiskii/rossiianin*).[1] The second term is more bureaucratic, but it reflects the reality of the Russian Federation as a multiethnic state whose majority ethnicity is Russian. Thus one can be "from Russia" (*rossiianin*) but not ethnically Russian (*russkii*). Or, if you are an ethnic Russian living in, say, Estonia, you might be *russkii* but not "from Russia" or a "Russian citizen" (*rossiianin*). But whenever we are dealing with questions of culture, *russkii* is still the adjective of choice. The "Russian World" (*russkii mir*), Putin's recent emphasis on a common Russian cultural space, may smack of cultural imperialism, but it would be both more threatening and more confusing if it were *rossiiskii mir*, stressing the geographic entity and the state rather than the language and the culture.

Given the current Russian emphasis on "traditional values," there is something supremely satisfying about the fact that "Russophobia" looks like a homology of "homophobia." The "phobia" part of "homophobia" presumes that anti-LGBT animus is based primarily on fear (rather than on, say, moral outrage or disgust) and suggests a connection to a fear of the "homo" within oneself.[2] While Russophobia can have a strong component of self-hatred as part of internal Russian debates, it's a safe bet that foreign hostility toward Russia or Russians is not rooted in an anxiety about latent Russianness.

If there is any connection between Russophobia and homophobia currently, it would be that the two concepts function as implicit opposites in contemporary Russian discourse. Homosexuality, framed as both a foreign infection and the result of "gay propaganda" and predation, is a failure in the proper traditions and patriotic education of youth; it is a defect of Russianness. By contrast, Russianness is something essential and unconstructed, a transcendent value that is as much a matter of metaphysics as of genetics and language. And yet Russianness, like heterosexuality, is posited as fragile: always under attack by Russophobic forces, it can be subverted and suppressed through the promotion of foreign values and liberal propaganda. As the popular nationalist saying goes, "Russians aren't born; Russians are made" (*russkimi ne rozhdaiutsia, russkimi stanoviatsia*). No one, apparently, is "born this way."

Assessing the validity of Russophobia, whether as an overall concept or as an accusation regarding discrete incidents, is a minefield, since there is no way to occupy a secure position. My status as an outside observer is something I wrestle with throughout this book, precisely because of the real danger of oversimplifying or orientalizing Russia. Certainly, the last thing I want to do is to reduce Russia to some sort of basic essence; quite the contrary, most of the (Russian) ideas I critique are themselves examples of essentialism.

Yet there is something distasteful about an outsider dismissing someone else's claim of discrimination, belittlement, or hostility as simply the product of an overactive imagination. Majority status does not grant automatic neutrality; instead, it accords the privilege of erroneously assuming one's position is universal, a privilege that operates most effectively when it is never subject to question. The problem is mistaking privilege for neutrality.

The key here is the question of personal experience and its relevance to claims of Russophobia. When Russophobia is deployed in either the English-language or Russian-language media, it rarely refers to the personal. That is to say, while there are no doubt many instances when people identified as Russian are treated badly by non-Russians, these have not played a large part in Russophobia discourse (with the status of ethnic Russians in the Baltic countries and Ukraine being the obvious, glaring exception). This imaginary scenario also exposes the weakness of Russophobia as personalized discrimination against Russians outside of Russia, since it has nothing to do with what Russians consider Russian ethnicity. Outside of Russia and Russia's traditional sphere of influence, it is highly unlikely that the distinction between an ethnic Russian and a Russian-speaking Jew or a Russian-speaking ethnic German would be at all comprehensible. We don't know enough to be properly bigoted.[3]

While we have yet to reckon with Russophobia as it plays out discursively within Russia's borders, it is clear that the term's deployment in relation to Western countries is far less about the personal experience of discrimination (this is also how Russophobia differs from Islamophobia, which attaches as much to individuals as it does to a religion). This does not mean that this sort of bias is absent, but simply that it is not what we are talking about when we talk about Russophobia. Instead, the victim of Russophobia is usually construed not as Russians but as Russia itself. The offended party is the state.

If we accept the increasingly common emphasis on statehood and sovereignty in contemporary Russian discourse, then perhaps viewing "the state" as an abstract, impersonal idea immune to offense is, in itself, Russophobic. That is, if more and more Russians identify proudly with the state, then shouldn't their pride be just as respected as the more personal sensitivities associated with race? This is not a position I can comfortably adopt, even if its rejection is difficult without invoking the old Marxist accusation of "false consciousness." There has to be room to see the state as a political actor whose choices are subject to rational critique. We can get a better handle on Russophobia if we remove it from the set of terms it resembles etymologically (such as homophobia) and see it in a more familiar context of geopolitics. Russophobia makes sense when compared to anti-Americanism.

Since the term has been with us for so long, there is a much richer literature available on anti-Americanism than there is on Russophobia.[4] This does not mean that anti-Americanism is any less problematic than Russophobia, but rather that the two phenomena share many of the same deficiencies. Moreover, as Max Paul Friedman convincingly elaborates, anti-Americanism's prominence during the Cold War cannot (and should not) be disentangled from the Cold War adversary. The very existence of the Soviet Union made charges of anti-Americanism all the more potent, since the same people who were comfortable throwing the term around were equally at home in the Cold War's schematic, binary worldview.

Like Russophobia, anti-Americanism could conceivably target the country and its policies, or simply Americans as a particular type. Unlike Russophobia, however, anti-Americanism rarely refers to individuals and their foibles. Where Oleg Nemenskii distinguishes between "everyday" (*bytovaia*) Russophobia and "ideological" (*ideologicheskaia*) Russophobia, anti-Americanism has little need of this distinction. Instead, charges of anti-Americanism assume the same identity between the country and its government's policies that characterize accusations of Russophobia. Internally, then, both anti-Americanism and Russophobia are construed as disloyalty or lack of patriotism, while externally, they substitute an emotional or ideological hatred for actual evaluation of a given policy or action.

Whatever one might think of the idea of anti-Americanism, it is a term that has proven vigorous and adaptable over a long period of time. The Russian counterpart is more complicated, since "Russophobia" could never have been an adequate term during the Cold War, even if we allow for the common Western confusion of the Soviet Union with "Russia," technically only one of fifteen constituent republics. For Western cold warriors, the enemy was communism itself. Within the Soviet Union, opposition was "anti-Soviet" rather than "Russophobic"—and unlike anti-Americanism in the United States, "anti-Soviet activity" was recognized as a crime by the Soviet legal code. The reintroduction of "Russophobia" by Igor Shafarevich was well-timed, since it reconfigured foreign hostility for an eventual post-Soviet era while accounting for interethnic rivalry in the Soviet and post-Soviet space.

As the Soviet Union fades into memory (a memory increasingly rose-tinged with nostalgia), the ideological distinction between anti-Sovietism as a manifestation of anticommunism and Russophobia fades with it. This allows contemporary conspiracy theorists and Russian nationalists to see Western anti-Sovietism as nothing more than disguised Russophobia. Throw in some poorly digested historical factoids and Russia, rather than the Soviet Union, is the object of twentieth-century Western animosity.[5]

Indeed, it is the demise of the Soviet Union, which both was and was not Russia, that makes Russophobia such a compelling idea. Though Russophobia would not be routinely invoked by politicians and pundits in the 1990s, the first post-Soviet decade laid the groundwork for the concept's postmillennial appeal. The role of the 1990s is crucial: first, its experience and subsequent discursive construction as an era of total collapse inevitably led to a search for the culprits behind Russian misery; second, the ongoing sense of collapse often manifested itself in representations of a "lost," "vanishing," "weak" Russia whose connection to Russophobia is explored below; and, finally, the chaos of the 1990s became the cornerstone of specifically post-Soviet conspiracy theories, nearly all of which will find in Russophobia an easy framework. To understand the key role that Russophobia would play in the political discourse of Putin's third term, though, we need to step back a bit and examine the evolving ideological context of post-Soviet Russia.

Ten Years That Shook the World

The 1990s are the first of three phases of ideological restructuring in the post-Soviet era: here ideology recedes while conspiracy theories multiply on the margins. Next comes the era of Sovereign Democracy, roughly coextensive with Putin's first two presidential terms. Now conspiratorial structures of thought come to greater prominence, but in a context that minimizes ideology. Finally comes Putin's third term, when the conspiratorial structures of Sovereign Democracy are filled with explicit, allegorically inflected ideological content. In each of these phases, the place of conspiracy and allegorical thinking shifts significantly, as does the place where one can most easily find the expression of conspiratorial thought. Appeals to Russophobia increased over the course of these three phases.

The only thing that united the discursive landscape of Russia in the 1990s was the common perception that Russia had reached a truly terrible state of affairs. It is this cultural logic of pessimism to which I devoted most of my previous book, *Overkill*: Russia was the train wreck that compelled all eyes to stare at it. To the extent that a common Russia narrative existed, it was one of downfall. But the culture had not developed a unifying story to tell itself about the ruins of the USSR.

Yet this lack of a metanarrative, while lamentable to so many, was also intellectually and artistically liberating. From the outside, the collapse of the allegorical imperative looks very much like what Westerners expect when discussing liberalism and pluralism: various new or revived narratives were competing for primacy in a market of ideas that was so open as to be practically devastated. The very notion of a "free market" of meanings, especially one so heavily influenced by Western imports (be they translations of cultural theorists, the ubiquitous Western advisers, or even the trashy movies and shows that filled the television schedule), could be interpreted as the erasure of anything distinctly Russian, not to mention a revival of an ideological malaise to which Russians first gave a name: nihilism. Nihilism and self-determination as to the meaning of one's life can easily be confused. By no means did life have to be meaningless, but, in a strange, implicit cross between the Protestant ethic and French existentialism, if you wanted meaning, you had to work it out for yourself. Those who expressed anxiety over the lack of a unifying idea reflected a deep discomfort with this state of affairs: it was not enough for people to find meaning for themselves; meaning was only meaningful if it was for *everybody*.

Hence one of the developments that, with the benefit of hindsight, proved to be crucial for the subsequent emergency of Putinist Russia:

the state's growing intolerance of religious pluralism. The collapse of the
USSR did not immediately lead to a wide-scale embrace of the Russian
Orthodox Church (ROC). Instead, missionaries for a whole range of Protestant denominations and new religious movements (NRMs, more commonly called "cults" in English and "sects" in Russian), competed for
post-Soviet hearts and minds. A series of panics about so-called "destruc-
tive" or "totalitarian" sects—particularly the Great White Brotherhood of
Maria Devi Khristos in 1994 and Aum Shinrikyo, a group that had been
very active in Russia before its 1995 sarin gas attack on the Tokyo subway
system—exacerbated by the sensationalist media and active opposition on
the part of representatives of the ROC, would justify increasingly harsh
strictures on "foreign" religious activity.[6] In 1997, the Duma passed the
Law on Freedom of Conscience and Religious Associations, which officially recognized Russian Orthodoxy, Judaism, Islam, and Buddhism as
traditional religions and required all other religious organizations to go
through a registration process that became increasingly onerous over the
years.[7]

Falling far short of an official establishment of the ROC as a state
church, the law nonetheless represented a significant narrowing of the
religious field. By the same token, it was in the 1990s that a variety of
relatively secular Russia narratives would compete with each other, particularly the various conspiracy theories that are the subject of chapter 2.
All of them treated the ideological fluidity of the 1990s as a problem to be
solved. As we shall see, each offered its own allegorical reading of Russia's
history and fate, and each either predicted or advocated the resolution of
the country's cultural crisis through the institution of a strong, centralized
leadership with a single ideology. While these trends were visible enough
in the 1990s, they are simply obvious in 2018, thanks to the retrospective
narrative that began in Putin's first term: the 1990s have become the terrible time of troubles from which only Putin could save Russia. Nearly a
generation later, the 1990s are no longer simply a decade. They are a story,
a shorthand explanatory device.

The demonization of the 1990s can be found in the culture almost
at random. Let's take as our example the bestselling novelist Polina
Dashkova's 2004 novel *The Prize*—a thriller involving talk shows, international espionage, Russian neo-Nazis, and, of course, cold-blooded
murder. In this scene, a former KGB officer-turned CIA agent-turned

FSB informant is listening to a slightly stoned, gay ex-East German spy-turned-avant-garde impresario:

> With baited breath, Germans followed the spectacular trials of predators and vampires. The newspapers described the murders in the most horrible detail. Cruelty became a kind of national narcotic. Everything strange, perverted, and pathological was hailed, while everything normal and healthy was declared dull and boring. Doesn't this remind you of something? Germany after WWI and Russia after the collapse of the USSR are as alike as sisters.

To which the KGB/CIA/FSB agent replies:

> In the early 90s, yes, everything in Russia was bad . . . but now a kind of stability has taken hold. [. . .] And anyway, I'm sick of all this talk about Russian nightmares, frankly. For seventy years of Soviet power, Russians were told about the decay of Western society: rampant unemployment, drug addiction, prostitution. People are shooting each other on the streets, and everything is run by the Mafia. [. . .] For the past fifteen years the Western media have been saying the same thing about Russia. And Western society believes it, with a moronic earnestness. (Dashkova, chapter 11)

Here Dashkova is exploring the pitfalls of facile historical parallels even as she indulges in them (the novel is held together by connections between Nazi Germany and Russian neofascism that are as mystical as they are political). Dashkova's example suggests a preoccupation with a real-time periodization of Russian history and culture, a periodization on the fly. Dashkova's character attempts to understand the present moment not only in its immediate context, both past and future, but also in terms of historical parallels that are tantamount to value judgments. In addition, Dashkova's fed-up spy makes the connection between the "reality" of the miserable 1990s and the West's never-ending delight in portraying a weak, chaotic Russia.

The Yeltsin era, both during the 1990s and in the Putin/Medvedev years that followed, has served as a particularly effective caricature of "Russia on the brink." Here I have in mind not the real, lived experiences of people who lost their jobs, saw their savings vanish, or became the victims or perpetrators of violent crime and sexual trafficking. By no means do I wish to minimize their suffering, but, as I find myself saying again and again, this is not their story. Rather, it is the story of their story, the story of their representation. Note that Dashkova's pot-smoking ex-spy deploys them only within the context of a double story: first, that of social decay in Germany, itself a set of generalized ills to be invoked rather than a collection of specific examples; and second, the equivalent phenomena in "Russia today." Indeed, historical comparisons and fears of incipient fascism aside, and the assemblage of social ills as a list of usual suspects appears to be a continuation of what Nancy Ries identifies as a fundamental perestroika-era speech genre: the litany (83–85).

The demonization of an entire decade is the temporal cornerstone of Putinism, and it is one that was so often prefigured during the 1990s themselves that the period's rejection looks almost like a foregone conclusion. Thriller after thriller (most notably Norka's *Inquisitor* novels) postulates that the only possible solution to criminal lawlessness is government lawlessness: state bespredel. In *Overkill*, I am at great pains to emphasize that the discourse of lawlessness, criminality, and ultraviolence summed up in the Russian term *bespredel*, though experienced by many as reality, should not be seen as coterminous with reality (214–24). But in the Putin/Medvedev years, it is as though the vast array of horrifying products of the media/culture industry have, in a deliberately naive reading, *become* the reality of the 1990s now that the decade is no longer with us. What was discursive is now true: the country was on the verge of total collapse. Just as liberals during perestroika would repeatedly invoke the specter of stagnation in response to any challenge to reforms, Putinists parry any critique of their system by reminding the public just how bad things were under Yeltsin, and how the danger of collapse still remains. In the runup to the recent presidential elections, the filmmaker Nikita Mikhalkov served as Putin's proxy in a televised presidential debate with Irina Prokhorova, the proxy for her brother Mikhail. When Prokhorova tried to make the case for her brother's candidacy and highlight the flaws of Putin's regime, Mikhalkov responded with categorical assertions about the fate of Russia itself: for Mikhalkov, the choice was between Putin and the collapse of Russia (Mavronchik). Weeks later, during his teary-eyed victory speech on election night, Putin himself declared: "We showed that our people can distinguish between the desire for renewal and a political provocation that has only one goal: to destroy Russian statehood and usurp power" (Flintoff).

From this viewpoint, Putinism is the only hedge against bespredel. Literally meaning "without limits," *bespredel* as a lexical item follows the same trajectory as the phenomenon it purports to describe: initially localized to the criminal world, where it signified criminal practices that violate the norms of "lawful" criminality, by the mid-1990s it had taken on political significance. That is, the term itself recognizes no limits to its possible applicability. It has become the black hole of Russian symbolic geography, a vision of Russia in which all borders (literal, behavioral, symbolic) are always approaching collapse but never quite reaching it—ironically, like a logarithm never reaching its limit, that is, its border. Nor can one forget that bespredel's supposed threat to the nation unfolds against the backdrop of the repeated border violations and erasures that constituted the collapse of the USSR, in Putin's words, the greatest tragedy of the twentieth century—or one of the greatest. As former Soviet citizens were confronted by the transformation of the largely notional internal borders of the USSR into the bureaucratic obstacles to mobility that true borders constitute, the 1990s saw a proliferation of alternative imaginary geographies to compensate for the grievous loss of a great superpower: the Commonwealth of Independent States (CIS), the ruble zone, the near abroad, the common cultural space, and the Russian abroad, not to mention the revival of words that had previously been the near-exclusive domain of specialists such as *rossiianin* and *russkoiazychnyi* (Russian-speaking).

The Russia We Can't Find

Meanwhile, Russia itself seemed to be undergoing a strange drama of object impermanence: endless riffs on the sensational perestroika film title *The Russia We Have Lost* (Rossiia, kotoroiu my poteriali), along with repeated invocations of *gibel'*, *krakh*, and *konets Rossii* (the demise, downfall, and end of Russia), played themselves out in headlines, pamphlets, and apocalyptic books. At the same time in the United States, factions in and around the State Department pointed fingers at each other, trying to resolve the burning question, "Who lost Russia?" It might seem like a cheap shot to take this question literally and respond that the country is still there, taking up prime Eurasian real estate, but the question of this "lost" or nearly lost Russia sets the scene for the symbolic geography of the following decade. It is as though the first two decades after the collapse of the USSR have been an elaborate variation on Freud's famous *fort-da* game.

For it is more than an appeal to patriotism and boosterism that explains the insistent repetitions of the country's name in post-Soviet political movements; among the parties that have come and gone in the last two decades one finds The Democratic Party of Russia, The Russian Ecological "Green" Party, The United Socialist Party of Russia, The Russian Party of Retirees, The Russian Party of Life, The Agrarian Party of Russia, Our Home Is Russia, The Fatherland/All Russia, and of course United Russia. In the case of the Greens and the Democrats, one can concede the need to distinguish Russia's homegrown version from the many parties throughout the globe that bear the same name, although the chances that anyone would have thought they were voting for German Greens or American Democrats in Russian elections must be slim. Victor Chernomyrdin's defunct Our Home Is Russia party has the distinction of being more than a name: it's an entire sentence, and a declaration of the patently obvious (any plans to pick up stakes and move the population to, say, Spain would have been impractical). But Our Home Is Russia proves to be the deep structure to nearly all these party titles, precisely because of its ambiguous status as a speech act. On the surface, it is an entirely constative statement, the patriotic equivalent of that favorite example of English-speaking linguists, "the cat is on the mat": it is either true or false. But the very banality of the phrase *Nash dom—Rossiia* as a truth statement suggests that its greater locutionary value is as a performative utterance. But what does it perform? It performs the circular function of (re)affirming the country's existence and the population's residency in it. It does what nearly all these Russia-affirming parties' names do: provide an opportunity to say the country's name and thereby, once again, confirm its existence. More than merely patriotic, these party names are *phatic*. And in some cases, they are also deliberately proleptic, as if they are trying to call into existence a desired state of affairs, as in an incantation or magic spell. Nearly all the parties I have listed merged with each other or swallowed each other up, becoming the ruling party whose name is the antithesis (and perhaps antidote) to the post-Soviet anxieties over a lost or fractured Russia: United Russia.

It is here that any considerations of post-Soviet symbolic geography threaten to collapse, due to a conflict of terms from overlapping traditions. Symbolic geography suggests the ways in which geographical notions and conventions create a discourse about the country that is eventually unmoored from actual physical geography. When we look at the names of these Russian parties, in the context of a decades-long discourse of Russian loss, they appear in Lacanian terms to be an Imaginary solution to a Symbolic problem. These are Russias whose primary function is the assertion of an identity, rather than a framework for understanding what that identity might signify. It doesn't matter what Russia is, but whatever it is, it is whole, integral, and extant. These are Russias that are not up for discussion, only for affirmation. We have not yet reached the heights of self-defensiveness obtained by the state media's subsequent insistence on the threat of Russophobia, but we have arrived at a key contributor to the embrace of Russophobia-as-threat: the truly existential terror represented by what we might call "Un-Russophobia"—the fear that Russia itself is on the verge of disappearing.

These imaginary Russias are short-term remedies that both facilitate and result from an equally imaginary model of sovereignty. Sovereignty and its close cousin, statehood (*gosudarstvennost'*), are the lens through which the Putin regime looks at Russia, a framework that suggests a particular set of solutions. "Sovereignty" is something of a curse word in contemporary cultural studies, uttered with a venom surpassed only by that accompanying the word "neoliberal." Sovereignty and statehood are an imaginary, rather than a symbolic, geography: they confuse the social constructs of borders and citizenship with the prediscursive world on which they are built. For example, Peter Nyers, in his intriguing study *Rethinking Refugees: Beyond States of Emergency*, argues that the refugee exists only as a function of state sovereignty: in the absence of a border/citizenship regime, refugee status is irrelevant and unthinkable (3–4). The modern nation state assumes sovereignty as a matter of course, but Russia (which, you may recall, we had lost), would make sovereignty something of a fetish object.

It is, of course, an accident of history that Putin's turn to sovereignty as a substitute for an idea should coincide with the Western academic Left's rediscovery of sovereignty as a bête noire. Scholars in cultural studies have had their attention turned to sovereignty largely by the work of Giorgio

Agamben, whose books *Homo Sacer* and *The State of Exception* build on Foucault's ideas of biopolitics as a way to define precisely how the sovereign state operates. Central to his critique is his use of Carl Schmitt's definition of sovereignty as the power to declare the state of exception (that is, to suspend the rules that supposedly constitute power) and to distinguish between "civic" or "qualified" life (the Greek *zoe,* here the political life of the citizen) and *bios* ("bare" life, the human being as nothing but a living body). The modern state has become particularly preoccupied with the deployment of bodies, from the Nazi concentration camps at one extreme to the seemingly innocuous collection of biometric data on the other, thus making "bare life" a central component of the state's operations. While there is no doubt that the sovereign state under Putin exerts its biopower in multiple fashions, army conscription being an obvious one, Putin's notion of sovereignty was curiously divorced from sovereign operations on the population. Instead, we have a kind of "bare sovereignty," which might just as well be termed "phatic sovereignty," "autochthonous sovereignty," or even "performative sovereignty": sovereignty whose entire purpose is sovereignty itself. Instead of a state ideology, as in the USSR, there is an ideology of statehood. Again, this approach to sovereignty belongs, in Lacanian terms, to the Imaginary Order. This is not a cultural space to be discussed, articulated, or contested: for Putin, it is the country's Ego Ideal.

Bare Sovereignty: Ideology's Event Horizon

This was made crystal clear in 2006 by Vladislav Surkov, then Putin's deputy chief of staff, subsequently personal adviser to Putin, and always gray cardinal. In a February 2006 speech to United Russia's Center of Party Training and Cadre Preparation, Surkov acknowledges the belief that globalization renders sovereignty increasingly obsolete, only to reject the idea in the strongest terms. Globalization threatens Russia's very independence no less than military occupation by a foreign power: NGOs and multinational corporations can take control of a weakened state, so Russia's only option for survival is strong state sovereignty with full control over the country's borders and territory. Russia, according to Surkov, is a state-forming people, and therefore cannot find its destiny in such transnational entities as the European Union. Internally, the greatest threats to Russian "sovereign democracy" are the oligarchs, who would bring us back to the 1990s, and extreme nationalists and communists, who would bring us even further (Smith and Conflict Studies Research Centre, 3).[8]

Surkov's identification of extreme nationalism as an enemy underscores the difference between bare sovereignty and mere nationalism, which on the surface would seem to have much in common. Nationalists are easily coopted into bare sovereignty, but they are ultimately being sold a bill of goods. Nationalists are invested in blood-and-soil, essentialist identifications of a Russian ethnos with a set of identifiable Russian cultural values. Nationalism means to save the Russian people, the Russian nation. Bare sovereignty sees both the source and the object of salvation as the Russian state. It is the latest, and most effective, response to the post-Soviet anxiety over the loss of great power status. In the 1990s, the mourning over great power status verged on the melancholic; by contrast, Putin has leveraged the shaky prosperity brought by high oil prices into a cure for what ailed his country. The most reflexively cynical critique of this admittedly cynical system would be to see bare sovereignty as power only for the sake of power. That would suggest something along the line of Orwell's definition of power at the end of *1984*: the boot that is constantly coming down on the subject's face. But Orwellian power is pure biopower, ensured and enjoyed through its exertion on the bodies of the people. Bare sovereignty hardly needs the people at all.

The genius of bare sovereignty lies in its very emptiness. Eurasianists like Alexander Dugin found it a convenient repository for their ethnographic fantasies, without needing the regime to endorse them. A huge cultural space is left open, one that has proven quite creative both for Putin's supporters and his opponents. In the past decade, there have been several prominent literary works that treat contemporary Russia and its historical past as the subject for works of fantasy, describing an alternative-universe Russia much like our own. The past master at this particular genre is Vladimir Sorokin, whose *Day of the Oprichnik* and its sequel, *The Sugary Kremlin*, paint a world that is technologically and politically our contemporary or near future, but with a restored Russian monarchy and a state security apparatus modeled on its precursor under Ivan the Terrible.

Despite the vast political chasm that divides Bykov and Sorokin from Dugin, all of them were essentially content providers under the empty regime of bare sovereignty. Ideology proves to be nothing more than a sideshow next to the real drama of state power. We are approaching the Marxist critique of (non-Marxist) ideology as false consciousness, Slavoj Žižek's equation of ideology with fantasy, or at the very least an understanding that ideology is simply a distraction. It doesn't matter what story the sovereign tells his countrymen; the crucial fact is that he stands there, speaking from a position of power.

As in the 1990s, the content-free ideology of bare sovereignty did not put an end to the culture of conspiracy. To the contrary, philosophers, pundits, and novelists continued to spin their tales of a Russia besieged by the West in general and the United States in particular. But the government, while tightening its control on broadcast media, still kept its distance from the larger cultural sphere. To be sure, nationalist, antiliberal youth groups such as Idushchie vmeste (Moving Together) and Nashi (Ours) were rightly seen as Kremlin confections: they wanted to be perceived as a grassroots movement, but were easily dismissed as astroturf.[9] Yet even astroturf is an attempt to manipulate civil society rather than reject it. And in keeping with the corrosive cynicism so commonly associated with Surkov and his projects, astroturf also cultivates a useful habit of suspicion: the fraudulence of Nashi ultimately reinforces the message that any group's claims to nongovernmental initiative are most likely a sham. By the time Putin was elected to his third term, media figures had developed a reflexive response to any apparent manifestation of antigovernment sentiment: "Who is [really] behind this?" (Kto za etim stoit?). We are back to the logic of deferral so essential to allegorical and conspiratorial thought.

Surkov was notorious for dismissing facts and viewing reality as an easily manipulated media construct, for weaponizing postmodern theory as propaganda. The messages that such a simulacrum were to convey may or may not have reached their target audience, but it was the metamessage that met with great success: we are all subject to media manipulation, and every expressed motive probably hides the hidden, real one.[10]

By this logic, the Surkov era should have produced a nation of unusually savvy media consumers, who could therefore be expected to have developed a rugged immunity to the stories told to them on television. Yet this is clearly not the case in Putin's third term. Poll after poll attests to a high level of trust in the state media and a widespread commitment to the narrative reinforced every night on the news.[11] The reasons for this are complex, and I discuss them in more detail in chapter 6. But the answer inevitably involves conspiracy. Not so much conspiracy on the part of the government or the media, but rather the wholehearted commitment to the kind of conspiratorial thinking that had been developing in the wider culture for decades. Sovereign democracy and increasingly tight media controls had already created a set of structures that would be the ideal vehicles for conspiratorial thought: the emphasis on the primacy of the state, the reinforcement of the sense that Russia has always been besieged by hostile powers, the reflexive distrust of civil society, and the habit of seeking hidden motivations and secret puppeteers. In response to the 2012–2013 street protests, the media clearly endorsed a quasi-Eurasianist, quasi-nationalist narrative that ascribed all of Russia's ills to hostile alien forces, whether they be Maidan activists, resurgent Ukrainian fascists, US and NATO schemers, or the "fifth column" of "national traitors" so famously invoked by Putin (only once, but once was enough for these words to gain currency in the contemporary media vocabulary).[12]

Adopting conspiracy has entailed a fascinating compression of historical time. If so many of the prominent post-Soviet conspiracy theories detail a long history of Western betrayal, now the media declare both new treachery on the part of NATO and the United States while simultaneously invoking that very conspiratorial history with which the audience might not have been entirely familiar. Just as Ukrainian nationalists must always be described in terms of the fascist World War II-era Ukrainian Resistance Army, so too must the West's alleged undermining of Russia in its "near abroad" be seen as simply one in a long list of similar underhanded actions by Europe and the United States. Of course, the West is the enemy; all its actions are construed as motivated by Russophobia.

Russophobia provides the largely empty ideology that unites virtually all of the conspiratorial narratives of plots against Russia, and, by virtue of a structure shared with *The Protocols of the Elders of Zion*, allows the enemy either to be the Jews or to occupy the position previously allowed to Jews. As the scholarship on both antisemitism in general and the Protocols in particular show, mythical Jewish conspirators are the condensation of ambient anxieties about modernity (capitalism and cosmopolitanism). The Jewish conspirators' modus operandi always amounts to the destruction of traditional values, suppression of national spirit, and the dismantling of family hierarchies. If all that is solid melts into air, it is the Jews who are blamed for turning up the thermostat.

Thanks to the diaspora, Jews also represent an enemy both internal and external. A hard-core anti-Jewish conspirator could therefore chalk up all foreign anti-Russian sentiment to the Jews and call it a day, but it would be a mistake to think that antisemitism is the discursive framework for all (or even most) non-Russian Russophobia; antisemitism is certainly not the motivation for Russian governmental officials' allegations of Russophobia on the part of Western powers. The external enemy need not be under the thumb of the international Zionist conspiracy to be Russia's enemy, nor is belief in this particular conspiracy a prerequisite for assuming a hostile, anti-Russian world. How, then, does Western Russophobia fit into the plots against Russia narrative?

As with the Jews, the answer lies with modernity, but in this case, with intensely mixed feelings about modernity. North America and Europe exemplify the lure of the modern, but also serve as a cautionary tale, while Russia's relations with both depend on a vicious circle of rejection: Russian hostility to the United States and, by extension, Russian perceptions of American Russophobia, are rooted in profound disappointment. Pundits in the West anxiously wring their hands over the rise of Russian "anti-Americanism," a notoriously vague term whose main effect is to make Americans feel besieged. Russia has become the latest focus for the naive question we never get tired of asking: "Why do they hate us so much?" In this case, though, the hostility toward America (as well as Europe) comes from a place of love. Angry, spurned love.

The Slash of Civilizations

Europe and the United States are, of course, obvious choices for Russia's enemies: the continued existence of NATO, not to mention its expansion to Russia's borders, has prolonged the binary oppositions of the Cold War. But it would be a mistake to see the United States' and Europe's role in Russian conspiratorial and extremist thought simply in terms of ordinary international politics. There is far too much emotional—indeed, libidinal—investment in these particular enemies to be merely a matter of current events.

Russia's love of America is an old story, one that is worth recalling precisely when relations have gone so sour. Like Humbert's Lolita, America had a precursor (she did, indeed she did): an older, and still simmering, affair with Western Europe in general and France in particular, on which more below. But in the twentieth century, Russia was preoccupied with modernity and with the future. An infatuation with America was inevitable.

To those who lived through World War II, America was the Lend-Lease program. To the generation who came of age in the 1960s, America was the enchanted kingdom that gave birth to jazz (broadcast on Voice of America for years), Ernest Hemingway, Kurt Vonnegut, and blue jeans. For most people, this love was political only to the extent that turning one's attention to the "enemy" was a politicized gesture. The appeal was not the United States' economic system or democratic institutions; US boosterism to the contrary, Russians were not seeking "freedom" or the "American Dream." They were simply charmed.

Nonetheless there was a gap in their knowledge about America that would prove disastrous: the Soviets did not know that their love for America was unrequited. And, really, how could they? The conflict between the two superpowers defined the entire era, and the limited contacts between them nearly always involved Americans who were emotionally or intellectually invested in Russia (otherwise, they wouldn't bother). This is not to say that Russia and the Soviet Union played no role in the American psyche: the Soviets made great movie villains. The ideological divide allowed for a reductive, functionalist approach to Russia and its culture, turning the Soviet Union into something of a totalitarian Disneyland for the American media/entertainment complex. What else could Russia have to offer?

Russia has a long history of preoccupation with its image on the world stage. America, on the other hand, is notoriously self-absorbed—indeed, self-satisfied—with little interest in other countries. The United States does, of course, get involved in foreign wars on a regular basis, but, really, its relationship with the rest of the world is one of benign neglect punctuated by the occasional recollections that other countries do exist; then, like a guilty but dutiful child picking up a Hallmark card on Mother's Day, the United States remembers to drop a bomb or send a drone to show that it cares.

America was briefly infatuated with Russia and the Soviet Union during Gorbachev's perestroika, a period that proved as anomalous for the United States as it did for its home country. The damage, however, was done: for at least five years (late perestroika through 1993), citizens of the (former) Soviet Union could justifiably convince themselves that we actually cared. America sent them McDonalds and Pizza Hut, and eventually humanitarian aid. More ominously, it sent its "experts" to reform/ruin the national economy and acted as indefatigable cheerleaders for the country's new democratic institutions (even when Russia's president disbanded and then shelled the country's parliament in 1993).

Love Will Tear Us Apart

In retrospect, the turn against America should have been predictable. When US leaders put their stamp of approval on a neoliberal, "democratic" regime that saw incomes plummet and crime run rampant, the United States became complicit in its failures. Even this could have been remedied, but America added insult to injury through neglect and lack of respect. Rather than seeing Russia as a partner, or even an antagonist—at least enemies get attention—it moved in the international arena as if Russia didn't matter at all.

The 1999 NATO bombing of Yugoslavia was a well-known turning point for Russia, when the media and popular opinion portrayed the Serbian people as victims of an overreaching predator. Russia's then prime minister, Yevgeny Primakov, was flying over the Atlantic on an official visit to the United States when he heard that NATO had commenced its bombing; Primakov briefly achieved cult hero status by ordering the plane to turn around immediately. This move was quickly dubbed "Primakov's Loop," an ironically appropriate term for a decision made because of the information loop from which Primakov had been excluded.

Russia's anger over the bombings was cast, both internally and for export, in terms of the long-standing brotherly ties between two Orthodox Slavic nations. But these ties were only (re)discovered in the 1990s; the Russian media and political elites emotionally reinvested in Serbia precisely when Yugoslavia was collapsing. The implicit homology between Serbia and Yugoslavia on one side and Russia and the Soviet Union on the other meant that Serbia's struggles were seen as a proxy for Russia's. What the US media cast as a human rights and European security problem was, in Russia, presented as a test case for America's plans for Russia itself.

If America is the enemy (indeed, if America is hell-bent on wiping Russia from the map), its aggressive role in the plots against Russia must have a reason. Even a desire for world domination goes only so far, while the resource-based arguments made in the Houston Project are ultimately too pragmatic to be compelling on their own.

As the 2016 US election campaign so sadly demonstrated, Russia and the United States are trapped in a game of discursive doubling. For years, the Russian media have been driving home the message that America is the cause of nearly all its problems—funding the opposition, masterminding Maidan, ruining Russian higher education through a nefarious system of grants—and now the American media are having a field day, blaming Vladimir Putin for Donald Trump, a xenophobic disaster that has more than earned the "Made in America" label. So, too, do Russian explanations for Western Russophobia echo the most banal American explanation for hostility to the United States around the globe: "They hate us for our freedom." In the case of Russophobia, the answer is "They hate us for our spiritual values."

What we see is the mirroring effect alluded to earlier in this chapter, a conception of Russian and/or Western (American) culture constructed in a dyadic relationship with a hated, yet somehow beloved, Other. Some of the recent advocates of the Russophobia hypothesis find themselves making one-way assertions that could easily be turned in the other direction: Oleg Nemenskii, in "Russophobia as Ideology," writes:

> This, on the whole is the Russian metanarrative of Western culture: Russia is a large country, with an entirely backwards civilization populated by a slavish people, or un-people, who blindly follow their all-powerful leaders, a country of omnipresent cruelty and violence, aggressive towards the rest of the world, to which it wants dominate while destroying all that is good in the world, it is an Evil Empire—this is a very precise formulation of the Western perception of Russia. . . . The basic manifestation of Russophobia are the projection all negative human characteristics onto Russians, the attempt to saddle Russia with a sense of blame for all of Russia's historical heritage . . .

Projection, of course, is a double-edged sword, and, while there are plenty of instances of Western hostility toward Russia, the Russophobia hypothesis turns them into part of an overall system based on an evil intent projected on the (non-Russian) enemy. Guy Mettan, the author of *Creating Russophobia: From the Great Religious Schism to Anti-Putin Hysteria*, makes an argument similar to Nemenskii's: "Russia upsets the image the West has of itself and of the world. The clash between the West's idealized image of itself and its harsh reality as viewed by Russia clarifies the Western psychological need for demonization of Russia. And vice versa, when the West is in a period of doubt, it tends to idealize Russia. For the West, Russia, with her blue-eyed white population and her own religion and culture, represents one facet of the Same" (98).

Could there not also be a "psychological need" (a problematic term, given the implication that an entire culture or civilization can be said to have a psychology) in some segments of the Russian elite to see their country as demonized by the West? No doubt there is political expediency, as nothing unites a population like an external enemy. But on a fundamental level, the West—whether NATO, the United States, or Western Europe— let Russia down. The wild optimism of the perestroika years, when "The West will help us" became both a mantra and an in-joke, was followed by neglect, by NATO expansion, and a long-term resistance to conceiving of Russia as an actual partner in world affairs. Just as in the 1990s understanding Russian misery as a result of conspiracy was sometimes preferable to ascribing everything to pure chaos, Western hostility is ultimately much more affirming than Western indifference.

At times, the very nature of imagined Western or US objections to Russia and Russianness is paradoxical, predicated on concerns that one would be highly unlikely to encounter in Western media or scholarship. Instead, such objections have far more to do with both Russian self-regard and self-consciousness. In a rather tedious book by Bardan Bagdasarian, *Anti-Russian Historical Myths* (Antirossiiskie istoricheskie mify), Myth no. 2 (of seventy) concerns the "'incorrect' religious choice made by Prince Vladimir." I hope I'm not spoiling anyone's surprise by revealing Bagdasarian's argument that the choice of Eastern Christianity was not only correct but vital to Russia's success as a civilization. The same argument appears in episode 7 of the first season of the Russian spy drama *Sleepers* (Spiashchie, 2017), when a US spy tells his Russian counterpart that

Russians are a "talented people. But you should stop being Orthodox. You should be Protestants."

The Russian chattering classes can't get enough of Samuel Huntington's "clash of civilizations," a notion that, whatever merits Huntington's book might have, easily lends itself to facile essentialism.[13] The adoption of "traditional values" as fundamental to Russian ideology in Putin's third term is the culmination of years of resentment and skepticism toward "European" or "Western" values. By no means do I endorse the "clash of civilizations" model, which I find in practice to be little more than an ideological prop; instead, I am arguing that this model has obtained such widespread currency in contemporary Russian discourse as to be all but taken for granted. Moreover, this model fits perfectly with the ideological tract that reintroduced "Russophobia" to late and post-Soviet Russia: a short, scandalous book by Igor Shafarevich.

Shafarevich's Clash of Civilizations

When Igor Shafarevich presented the term "Russophobia" to a new generation, he could not have known just how perfectly timed this reintroduction was.[14] Shafarevich, a world-renowned mathematician and dissident, wrote *Russophobia* (Rusofobiia) in 1982 as samizdat, but only seven years later, his (abridged) text would be published in *Nash sovremennik*.[15] Shafarevich's elaboration of Russophobia would prove useful not just as a term waiting the wings to replace "anti-Sovietism," a concept derided by Shafarevich himself, but as a possibly inadvertent contribution to Russian conspiracy theory in the wake of the Soviet collapse only two years later.

The debate surrounding *Russophobia* is partly based on the question of revealing the nation's "enemy" by name or inference; the term that gives the book its title allows for the "enemy" to be renamed, expanded, or inferred in a manner far more productive than traditional Russian conspiratorial thought provided. Critics of *Russophobia* accuse Shafarevich of framing the Jews as Russia's enemies, a charge Shafarevich roundly rejects. But whether or not *Russophobia* is antisemitic in content, it proves to be antisemitic in structure. The Jews may or may not be Russia's enemies, but, thanks to the framework of *Russophobia*, all of Russia's enemies can essentially occupy the discursive space traditionally carved out for Jews.

Shafarevich begins his tract with a critique of the most extreme "anti-Russian" historians and polemicists, those who argue that Russian culture and the Russian people are, by nature, slavish. His most frequent targets are the émigré historian Alexander Yanov, whom Shafarevich accuses of desiring Russia's "occupation" by foreign powers, and Vasily Grossman, the author of *Life and Fate* and *Forever Flowing*. Both men are Jewish, which could be chalked up to coincidence, but, since Shafarevich himself sees something significant wherever two or more Jews are found, there's no need. In any case, his argument is with their ideas: Yanov's rejection of Russian nationalism and embrace of Western liberalism, and Grossman's identification of Russia with the figure of the slave.[16]

The crux of Shafarevich's argument involves the notion of the "Lesser People" (*malyi narod,* sometimes translated as "Small People," a term he borrowed from Augustin Cochin). For Shafarevich, the Lesser People are an elite group who look at the larger masses (the Great People) with disdain and therefore see their own role as guiding the Great People's historical development.[17] In Russia, the Lesser People are the Russophobes, whose liberal ideals are based on their hatred of Russia. Who, exactly, are the Lesser People, the Russophobes?

Yes, it's the Jews. More specifically, the Jewish intellectuals whom Shafarevich sees not only as the core of dissidence and of émigré politics (strangely, their concern for the plight of other minorities gives them away) but as the people directly responsible for the disastrous October Revolution and the triumph of Bolshevism. Shafarevich is quick to defend himself against charges of antisemitism, both within *Russophobia* and in subsequent interviews.[18] His main defense is to reject antisemitism as a category:

> But no one has ever explained what one should seemingly begin with: what is antisemitism, and what does the word imply? In essence, what is involved here is that same ban: do not allow even the hypothesis that the actions of certain Jewish groups, tendencies, or individuals could have negative consequences for others. But one cannot, of course, formulate it so openly. Therefore, it is also vain to try to get an answer; none will be given, for herein lies the explosive power of the atomic bomb: in the fact that the question is removed from the sphere of reason to the realm of emotions and suggestion. We are dealing with a symbol, a sign whose function is to mobilize irrational emotions and arouse, on signal, a tide of aggravation, indignation, and hatred.

My point here is not to make an argument about Shafarevich's anti-semitism; it seems self-evident to most Western and Russian liberal critics. Robert Horvath provides a good overview, while Krista Berglund wrote an entire book in defense of Shafarevich, with particular attention to the question of antisemitism.[19] Berglund rejects the label, both because Shafarevich himself claims not to be antisemitic, and because she does not find explicit antisemitism in Shafarevich's writings.[20] While it is certainly true that *Russophobia* is exceedingly careful in its terminology, it is none-theless rather clear in its intent. Berglund has a keen eye for the literal meaning of words, and a tin ear for dog whistles.

Instead, Shafarevich's own preoccupations, when it comes to both Jews and Russophobia, demonstrate how a basic conspiratorial structure can simultaneously reinforce an existing prejudice (antisemitism) and become so portable that it no longer relies on the initial target of its hatred as the source of its power. Shafarevich's critique of the Jewish people is based on a set of misguided notions familiar to anyone who has followed the history of Russian antisemitism, the most important of which is the idea of the "Chosen People." Before the Jewish Enlightenment (Haskalah) movement, Jews were often denounced as "tribal"; if they kept to themselves, it was out of disdain for gentiles (see the emphasis on the goyim in the *Protocols*). The "Chosen People" works as the perfect rhetorical contrast to Christian ecumenicalism: Christians proselytize (welcoming the stranger), and Jews do not (keeping strangers out). Shafarevich seems to assume that the idea of the "Chosen People" is key not only to the development of Judaism but to Jewish attitudes toward others in virtually any context.

The irony here is that, in his attack on Jews and his critique of anti-semitism, Shafarevich emphasizes "chosenness" because he clearly has "Chosen People envy." This is how he responds to "Russophobia" attacks by Jewish writers:

> But here is what is striking: although the authors are for the most part Jews, they NEVER try to apply to their own people and its state the criticisms that they level at Russians and Russia. For example, practically all the authors accuse Russians of "messianism" and of the arrogance of feeling themselves to be a "chosen people." Whether Russians have such feelings and how strongly they have manifested themselves is a debatable question. But after all, "Messiah" is not a Russian word!

Yet Shafarevich's entire project is based on the "specialness" of Russia and Russians, in terms of both their historic destiny and their function as an international scapegoat. We saw that Shafarevich views antisemitism as a much-publicized myth, while Russophobia is the unspoken reality. Not only can Shafarevich not conceive of Russian history without the Jews as villains, he cannot imagine Russophobia without antisemitism (myth or not). If all references to "Russophobia" in Shafarevich's book were replaced with "antisemitism," the argument wouldn't suffer.

Shafarevich doesn't merely want to appropriate messianism on behalf of Russians; he wants ownership of antisemitism as well. Not to own up to antisemitism, but to reject it and then seize all its attributes for the construction of Russophobia. If I could speak on behalf of all Jews, I'd be tempted to let him have it—it hasn't done the Jews any good. Still, if we look at the Lesser People not in terms of ethnography, but in terms of Vladimir Propp's plot functions, we find a role open to an infinite variety of substitutions. As presaged by Shafarevich's own disdain for Jewish support of other minorities, the Lesser People is a model for the subsequent figuration of minority rights as "minority tyranny," on which more in the next chapter. More important, it takes the all-important trope of the cabal, so crucial to *The Protocols of the Elders of Zion*, and deracinates it. Any group can serve this function for a conspiracy theory. As the title of the old American comedy album put it, "You don't have to be Jewish."[21]

Structurally, antisemitism works just fine without Jews. The problem is: does antisemitic content haunt the antisemitic structure? If, for example, the villains of a popular thriller have all the traditional demonological attributes of Jews and Masons, but are never identified as such, are the stories advancing an unspoken chauvinist agenda—itself a conspiracy hidden behind the text—or has the representation of the enemy been so conditioned along classic conspiratorial lines that he is virtually unimaginable in any other way? Can popular narratives borrow the trappings of neofascist storytelling without opening the door to neofascist content?

Fascism with a Human Face

While the proliferation of hardcore conspiratorial narratives cannot help but reinforce and intensify conspiratorial thinking, it is the more mainstream entertainments that naturalize and domesticate conspiracy, borrowing compelling or locally useful elements to advance the plot and pique interest. When conspiracy trickles down into novels and films marketed as pure entertainment, the reader or viewer is not obligated to buy into an entire conspiratorial worldview; yet the boundaries between the extreme and the mainstream become harder to identify. Mark Lipovetsky ("Postmodern Crises") identifies a trend in contemporary Russian culture he calls "Post-Sots": the appropriation of the socialist realist aesthetic, apparently devoid of both Soviet ideology and Sots-Art irony. At issue is a question of cultural memory: can socialist realist art be reinscribed in popular entertainment without threatening to smuggle in totalitarian content?

The mainstreaming of conspiracy poses a similar problem: can the trappings of right-wing conspiratorial narrative be incorporated into popular entertainment as "good, clean fun," or do history and ideology so haunt them that the books and films become "fascism with a human face"? The question itself verges on the conspiratorial, for one imagines a collusion between extremist ideologues and mass publishers such as Vagrius and AST to bring fascism into the mainstream—"The Protocols of the Elders of Vagrius." Yet the answer is decidedly anticonspiratorial, for it rejects simplicity in favor of complexity and contingency.

Conspiracy has long served as a toolbox full of useful plot devices that can be particularly effective in stories involving action, adventure, and crime. Arguably any plot relying on mystery and disclosure has a clear affinity for conspiracy, although this is less the case in stories revolving around individual cases of murder committed by one felon. In Russia, the genres that most frequently avail themselves of conspiratorial plots are science fiction, fantasy, and the boevik. Authors of science fiction and fantasy have a wide range to work with when they imagine their villainous plotters: from alien races (Zvyagintsev), to supernatural forces (Lukianenko) to top secret government agencies (Lukianenko again). By no means do I wish to argue that their choice of villains is somehow neutral or unmarked; science fiction and fantasy lend themselves quite easily to allegory. The rival supercivilizations using earth's history as a battlefield in Zvyagintsev's *Odysseus Leaves Ithaca*, a series conceived before the advent of perestroika, are inevitably reminiscent of the opposing superpowers during the Cold War, while in Lukianenko's *Specter* (Spektr), the intergalactic network of stargates that threatens to unite alien civilizations too closely can be seen as a projection of globalization onto the cosmos as a whole.[22]

Moreover, the genres' strong reliance on idealistic metaphysics—Daniil Andreev for Zvyagintsev, the reification of such concepts as "Art" and "Power" in Lukianenko's *Autumn Visits* (Osennie vizity)—reinforces the Manichaean approach to good and evil that also characterizes conspiracy. Nonetheless, the conventions of science fiction and fantasy allow for the creation of villainous groups that can be so far from ordinary earthly experience as to not resemble the "usual suspects" of conspiracy. While the reliance on the notion of "evil races" in fantasy and space opera has chilling political implications, it is easier for science fiction and fantasy to create a conspiratorial enemy who does not resemble the Jews, Masons, or the International Monetary Fund. The boevik has fewer options, and on the whole, the authors of the boevik show little interest in exploring them.

Jews, Masons, and Mad Dogs

To see how the boevik handles these issues, I turn to a series I discussed in *Overkill*: Viktor Dotsenko's Mad Dog novels, which evolved over the course of decades, highlight an important cultural dynamic.[23] Just as Norka managed to repackage Klimov without the virulent antisemitism and homophobia, Dotsenko's work in the 1990s offered up tales of the struggle against evil secret societies as guilt-free entertainment even for liberals. Mad Dog's first recurring villain was ex-KGB General Arkady Rasskazov—who first appeared in the third novel, *Mad Dog's Return*, in which he was revealed to be the secret mastermind behind the machinations described in Savely's previous adventure, *Number Thirty Must Be Destroyed!* Rasskazov continues to be prominent until the fifteenth novel, *Mad Dog's Island*, in which he is defeated by the scheming Shiroshi, but soon after Rasskazov's introduction to the Mad Dog mythos, he shared primacy of place in Savely's rogue's gallery with the Secret Order (*Tainyi Orden*). Introduced in Dotsenko's fifth novel, *Mad Dog's Gold*, the Secret Order is an extremely hierarchical, ritualistic secret society divided into lodges and led by the Great Master and his Magisterium. The Secret Order is hell-bent on world domination, relying on financial manipulations, political infiltration, and the occasional murder to reach its goals.

Most of its leaders are of Russian descent, and even Rasskazov got his criminal start as a member of their organization. Moreover, Russia is an important target of the order because of its key role in world civilization.

The most remarkable feature of the Secret Order is that it is so completely generic. In structure, form, and ritual, the Secret Order is clearly modeled on the Masons, who have long been one of the most hated groups in Russian conspiratorial circles, and who are usually equated with Jews—hence the popular term *zhidomason* (Jewmason) as an umbrella term for the conniving enemies of Russia.[24] But when Dotsenko introduces the Secret Order, he is still a "liberal" writer, inveighing against the Communists, praising Yeltsin, and calling for a strong Russia based on democratic principles. The United States is more often an ally than an antagonist, and the occasionally stereotyped portrayals of individual Jews are mild in a cultural context that is highly tolerant of national and ethnic clichés. With the Secret Order, Dotsenko manages to have it both ways: he creates an organization with all the trappings associated with the villains of xenophobic fantasy, but stripped of the particular ethnic and religious context that would put his work in unwelcome company.

In 1999, however, with the NATO bombings of Yugoslavia, the national mood changed drastically. For years, the Russian media coverage of the wars of Yugoslav succession was virtually the mirror image of their presentation in the United States: pro-Serb sentiment ran high, despite the fact that brotherhood among the Slavs had been largely forgotten throughout the Soviet period. Moreover, the parallels between the dissolution of Yugoslavia and the collapse of the Soviet Union were easy to make, allowing many to see both Russia's and Yugoslavia's problems in terms of a clash of civilizations (Eastern Orthodox Christians versus the Islamic world). Russian and Serb television organized a "space bridge" to unite the two peoples; leading Russian cultural figures declared their solidarity with Serbia, and the boy band Na-Na declared its intentions to perform in beleagured Belgrade. But most important of all was the opportunity to condemn an act of NATO "aggression." After years of being lectured to by the United States about democracy, human rights, and reform, it was Russia's turn to accuse the Western allies of atrocities and arrogance.

The NATO bombings were a turning point in popular culture and the discourse of Russian nationalism, releasing pent-up resentment against the remaining triumphalist superpower. They also inadvertently aided the mainstreaming of conspiracy. The Mad Dog series, a multivolume serial narrative whose quick production had already allowed it to react rapidly to current events, embraced this new direction immediately. In early 2000, Vagrius published Dotsenko's twelfth Mad Dog novel, *Mad Dog's Justice*, which inaugurated Savely's association with Serbia and his blood-brotherhood with a Serb fighter. Not only are the Kosovar Albanians depicted as a Yugoslav version of the Chechens, but both the Albanians and the Chechens are part of an international Islamic terrorist organization headed by Osama Bin Laden. The Kosovar Albanians despise Russians, while Chechens are involved in a plot to destroy Orthodox monasteries on ethnic Albanian territory (171).

Given the circumstances, it should come as no surprise that Americans are the target of particularly harsh invective in this novel. What is far more startling is that the abrupt, but understandable, shift toward Russian nationalism and anti-Americanism is accompanied by undisguised antisemitism. Savely's counterpart, a colonel who "does not mince words," complains about "that Jewish bitch [Madeline] Albright." Meanwhile, the Secret Order counts on the support of a Moscow businessman who has established a charitable foundation called the Association of the Jewish People, which pays journalists to make accusations of state antisemitism (122). The businessman bears the Georgian name Nuzgar Dzhanishvili, but, since his mother was Jewish, he is as well: "Nuzgar himself sometimes admitted that he had a lot of negative features of the Jewish character. He even looked like a classic Jew; only his noticeable Caucasian accent ruined everything" (121). The Secret Order works with Jews like Nuzgar because "it is a known fact that almost 90 percent of the leading bankers in the world are Jews" (122), which makes them useful. From this point on, Jews are constantly causing trouble in Savely's world, working with the International Monetary Fund to ruin Russia.[25] In *Mad Dog's Kremlin Case* (231), Yeltsin nearly falls victim to a "Doctor's Plot," masterminded by a cabal of oligarchs whose Jewish roots are emphasized at every turn, one of whom is even the grandson of a Hassidic rabbi (273). In *Mad Dog's Island*, the fifteenth book, Jews are also responsible for the anti-Russian policies of George Bush's administration (even Condoleeza Rice's fictional stand-in, the "mulatto" Condoleeza Gatti, is Jewish on her father's side) (104).[26] Out of the blue,

Savely's beloved Roza suddenly decides to change her name to "Julia," because she is so tired of explaining to everyone that, despite her name, she is Russian, not Jewish (*Sled*, 20).

At the same time that the United States and the Jews become Russia's enemy, one of Mad Dog's oldest enemies reveals its true nature. Without any fanfare, *Mad Dog's Justice* adds one more word to the Secret Order's name. From now on, the organization is called the "Secret Order of Masons," or, for simplicity's sake, just "the Masons." It is as though the conspiratorial form had simply been waiting for its traditional content. For Dotsenko, at least, conspiracy ultimately discovers old answers to new questions.

Perhaps an inverted case can be made for Shafarevich: the mere fact that he is focusing on the Jews as a minority (a "Lesser People") puts them in a position familiar from *The Protocols of the Elders of Zion*: that of the conspiratorial cabal. Shafarevich's case is complicated because *Russophobia*, while devoted to the proposition that Russia is the constant target of hatred from internal and external enemies, does not precisely constitute a conspiratorial text. No one in *Russophobia* is hiding what they are doing; any reluctance to talk about the "true" role of Jews is the result of self-censorship based on the "myth" of antisemitism. Here it is the antisemitic *content* that pushes *Russophobia* closer to the world of conspiracy. If Dotsenko possibly alluded to Jews by invoking conspiratorial structures, Shafarevich gestures toward conspiracy by invoking the harmful role played by Jews.

Russophobia and the Generic Villain

At this point, we are at the intersection of form and content, structure and ideology. In chapter 1, I argued that conspiracy doesn't have to be defined only in terms of a full-fledged plot, in both senses of the word; conspiracy can be a (paranoid) mode, a subject position adopted and discarded at will or unconsciously. But these last three chapters look at the interdependence of conspiracy and plot, particularly the plot structures such as apocalyptic/disaster narratives and action-packed thrillers that can so easily be filled with conspiratorial content. Arguably, the entire notion of the "plot against Russia" is one such structure.

The different instances of conspiracy discussed in this chapter vary significantly in terms of both ideology and the identity of the enemy. Most of the time, though, the enemy represents some form of cosmopolitanism, globalism, or simply modernity. Traditionally, this has meant the Jews. Even if we set aside the long history of antisemitism throughout Europe, a particular conception of Jews (as an all-powerful, antinational cabal) is at the heart of the document on which modern conspiracy is founded: *The Protocols of the Elders of Zion*. Even when the enemy isn't Jewish, the structure in which the enemy is inscribed is one that places him in the "Jewish" position. Thus conspiracy by no means always has to be antisemitic, but should there be any desire to add antisemitic content, the structure of conspiracy makes the addition effortless.

This is where Russophobia comes in, first as Shafarevich's book, then as the broader concept described by its title. The very fact that there can be any controversy at all over the text's status as an antisemitic tract says something about modern conspiracy. Even if we agree with Berglund that *Russophobia* is not antisemitic because it does not make antisemitism explicit, then the antisemitic misreading is the result not simply of (justifiable) Jewish paranoia but of the similarity all such enemies have to the role of the Jews. Shafarevich doesn't occupy a position on antisemitism and the plots against Russia but rather a *superposition*, where the enemy is both Jewish and not necessarily Jewish at the same time: Schrodinger's Jew.

Russophobia, particularly when released from the confines of Shafarevich's writings, becomes an all-purpose, blanket explanation for any disapproval of anything done by Russia or Russians. Russophobia need not be explained or proven to be invoked and possibly believed. It turns a basic paranoid subject position (the world is against us) into both an affirmation of the paranoid stance and the motivation for the enemy's attack. As a concept, Russophobia does not require a full-fledged conspiracy theory to justify its invocation, but what it does provide is, if not an ideology, than an ideological placeholder that covers all "anti-Russian" sentiment or activity. Thus Russophobia is immensely convenient for Russian conspiratorial thought, occupying the all-important "enemy" space in a banal, underdescribed manner.[27]

Russophobia is an example of the semiotic deferral Jacques Derrida calls *différance*: it is a signifier that points not to an exact signified, but

rather to a possibly endless series of signifieds. As such, it needs no explanation when invoked but is available for explanation by pointing to other,
better developed theories of the enemy.[28]

Russophobia is the explanation that explains nothing. Which brings us
back to where we started: the apocalyptic narrative of Russia's destruction
by malign forces. Why are the Enemies trying to destroy Russia? Because
they hate Russia. Why do they hate Russia? Because they are Russophobic. Recall that the apocalyptic narrative has the positive benefit of con-
firming Russia's crucial role in world history. Russophobia is the abject
Other of Russia's messianic mission; they are based on the same binary
opposition (Russia/the world), but with the balance of power reversed.[29]
Russophobia makes Russia both the victim and the explanation: Russia's
enemies hate Russia because Russia is Russia.

For the Russian conspiracist, all roads lead to Russia. And they bring
the Enemy with them.

One Hundred Years of Sodom

Dystopian Liberalism and the Fear of a Queer Planet

The word "liberal" has become a synonym for the word "enemy."
—Andrei Arkhangelskii

The Phantom Menace

If, in the clash of civilizations à la russe, Russia represents "conservative," "traditional," or "spiritual" values, what does America represent? The antithesis of these values, framed as fundamentally anti-Russian: liberalism. Liberalism is a notoriously tricky word, and not just in Russian. Depending on the context, it can refer to proponents of free markets, procedural democracy, or inclusive social policies designed to minimize discrimination on grounds that now include race, class, religion, gender, gender identity, and sexual orientation.[1] Perhaps the only thing all of these forms of liberalism have in common is how despised they are by significant portions of a given population.

The term has been effectively demonized in the United States since the Reagan era, even as liberal social views have gained a stronger foothold throughout the culture. As is so often the case when we talk about late

and post-Soviet culture, its delayed arrival as an everyday word creates new, quite specific contexts that might not be readily apparent to
Westerners.

In an interview about the opposition to Putin, Ilya Budraitskis claims
that the very term "liberal" has "completely lost touch with its real meaning," arguing for the importance of distinguishing between proponents of
"economic freedoms" and "civil liberties and human rights":[2]

> The very word "liberal" has become a synonym for the internal enemy.
> Of course, this phantasmagoric figure is necessary for the ruling power. In
> order to insist on the organic unity of the people and government, it is nec-
> essary to point to those who are trying to destroy that unity. . . . From the
> point of view of power, anyone who opposes new repressive laws, attacks on
> human rights, or restrictions on freedom of speech, is automatically num-
> bered among liberals. (Budraitskis, "Putinist Majority")

Budraitskis is correct: in Russia, the term "liberal" is largely a term of
abuse, linked to the excesses, failures, and privations of the Yeltsin era. Still,
what we really need to know is (1) what do people in Russia mean when
they call someone a liberal? and (2) why liberals are so despised.

While much of the animus toward liberals is based on economic
grounds (the Thatcherite economic liberalism of the 1990s, which in the
West would be the work of "conservatives"), the discussion nearly always
moves to issues of culture and national pride. In right-wing tracts such as
Mikhail Leont'ev's *Fortress Russia* (Krepost' Rossii) and throughout the
collected works of the neofascist pseudohistorian Nikolai Starikov, the
liberal is understood to be the enemy of Russia.

A simple Google search ("Why they don't love liberals in Russia" [in
Russian]) leads to articles and blog posts that return to the same basic
propositions: liberals are Westernizers who don't love Russia, work on
behalf of Western governments either consciously or as dupes, and promote values that are inimical to Russian traditions. Some of this is predictable and understandable: since late Soviet times, it is self-identified
liberals who have been most willing, and perhaps eager, to point out the
flaws of the Soviet system, the crimes of the past, and the inadequacy of
the present. Not only is it easy to present such views as unpatriotic, but
the absence of a positive, specifically Russian-based message makes liberal
critics look like snobs at best and Russophobes at worst.[3]

With liberals out of power for over fifteen years, antiliberalism has caught up with its Western counterpart: in both the United States and the Russian Federation, those who hate liberals see themselves as defenders of "traditional" values. In Russia, this has been a slow process. For example, when homosexuality was decriminalized in 1993, gays and lesbians gained an unprecedented visibility. By no means was this development met with universal acclaim, but anti-LGBT sentiment was relatively restrained. As Lena Klimova points out in the first book edition of *Children-404*, LGBT themes in mass culture used to be met with mild disdain or indifference, as opposed to the homophobic campaigns of recent years (Klimova, 2015).[4]

There are many external factors to consider (not the least of them the proposition that, in the 1990s, people were too busy struggling to survive to care about social issues), but the conservative turn of Putin's third term has brought "values" to the forefront. If Russian values are defined as traditional or conservative, then those (liberals) who disagree are inherently un-Russian. Small wonder that an antiliberal slur coined by Ilya Smirnov in 2000 has become such a popular meme; Smirnov called his book manuscript "Liberastia" (Liberastiia), a combination of "liberal" and "pederasty" (which in Russian connotes male homosexuality rather than pedophilia). From *liberastiia* comes *liberast* or *liberas*, a term of abuse that has a handy 4chan troll equivalent in "libfag."[5]

Though the public campaign for traditional values is new, the framing of liberal values as an existential threat to Russia is the work of at least two decades. It started as a derisive look at developments in North America and Europe before turning into a clear and present danger for post-Soviet Russia. If liberalism is the enemy, its main weapon is political correctness.

In his 2013 speech to the annual Valdai International Discussion Club, which gathers politicians and intellectuals supportive, or at least not overly critical, of Kremlin policies, Vladimir Putin identified liberal values and political correctness as a "serious challenge to Russia's identity":

> We can see how many of the Euro-Atlantic countries are actually rejecting their roots, including the Christian values that constitute the basis of Western civilization. They are denying moral principles and all traditional identities: national, cultural, religious and even sexual. They are implementing policies that equate large families with same-sex partnerships, belief in God with the belief in Satan.

The excesses of political correctness have reached the point where people are seriously talking about registering political parties whose aim is to promote paedophilia. People in many European countries are embarrassed or afraid to talk about their religious affiliations. Holidays are abolished or even called something different; their essence is hidden away, as is their moral foundation. And people are aggressively trying to export this model all over the world. I am convinced that this opens a direct path to degradation and primitivism, resulting in a profound demographic and moral crisis. (Putin)

Putin's specific complaints, as we shall see, reproduce and amplify anti-Western talking points that were already familiar on Russian state television (not to mention Fox News). The invocation of political correctness as a menace, and, in particular, the nature of that menace, are the culmination of several decades of discourse based on an ideological caricature.

Politically Correct Scary Tales

I use the phrase "political correctness" with a great deal of trepidation. Most American academics my age and older remember the Culture Wars of the 1980s with as much fondness as most Russians recall the Yeltsin era of the 1990s. Bystanders and standard bearers on both sides of the barricades have very good reason to be war-weary. The huge fights over the "canon," multiculturalism, and "Western civilization" have settled into minor skirmishes, and the notion that any particular set of books, great or otherwise, will determine the course of civilization seems charmingly quaint in the age of 140-character tweets.

In academia, the afterlife of the Culture Wars plays itself out in separate but unequal walled-off graveyards. The engagé earnestness of parts of the annual Modern Language Association convention program is still good for a laugh, while the National Association of Scholars (a literary equivalent to the high-school anti-prom) still fulminates against cultural studies like some grandpa ranting about kids who refuse to get off his lawn. In higher education, the Culture Wars survive largely as the equivalent to an Eighties tribute band.

Only thanks to Donald Trump has political correctness (PC) been revived as a bogeyman, this time as the primary obstacle to "making America great again." Unlike the Culture Warriors of yore, Trump (unsurprisingly) does not offer a clear definition of PC; instead, he is performing a remarkable rhetorical service by reducing the opposition to PC to the same level of caricature that the Culture Warriors imposed on progressives in the 1980s. In any case, even when we take into account all of the overheated allegations of a Putin/Trump bromance, Trump's demonization of political correctness has little to do with Russia.

In fact, it is hard to imagine what link could be possible between PC and Russia, even if we recall the American Right's characterization of political correctness as liberal totalitarianism. Given all the terrible traumas that Russia has endured in the past twenty-five years—from the Soviet collapse through banking crises, wars with separatists and neighbors, the impoverishment of the majority of the population, and domestic terrorism—one could be excused for not expecting "political correctness" to be a viable scourge on the motherland. And even when one recognizes the utility of invoking such a peril—much like Fox News' hysteria over the so-called "War on Christmas," which, like an angry mistletoe, has become a reliable fixture of every holiday season—it would be a mistake to dismiss the rhetoric of the perils of PC as mere cynicism or political expediency.

Rather, the discourse of political correctness in Russia has, in the two decades of its evolution, moved from the realm of smug satire to clear and present danger as a compelling framework for renegotiating Russia's relationship with Western liberalism. When combined with increasing anti-Western sentiment after the 1999 NATO bombings and the forced self-reliance of Russia's culture industry after that same year's financial collapse made imports too costly, political correctness and *tolerantnost'* (tolerance), the liberal term that came to be associated with it, enabled the portrayal of a self-sabotaging multicultural Europe and North America as a nightmare of liberalism run amok.

This nightmare in turn found a comfortable narrative home within the genre of the literary dystopia (particularly of the post-Huxley variety), giving rise to a new subgenre of Russian science fiction called "liberpunk." While liberpunk itself is a marginal literary phenomenon, it has had a role in elaborating the political vocabulary that has come to prominence in the wake of the annexation of Crimea: the straightforward rejection of tolerance itself as an alien, anti-Russian value that can cause only harm.

As a weapon in the discursive ideological arsenal, political correctness has had a peculiar trajectory of deployment. According to one prominent (and oppositional) etymology, the adoption of the term in post-Soviet Russia is less a question of cultural importation than it is of a return home. Geoffrey Hughes joins a number of scholars on the right in tracing political correctness back to Leninism and the party line, with a bit of subsequent help from Chairman Mao. This etymology delegitimizes PC from the outset, both among conservatives in the West and many of the pundits who deploy the term in Russia. This origin story thus clears away any obstacle to caricature.

A counternarrative, championed by Stanley Fish among others, is that the term "politically correct" and its abbreviation "PC" do not so much represent an Orwellian shorthand employed by rigid dogmatists as they exemplify a self-deprecating progressive irony that gets lost in the right-wing caricature. Progressives have a tendency to compile laundry lists of noble causes and oppressed groups, and, because they typically put a premium on coalition building, feel the need to represent all of them at all times. The potential comedy of the situation is immediately apparent to many on the left: in the 1980s, protesting apartheid while arguing for the rights of gays and lesbians and being sensitive to the gender dynamics of a group's leadership could seem like the equivalent of patting your head and rubbing your stomach while hopping on one foot. But for a good cause. In this view, "politically correct" was an insider's term that mocked the standard leftist inventory of good causes at the same time that it affirmed it. It could also be used internally to express frustration at a fellow progressive who was guilty of being "leftier-than-thou."

But in an age otherwise saturated by irony, the relationship between irony and PC is surprisingly complicated. Any irony in the leftist use of the term "PC" is either missed or deliberately ignored in the caricature created on the right. This is particularly true about what nearly everyone seems to agree is the key feature of political correctness: concern for language and nomenclature. Part of the reason that PC terms were so vulnerable to parody has to do with the awkwardness of novel terminology. In some cases, when the novelty wears off, so too does the PC stigma.

Novelty alone, however, cannot explain the entire anti-PC linguistic backlash. Progressives in the 1970s and 1980s proposed a number of terms that never really took off, such as "wimmin" and "differently abled;"

in other cases, words that were deployed for their polemical value, such as "herstory" for "history," get (perhaps deliberately) misconstrued as proposals to replace the accustomed term. That is, the rhetorical is mistaken for the prescriptive. Finally, there are the patently ridiculous coinages that, if they appeared here and there in leftist literature, were never taken seriously by more than a few people at most. And it is these terms out of which anti-PC critics got their most mileage. If you read *National Review* or *The New Criterion* in the 1980s or 1990s, you might believe that the replacement of "short" with "vertically challenged" was a fundamental plank in the progressive platform. The excesses of PC terminology were passed off as the PC norm. All of this reached its apotheosis in James Finn Garner's bestselling 1994 *Politically Correct Bedtime Stories,* a hilarious retelling of folk tales using stereotypical PC terminology and values ("Little Red Riding Hood" ends with the grandmother taking revenge on the woodchopper, who "assumes that womyn and wolves can't solve their own problems without a man's help").

For the American Right, PC represented an Orwellian nightmare for our times, in which an ideologically motivated thought police enforced linguistic discipline in the name of creating an allegedly utopian reality. In this sense, PC was a postmodern, nonstatist variation on a familiar totalitarian enemy. It is this vision of political correctness, as a dystopian caricature with built-in lessons about liberal excess rather than in any way a part of a complex, evolving political discourse, that would be exported to Russia in the 1990s.

American Idiot vs. Russian Cynic

In what must be an accident of history, the Culture Wars in the United States unfolded at roughly the same time as perestroika did in the USSR. The two phenomena have little in common, save perhaps a renewed attention to ideas and ideology in the public arena. But one of the things that glasnost and the subsequent fall of the USSR did facilitate was the growing number of informal Russian "reports from the front": that is, polemical, amusing, quasi-ethnographic accounts of life in the West in general and the United States in particular.

From sociologists such as Ada Baskina to writers and intellectuals such as Tatyana Tolstaya, popular journalistic ethnographies ranging from short opinion pieces to book-length studies occupy a niche that should be familiar to anyone who has ever read *The New Yorker*. The arch intellectual observer of foreign mores is a recognizable figure in the world of nonfiction, and the observer's conclusions have at least as much entertainment value as they do truth value. If readers of Adam Gopnik's *Paris to the Moon* come away from the book concluding that all French obstetricians wear black jeans and black silk shirts while delivering babies, they are missing the point.

At the height of her popularity in the West, Tolstaya played this role in both directions: peppering her essays in *The New York Review of Books* with anecdotes about Russia's high culture and low civilization, Tolstaya was scathingly funny when writing in Russian about America. I want to look briefly at one particular essay by Tolstaya, because it is a fairly comprehensive summary of anti-PC stereotypes that appeared at a crucial moment (1998).

Tatyana Tolstaya's article "Political Correctness" (Politicheskaia korrektnost') did not introduce PC to Russian readers; quite the contrary, one reason for presuming it would get an audience was that the topic was already on people's minds. Writing from the privileged position of a Russian intellectual who had spent many years in the United States, Tolstaya immediately translates PC concerns into a Russian linguistic and cultural context, as witnessed by her first sentence: "The president received a delegation of *chuchmeki* [a racial slur] is an impossible headline."

That is, she eases her reader into the idea by pointing out how even the Russian media have their limits when it comes to the linguistic etiquette of dealing with race and ethnicity. By her third paragraph, however, she sets the stage for a familiar critique of political correctness: the naive assumption that changing people's words will change people's behavior: "for the word is the deed. And it's easier to correct the word. One must speak and think *politically correctly.*"

Much of Tolstaya's essay repeats the familiar tropes of PC-bashing. For the most part, she picks the lowest-hanging fruit—that is, the perceived terminological excesses of political correctness. By her fourth paragraph, she pretends to take herself to task for using the "sexist" term "brotherhood," a term preconditioned by her own status as a pathetic, blind victim of phallocentrism, unable to free herself from the shackles of (sic) male pig chauvinism (in English in the original); instead, she should have used the term *sestrinstvo* (never mind the fact that no such word exists in Russian).

She quickly moves on to proposing that the word "seminar" be replaced by "ovarium," and to claiming that feminists want to replace "history" with "herstory" and "hero" with "shero." Naturally, she trots out "vertically challenged" and "follicular challenged," and even works sheroically to develop Russian equivalents (after suggesting *vertikal'no ozadachennyi* for the first, she quietly gives up on any translation of the second). Imagining an anachronistic imposition of PC in nineteenth-century Russia, she suggests that Lev Tolstoy (whose last name is close to the Russian word for "fat") might have had to change his name to "Lev Polnovesnyi" (Lev the Heavy-Set). In an American context, this would already have been old news: to mix animal metaphors, what started out as shooting fish in a barrel had long since degenerated into beating a dead horse. But the Russian context is different: again and again, the idea behind "political correctness" is conflated with its own caricature as the concept is being introduced, making it virtually impossible to look at the phenomenon with anything but amusement, disgust, or horror.

To her credit, Tolstaya does make an exception for PC attitudes toward the disabled, interrupting her ongoing parody with what appears to be heartfelt appreciation of the American inclusion of people with disabilities into everyday life:

> No, political correctness is not as stupid as it seems. And when you see the care for invalids (a word you're not supposed to call them), all those widened doorways, special wheelchair lifts in buses, . . . I swear to God, you start to respect correctness and its uses, and think twice before blurting out:
> "That was lame"
> or
> "Only the grave can cure the hunchback."

In other words, we're back to caricature. By the end, she makes the dangers of PC clear. Yes, the ideals are, for the most part, admirable, but, when taken together, they smack of something all too familiar to anyone who grew up in the Soviet system:

> all of this raises no objections, save for the suspiciously familiar memories of certain verbal constructs that have yet to pass into oblivion: man of the future, builder of communism, friendship of peoples, the woman swineherd and the shepherd, the grandchildren of October. After all, in order to build the radiant future, someone must be vigilant.

PC, like Leninism, is an attempt to bring about a better world through force: "The liberal gendarmes, the political RAPP knows better, and sees all." All joking aside—or nearly all of it, because Tolstaya isn't Tolstaya without being snide—this is a clearly totalitarian threat. Hence her closing line: "Happy New Year 1948 or 1984, dear comrades."

Even in the hands of so discerning an observer as Tatyana Tolstaya, political correctness is presented to a Russian audience not as a debate, not as a process, and not even as anything more than vaguely defensible. Rather, the image of political correctness disseminated through the Russian media is virtually identical to its American right-wing critique. I emphasize this not to defend political correctness as such; as I hope I've already made clear, I consider the entire concept to be largely played out. But in a postsocialist Russia that has spent only a few years unsuccessfully grappling with the very idea of liberalism through an implementation that can be most charitably described as flawed, political correctness comes to represent the apotheosis of liberalism, the quintessence of everything wrong and alien about a poorly assimilated ideology. In both its manner of presentation and the timing of its entry into Russian public discourse, political correctness need not be used as a basis from which to extrapolate a dystopia. In this context, political correctness is already dystopian from the outset.

Tolstaya's presentation of political correctness follows the familiar right-wing narrative of an Orwellian movement that enforces ridiculous linguistic norms as a way of silencing dissent. The "free speech" argument against PC comes up frequently in the Russian media, often as an example of Western hypocrisy: the West claims to value liberty but punishes violations of linguistic etiquette with a totalitarian zeal. In 2011, Edward Snowden's future lawyer, Anatoly Kucherena, wrote a blogpost on *Ekho Moskvy* titled "Political Correctness: Totalitarianism for Dummies" that trotted out the usual unsourced horror stories about American victims of PC, arguing that PC is at least as insidious as traditional totalitarianism in that it retards the development of free thought and analysis and tries to reduce all of society to the level of its weakest, most flawed, and most complex-ridden members (Kucherena). A 2015 article on pravda-tv.ru claims that the public utterance of the word "n*gger" or even "calling a black-skinned person 'black'" can lead to court summons and fines ("Only "Afro-American,' nothing else will do") ("Bezumie"). On July 3, 2016, Dmitry Kiselyov began an editorial monologue on Brexit with familiar anti-PC clichés: "European political correctness has once again raised new questions. The attack can come at the most unexpected moment. And, really, the most trivial thing is given significance. You still open doors for women and hand them their coats? So you're against emancipation? And maybe you might also be a homophobe?" ("Kiselev rasskazal").

Never mind the lack of evidence, or even the complete ignorance about the US legal system (state law vs. federal law vs. campus speech codes); these stories work because they fit with the general (and, frankly, justified) understanding that, in comparison to Russians, Americans are hypersensitive about racial nomenclature and stereotypes. What is absent is any explanation of the actual reasoning behind such sensitivity.

Focusing on PC entirely in terms of speech norms would, however, limit the possibilities of political correctness as a clear and present danger to the Russian Federation. Polemically, one could engage in a bit of "whataboutism" and point out that recent laws against "hurting the feelings of religious believers" are far more Orwellian (and far more restrictive of free speech) than the PC paper tiger. The point is not to argue for different cultural policies but rather to see how certain arguments play themselves out.

In any case, the United States' racial concerns do not translate well when they cross Russian borders. Instead, there is another aspect of PC (and liberalism in general) that is often posited to be a direct attack on Russian values: issues of gender.

"Gender" is a more immediate threat because the male/female divide is presumed to be universal; as such, it moves liberalism and PC from a solely US-centered problem to an ailment of "old Europe." Gender also has the advantage of being both foreign and ubiquitous (presumably, everyone has at least a connection to gender, even the nonbinary or agender). When women's studies and feminist studies came to Russia in the late 1980s and early 1990s, there was no term readily available to denote "masculinity" and "femininity" as extrabiological, nonessentialist, constructed categories.[6]

So what did Russian feminists do? The same thing that Russian free marketeers did when they coined the word *vaucher* (voucher) during the first wave of privatization: they imported an English word, that, in Russian sounds clumsy and opaque. "Gender" became *gender* (pronounced with a hard "g"), an ugly—and, incidentally, masculine—noun that, like the "voucher," sounds like something Russians never used to have and have little use for now that they do.

The foreignness of *gender* plays a role in the opposition to feminism and LGBT rights throughout Eastern Europe. The title of a 2015 essay collection says it all: *Anti-Gender Movements on the Rise?* In an English-speaking country, the idea of an anti-gender movement would sound not just odd but radically progressive. But, as the authors of the articles make clear, "gender" is invoked not in its originally imported meaning of socially constructed category superimposed on biological sex but as an alien, pernicious movement designed to destroy the family as we know it. These anti-gender movements frequently refer to what they call "gender ideology," a phrase that encompasses a range of feminist and progressive attitudes toward gender and sexuality. Despite the frequent characterization of gender and feminism as a Western import, Russia's anti-gender movement proves to be quite cosmopolitan, sharing sources and strategies with like-minded groups throughout Europe (Kuhar and Paternotte). All of these anti-gender movements are united in their opposition to liberal values. As the emphasis on "traditional values" grows, Russian antiliberalism looks increasingly like gender panic.

All Happy Families

Tolstoy famously began his novel *Anna Karenina* with the declaration that all happy families are alike, and all unhappy families are unhappy in their own way. The anti-gender crusaders have yet to take this up as their motto, which is really a wasted opportunity on their part.

The idea of "gender" is disruptive to Russian conservative circles for the same reason progressives find it liberating: identity, behavior, and family structures are understood not to be natural or innate, but the product of social forces that obscure their own role in gender's construction.[7] Conservatives prefer to see all these phenomena as fundamental, yet still subject to perversion by unnatural influences. The result is itself quasi-constructionist: "proper" gender and sexuality are inherent and natural, while LGBT people and feminists have been reconstructed by malign forces.

The general conservative turn in Russian family and gender politics is not new. As feminist scholars have noted for decades, the alignment between feminism and socialism in the years immediately preceding and following the October Revolution narrowed the popular understanding of feminism in Russia (Holmgren). On one hand, the "woman question" was considered solved by bringing women into the workforce; on the other, nearly every difficult social problem involving the family could be blamed on "feminism," from the preponderance of single-mother-led households to juvenile delinquency. Moreover, the perennial complaint of educators and sociologists in the Brezhnev era that Soviet men were "infantilized" (deprived of their "natural" leadership role at home, marginalized within the family, and generally irresponsible) could be ascribed to the excesses of Soviet "feminism"(Borenstein, *Overkill*, 46–47).

In the 1990s, a hypermasculine business/criminal culture welcomed patriarchal norms, while demographic concerns (as well as a growing role for the Russian Orthodox Church) led to increased calls for larger families with a traditionally gendered division of labor. Still, it was the 1990s: the media and culture industry featured too many diverse voices for the anti-gender narrative to go mainstream.

As in so many areas, the rise of Vladimir Putin would mark a turning point in the gender narrative, even if that turning point was clear only with the benefit of hindsight. And I am uncomfortable ascribing too much significance to the Russian president as an individual, since the US media's myth of an all-powerful Putin micromanaging a vast country is both pernicious and lazy.[8] Following on the work of Helena Goscilo and Valerie Sperling, I prefer to treat Putin as a phenomenon, a media/cultural creation that need not be identical to the actual man, nor reflect his personal intent (Goscilo, "Russia's Ultimate Celebrity"; Sperling).

Victor Pelevin notoriously suggested in his 1999 novel *Homo Zapiens* (*Generation "Π"*) that Yeltsin and his entourage were all figments of the media imagination, created by political technologists with access to cutting-edge CGI. Putin, by contrast, is a construct meant to project manly authenticity; Pelevin's novel went behind the curtain to turn the camera on the puppeteers, but the Putin phenomenon goes several steps further. A live-action simulacrum of his own self, Putin could join Pinocchio in a joyous chorus of "I've Got No Strings."

The first Putin/Medvedev decade, while definitely marked by an uptick in patriotic rhetoric and appeals to the national patrimony, nonetheless resembled the 1990s in the absence of any sort of national ideology championed by both state and media. Culturally conservative politicians were gaining influence regionally, but it was only with Putin's return to the presidency, the crushing of the protest movement, and the troubles in Ukraine that "traditional values" would become the foundation of Russian public culture and policy.

To the outside world, the triumph of "traditional values" in Russia can be summed up in two words: gay propaganda. On June 11, 2013, after a series of similar laws were adopted by local and regional authorities, the State Duma passed a law officially titled "For the Purpose of Protecting Children from Information Advocating for a Denial of Traditional Family Values" (Decker).

Technically, the law is meant to "shield" minors from any content that portrays homosexuality as normal or contains "propaganda of nontraditional sexual relationships." As the law's defenders are quick to point out, it does not recriminalize homosexual activity or ban gay clubs, and there are plenty of countries throughout the world that are far more punitive toward their LGBT citizens.[9] Moreover, if we look at the United States, the great strides toward LGBT acceptance and legal equality in the past decades means that anyone over forty can easily remember a time of far less tolerance. Russian supporters of the law argue that it is unreasonable to expect every country to follow the United States (and Western Europe) in lockstep on the march to progress.

But what is happening in Russia is not merely a question of "lagging behind," a concept that plays all too easily into stereotypes about Russia's relationship to the West. Nor is it a matter of the simple continuity of long-standing traditions and attitudes. The story is actually much more complicated. First of all, it is not as if any country in Europe or North America was a model of LGBT freedom until quite recently. Is there any modern nation that can't claim homophobia as part of its historical values? Second, while Soviet law stipulated prison sentences for men who engaged in same-sex activity and involuntary commitment to mental hospitals in the case of women, most Soviet lesbians and gay men led lives of closeted invisibility that kept them relatively safe from incarceration, though quite vulnerable to blackmail and coercion. The Soviet law against homosexuality worked like most Soviet and post-Soviet laws: while not universally enforced, they were always available as a weapon against anyone who became inconvenient.

LGBT invisibility resulted in a widespread naïveté about LGBT people in Russia. Essentially, the USSR never perfected gaydar technology. That is, it was understood that homosexuals and lesbians existed, but only as such rare, abject freaks that the designation couldn't possibly apply to an actual person one might know. The result was a queer invisibility whose uses are certainly familiar in the West ("If only that nice Liberace could meet the right girl . . ."), but rapidly dying out.

Virtually no one in Russia is in the habit of thinking of queer people as a legitimate political constituency, which at least partially explains the surprise expressed by Russian officials when Americans and Europeans keep "harping" on gay rights. Tatyana Moskalkova, Russia's top human-rights official, dismissed questions about LGBT people and political prisoners: "Is that really the most pressing [*nabolevshaia*] topic?" (Kanygin).

Her question has a strong populist overtone, in that she deflects these concerns in favor of issues that trouble "average" Russian citizens. Average citizens of the Russian Federation assume that they don't really know any actual gay people. That is, chances are, they do know someone who is gay, but they don't know that they know someone who is gay. To them, worrying about LGBT rights is like anxiety over the plight of leprechauns.

The current law against "gay propaganda" is a perfect fit with the casual disdain for "sexual minorities" that was prevalent in popular culture after the Soviet collapse. In the popular fiction of the 1990s, one could find frequent references to entertainers who claimed to be gay or lesbian just to "follow fashion" or "get attention" (the faux lesbian duet t.A.T.u. has a lot to answer for). In these stories, the media "turned" people gay.

Even the liberal writer Boris Akunin, whose novel *Coronation* can be read as sympathetic to homosexual men, resorts to crass caricature when setting his fiction in contemporary times: in a later novel, *FM*, Nicholas Fandorin's secretary, Valya, is a flamboyant, cross-dressing bisexual male who is always playfully hitting on his boss, before declaring himself a transwoman and having gender confirmation surgery, apparently on a whim (feeble comedy and misinformation all in one).

But playful ignorance and casual dismissal are a far cry from the 2013 law, which restricts a minority group's right to self-expression after years of freedom of speech. Moreover, the deployment of children as an endangered group is particularly insidious. All it takes to shut down a discussion of LGBT rights is the presence of a minor, or even the allegation that a minor is or could be present. This is not merely a limitation on LGBT rights; it makes the very argument in favor of LGBT rights potentially criminal.[10] Queer people and their supporters could now be violating the law if they argue against the law in hearing distance of someone under eighteen.[11]

But even as LGBT advocates and allies are silenced by the law, antigay stereotypes are deployed freely without any consequences. In the February 2018 presidential election campaign, an unattributed "get out the vote" commercial was posted on YouTube, featuring a husband and wife arguing about whether or not voting was worth the bother. The husband has no intention of going to the polls and falls asleep. The rest of the video features his nightmare: first, he finds out that the draft age was raised, and he's being called up. Then his young son asks for four million rubles to pay for security. But the worst is when the husband walks into the kitchen to find a distraught effeminate man sitting in his kitchen. According to the law, any gay man who has broken up with his boyfriend has to be taken in by a straight family. If he doesn't find a new boyfriend, the husband will be obliged to sleep with him. He wakes up, only to find the gay man next to him in bed. Then he wakes up again, this time for real. Not only is homosexuality such an obviously negative, deviant phenomenon in this video, but it is also immediately brought into the realm of the compulsory: straight men are "drafted" into servicing gays.

Whatever the intent of the law, the ban on "gay propaganda" has effectively declared an entire population within the Russian Federation to be deviant, with any positive discussion of their existence portrayed as a threat to families.

In the new era of "traditional values," queer people are the perfect internal enemy.

Vampire Gays of Sodom

Since the passage of the law on "gay propaganda," physical and verbal attacks on LGBT people in Russia have become all too common.[12] This book, like virtually everything else I write, is about media, culture, and discourse, not about "real life," but I would be remiss if I did not at least mention the numerous incidents of gaybashing in Russia's major cities, often recorded on video by the perpetrators themselves.

In December 2014, Human Rights Watch issued a detailed report, "License to Harm," which can be downloaded from its website ("Human Rights Watch"). While precise statistics are difficult to come by, Human Rights Watch found a clear and growing pattern of abuse:

> LGBT people in Russia face stigma, harassment, and violence in their everyday lives, and most people who spoke with Human Rights Watch said that this intensified in 2013. In some cases they were attacked by anti-LGBT vigilante groups that sprang up in late 2012 across Russia. These groups consist of a network of radical nationalist men who lure gay men and teenage children on the pretext of a fake date, hold them against their will, and humiliate and expose them by videotaping the encounter. Such encounters have often involved perpetrators pouring urine over their victims and in some cases forcing them to drink it. Assailants often hit and kicked the victims; in some cases they hit their victims with dildos or forced them to hold and pose with dildos; stripped them naked; painted and drew slurs on them; and/or sprayed them with construction foam in the genital area. Hundreds of such videos have been posted online.

I cannot speak with any authority about the lived experience of queer people in Russia today, nor do I have the training or interest in gathering empirical data through fieldwork. What I can speak to is the shrill, antigay hysteria that has found a welcome home in the mainstream Russian media, not to mention the Internet. I do not use the word "hysteria" lightly; given the media and government's construction of a lavender menace to all that true Russians hold dear, despite the general population's complete lack of awareness of interacting with actual LGBT people during their daily lives, I can only conclude that the homophobia that clearly existed before 2013 has been turned into an ideological weapon.

Current antigay rhetoric in Russia has a strong and disturbing basis in notions of social hygiene: more than just inveterate corruptors of Russia's youth, LGBT people are framed as an alien, virulent infection menacing the immune system of Russia's body politic. Consider some of the most notorious statements made in the wake of the gay propaganda law.

In August 2013, Dmitry Kiselyov, host of one of the country's most popular news programs, declared: "I think that just imposing fines on gays for homosexual propaganda among teenagers is not enough. They should be banned from donating blood, sperm. And their hearts, in case of the automobile accident, should be buried in the ground or burned as unsuitable for the continuation of life" (Broverman). His remarks were applauded by the studio audience. Four months later, Putin appointed him as head of the new state news agency, Russia Today.[13]

In December of that same year, Ivan Okhlobystin, star of the popular *Scrubs* rip-off *Interns*, went even further: "I'd put them all alive in the oven . . . it's a living danger to my children" ("Russian Actor"). Just a few weeks later, Okhlobystin posted an open letter to Vladimir Putin on Vkontakte urging the president to restore the old Soviet law stipulating prison time for homosexual activity.

Kiselyov later defended his remarks as being consistent with "internationally recognized practice" (referring to bans on blood and organ donation by gay men in the United States and Europe). Even if we set aside for the moment the dubiousness of such practices in the West, they are framed specifically in terms of combatting the spread of one particular illness: HIV/AIDS. Certainly, AIDS is behind both men's remarks, but what is noteworthy is that the illness need no longer be name checked. Rather, gay men are the source of infection by their very nature.

As Laurie Essig notes, Kiselyov's remarks implicitly make gay men the modern equivalent of vampires, recommending that their bodies be disposed in the traditional manner for fighting the undead ("Bury Their Hearts," 40). Okhlobystin turns gay men into Jews under the Nazis, fodder for industrialized destruction in crematoria. Both metaphors are revealing, in that each of them is rooted in the logic of social hygiene. Vampires are parasites as folk devils, while the Jews were explicitly labeled vermin by the Third Reich.

Two men do not make a statistic (at best, they make a domestic partnership, which in this case would be slash fiction I would happily pay for). Nor were their remarks exempt from condemnation by some in the Russian media. They represent something other than a verifiable trend. As so often happens on Russian television in the past few years, Kiselyov's and Okhlobystin's words show shifts in the boundaries not of the thinkable but of the sayable.

Such statements do not become the norm, but they do show what is permissible and make otherwise extreme statements that stop short of crematoria and vampire disposal more ordinary. The domestication of extremism is a slow and complicated process. In this case, we see it happening over gay men's dead bodies.

The Love That Dare Not Speak Its Name to Anyone under Eighteen

Everyone has a theory of gender and sexuality, but if you're lucky enough to be in the majority, you might mistake your theory for "nature."

In his 1996 travel memoir/lay-anthropological report *Cracks in the Iron Closet*, the journalist David Tuller's thirteenth chapter, "Theories, Theories, Theories," provides an amusing overview of the multifarious hypotheses about the origin of sexual orientation, as well as a case study of the Russian habit of theorizing. Twenty years later, the debate on sexual orientation in Russian public culture is virtually closed: yes, we were born this way, but this way is straight (and narrow).[14]

Even though the overwhelming scientific consensus is that people are not "turned" gay via seduction, propaganda, or Joan Crawford retrospectives, the "traditional values" crowd has followed in the footsteps of their American brethren in totally rejecting the data.[15] Instead, they have latched on to the occasional study, usually by right-wingers, that reinforces the idea of LGBT abnormality and danger.[16] As Lena Klimova notes in *Children-404*, Mark Regnerus's 2012 sociological study claiming that children raised by LGBT parents are at a greater risk of abuse and suicide attempts was widely trumpeted in Russia, despite its debunking by the scholarly community.[17]

Recall how tenuous was the connection between the violent homophobic remarks by Dmitry Kiselyov and Ivan Okhlobystin and any actual question of AIDS. This homosexual threat is often cast as demographic problem, but it is really the weakest of rhetorical gestures. If the LGBT presence in Russia is really so small (and so recent), how can it be responsible for depopulation? The primary engine of antigay panic is quite different.[18]

If gay men have long been cast as an AIDS risk group, who is at risk when gay men themselves are the pathogen? The answer is quite simple: children. Little work is required to make that connection in the popular mindset, since gay men and lesbians in Russia have long been assumed to recruit young people. Even the most common antigay slur (*pederast*) confuses the issue: this term is frequently and incorrectly given a literal gloss in English as "pederast," though it is best translated as "faggot." More to the point, it etymologically reinforces a common conflation of homosexuality with pedophilia (a conflation facilitated by appeals to the traditions of ancient Greece).

What is new, then, is not the association between male homosexuals and pedophiles, but the post-2012 construction of the endangered child. The innocent child is always a figure that demands protection and in whose name a great many otherwise questionable policies can be justified. Russia is hardly alone in using the rhetoric of child protection as a fig leaf for encroaching on individual liberties; what is noteworthy is how new this tactic is in the Russian Federation, as well as how widespread it has become. Since 2013, the Russian legislature has passed a string of laws whose ostensible purpose is to protect children, but whose effects appear to critics to be much less, well, innocent: bans on violence in cartoons, bans on a whole range of subject matter on television before 10:00 p.m., restrictions on Internet content (the final frontier of free speech), and, of course, the "Dima Yakovlev" law outlawing the adoption of Russian children by Americans.

The deployment of children in these debates might be sincere on the part of many of these policies' supporters, but when all of these repressive measures are examined side by side, it starts to look rather cynical. Taken as a whole, this is an extremely clever reappropriation of the liberal/sentimental tropes that have long served to critique Russian government policy. At the same time that the state trumpets the sanctity of the traditional family, it is more than happy to assume a protective parental role in the service of a broader agenda of social restriction.

In the case of the gay propaganda law, we are not merely talking about shielding children from pedophiles: after all, who could be against that?[19] To put it bluntly, the law's purpose is not to prevent child rape. It's to prevent child homosexualization. Gay seduction, it turns out, uses two vectors of transmission: adult men preying on children, which was already illegal, and adults simply talking about gay life when children are present.

In part, this is a return to the Soviet ethos of sexual discourse: sex should not be a subject for discussion. This idea is not mere prudery; when considered in the context of the other restrictive laws that use children as an excuse, the overall goal appears to be the restriction of discourse, period. The first ten years of the Putin/Medvedev era were governed by a tacit compact: if you stay out of the state's way, the state will, for the most part, allow you to talk about whatever you want and consume whatever media you want. As long as the commanding heights of discourse (television) were in state control, everything else was just empty chatter. This is clearly no longer the case.

But even if we look at the gay propaganda law in isolation, its basic premise suggests an intriguing, presumably unintended, theory of sexuality. Despite the professed belief in the natural and the traditional, the gay propaganda law betrays a fundamental uncertainty about heterosexuality itself. It is as though homosexuality were somehow naturally more attractive and more fun that anything the straight life could offer. If we let people talk about homosexuality, everyone's going to want to do it. In the final analysis, the law is offensive to straight people: heterosexual sex is the performance of one's duty to God and country, while homosexual sex is just nonstop fun. When did heterosexuality become such a drag?

Chasing Rainbows

A funny thing happened to homophobia on its way to being enshrined in Russian law: it stopped being about sex and started being about identity.

This is a familiar pattern in the history of homophobia; it's just that in the Russian case, the timeline has been so drastically accelerated. It has become something of a truism in sexuality studies that, before the end of the nineteenth century, the homosexual did not exist. Homosexual activity certainly did, but it took the combined efforts of the medical and legal systems (most notably in the 1895 trial of Oscar Wilde for "gross indecency") to generate the idea of the homosexual as a particular *type*, a person defined either in terms of medical dysfunction, legal violation, or both.

Persecution of male homosexuals could thereby be justified either in terms of the "disgusting" activities in which they engage or the everyday violations of gender propriety they commit simply by being themselves—or, if you prefer, performing their identity. In mainstream North America, the growing acceptance of LGBT people was often facilitated by the creation of popular LGBT characters who led all but sexless lives, as in the *Will and Grace* syndrome. This is obviously problematic, but it did make it possible to talk about and think about gay people without immediately picturing them naked and copulating (not that there's anything wrong with that).

The gaydar mentioned earlier doesn't mean the ability to somehow catch two men having sex, but rather the capacity to read behavioral codes. The gay propaganda law does something magical to homosexuality: it frames gay sex as a threat to be avoided, but, as its defenders repeatedly remind us, it does not criminalize homosexual activity. It purports to protect children, but it does not outlaw the adult rape of children, since that's already taken care of. Instead, such antigay lawmakers as Elena Mizulina and Vitaly Milonov have created the perfect Foucauldian legislation: it shifts the focus from homosexual activity to homosexual discourse.

The current antigay hysteria has drifted far from considerations of what actual LGBT community members are doing with other members. There's a certain logic here: man-on-man sex must be so vile as to be unthinkable (straight porn suggests that lesbian sex is more than thinkable, as long as it doesn't involve actual lesbians who know what they're doing). Instead, let's concentrate on everything else that may have to do with homosexuals.

Contemporary Russian homophobia is already couched in paranoid terms, since pro-LGBT activity is habitually blamed on the West. But in a country long familiar with the benefits of Aesopian language, the crusade to protect minors from homosexual discourse demands paranoid interpretive strategies. Consider the antigay manifestations that properly belong to the "news of the weird" category. For example, in late 2014, a St. Petersburg monument to Apple founder Steve Jobs was removed after the company's CEO, Tim Cook, came out to the public. A spokesperson for the consortium of companies responsible for the monument explained: "After Apple CEO Tim Cook publicly called for sodomy, the monument was taken down to abide to [sic] the Russian federal law protecting children from information promoting denial of traditional family values" ("Russia Takes Down").

Steve Jobs's offense, then, is not that he had sex with men (if he did, he never mentioned it to his biographer Walter Isaacson), but that he hired as his future replacement a man who does. The statue doesn't actually violate any statute, but its removal shows one of the law's worst consequences: it is an incitement to take every opportunity to affirm that LGBT people are anathema. The Jobs statue incident removes the last defense of the bigot: apparently, it is no longer acceptable to say, "Some of my best friends are gay."[20]

On its own, this case doesn't mean all that much; after all, Steve Jobs is (1) dead, (2) straight, and (3) not Russian. But it is consistent with the media campaign against anything even vaguely associated with LGBT people. And the biggest (symbolic) victim is the rainbow.

Because the rainbow is an internationally recognized symbol of LGBT pride, it has become an object of suspicion in the eyes of Russia's homophobes. Even some supporters of the gay propaganda law recognize that this has gone too far. Dmitry Belyayev, a proponent of the St. Petersburg law that served as a rough draft for the subsequent national legislation, admits that deputies who want to ban the use of the rainbow symbol are "deranged": "The rainbow itself . . . has nothing to do with pederasty [*pederastiia*]" (Beliaev). This is a defense to warm gay hearts, assuming that they haven't already been removed and burned, according to Dmitry Kiselyov's wishes.

The reliably unhinged Arkady Mamontov, star of the *Special Correspondent* talk show on Channel 1, showed a predictably homophobic documentary in November 2013 in the wake of the gay propaganda law. As the journalist Michael Bohm, Mamontov's regular American talk-show punching bag, describes it:

> The show started with a 30-minute documentary-style film that claimed an aggressive, well-financed and organized Western homosexual lobby was forcing its values on Russia. If the country failed to defeat the threat, we were told, the number of homosexuals would increase. The film ended with a collage of scenes depicting rainbows in Russia on a pharmacy, a supermarket, the covers of notebooks and on a sign in front of a business center. All of these rainbow symbols, it was explained, were part of an insidious Western conspiracy to propagandize homosexuality and corrupt Russia's fundamental moral and spiritual values.
>
> After the film, Mamontov asked me, the only foreign guest on the show, the first question: "Why do you stick your nose in our business?" he said. "Why do you try to impose your alien values on us?" (Bohm)

There is no need to explain patiently that rainbows can mean many different things. Instead, I like to recall that, in Soviet times, when the USSR put an emphasis on publishing Russian classic works in translation to be read around the world, the name of that particular publishing house was Raduga, or rainbow. Coincidence? Or were Pushkin, Dostoevsky, and Mikhail Sholokhov all part of the gay agenda? Perhaps we should go further back. When Noah and company sailed for forty days and forty nights, God sent a rainbow as a sign of his new covenant. Jewish tradition teaches that this meant God would no longer destroy the world when he was in a bad mood. But apparently, he was just advertising the world's first gay bar.

Gayropa, Gayropa

At the end of *The Notebook* (Le grand cahier, 1986), the first novel in an award-winning trilogy by the Francophone Hungarian writer Agota Kristof, the nameless, identical twin boys who are both the protagonist(s) and collective narrator(s) of the story, come to a crossroads: the boundary line between their unnamed but obviously Soviet-occupied country and its liberal democratic neighbor. One of the twins crosses the border literally over their father's dead body, while the other stays behind.

Stripped of all explicit historical and geographical referents, *The Notebook* reads as both fairy tale and allegory: the twins divided by this fortified border almost beg to be read as the embodiment of postwar Europe. Either they are Romulus and Remus, somehow unfairly separated, or they are one person imagining that they are actually two (one Europe allowing itself to be divided when it never should have been). Half of Europe pines for the other half, at the same time fearing that one twin has forgotten the other.

If so, it is an allegory very much of its time: while Eastern Europe yearns to rejoin its long-lost identical twin in the West, the boys (now men) are no longer identical, thanks to a crippling injury suffered by one of them. Granted, this allegory is delightfully subverted by the time the trilogy ends. I would submit, however, that it is still a valid reading, albeit a superseded one.

I bring up Kristof's trilogy mindful of its limited applicability to the Russian context because of what it suggests for our current conversation.[21] The whole idea of "Gayropa" (a portmanteau of "Gay" and "Europa") disseminated throughout the Russian media is a deliberate twist on what was once a nostalgic longing for the missing piece of a larger, European self. *The Notebook*'s sequels suggest that this lost wholeness can never be restored; the pieces have grown in their own, separate ways and no longer fit. To the extent that this allegorical reading works at all, it is also a tragedy. The Gayropa narrative is a fairy tale of a different kind: a tragedy for Europe that is a cautionary tale for Russia. Gayropa instructs the audience to be glad about its distance from (Western) Europe. Russia is not a part of Europe, and we should all thank God for that. This is not an opportunity lost, but a bullet dodged.

Gayropa is an even better straw man than politically correct America. Whatever else it was going to be, Russia was never going to be America. But Europe was aspirational. If we superimpose Gayropa on Kristof's tale of divided brothers, we end up with the gold standard of genetic studies: an examination of identical twins raised separately, in strikingly distinctive environments. The myth of Gayropa demonstrates what could happen if Russia should choose the incorrect path, showing why Europe, rather than being enticing, is dying and repellent. Structurally, Gayropa is the reincarnation of the Soviet cliché about the decadent or rotting West. But where the Soviets based their anti-Western caricature on a critique of capitalism (the decadent was synonymous with decadent capitalism), Gayropa is about culture, or even worse, civilization.[22]

Indeed, calling Europe "Gayropa" is only a short step from calling it "Sodom": the homophobic documentary I mentioned earlier was called *Sodom*, and the program's host insists on referring to gays as "sodomites" (*sodomity*). Just as Sodom's downfall is framed as punishment for male homosexuality, Europe can expect little better. In Greek mythology, Europa was a Phoenician beauty ravished by Zeus; Gayropa is the homophobe's nightmare: the monstrous drag queen whose deceptive beauty works best when viewed from afar.[23] She is the gorgon who must not be viewed. She is Freud's "phallic mother," striking just as much terror with the phallus's presence as she does with its absence.

Russia's gay panic is, however, framed in terms of children, and contemporary children's literature also proves instructive. The release of the trailer for an animated adaptation of *Children versus Wizards* (Deti protiv vol'shebnikov) in 2016 revived interest in this series of nationalist Russian novels that began in 2004. Like Kristof's trilogy, it purports to be a feat of linguistic border crossing: the alleged author, Nikos Zervas, is a Greek with a vast love of everything Russian, even if all evidence points to the novel's foreign authorship as its most fantastic fiction (Kachurovskaia). Here the world's children are seduced by none other than Pottermania: the widespread popularity of Harry Potter and other children's fantasy stories are actually part of a (primarily Jewish) international conspiracy to hand the world over to the forces of Satan. Only Russia has been spared so far, thanks to a mysterious, metaphysical "Russian shield" preserving the nation's morality. That shield turns out to be none other than Russian Orthodoxy itself.[24]

Gayropa is an even less inventive childish fantasy, but it relies on the same source of salvation: Orthodoxy is the shield that saves Russia from liberal Europe's horrible multicultural fate. The specifics of that fate are once again less about adult homosexuality than they are about children. There are two basic issues at hand here: the evils of the child welfare system and sex education, and the dangers of migration.

The Rape of Gayropa

On January 11, 2016, the parents of Lisa F., a thirteen-year-old Russian-German girl, told the Berlin police that their daughter had disappeared.

Thirty hours later, she came home with a horrific account of her absence: after being lured into a car by a "foreign man, who looked like he was from the Middle East," she was held captive in an apartment and raped repeatedly by three men over the course of an entire day and night ("Migranty v Berline").

Soon Lisa F.'s relatives would claim that the police insinuated that the girl had slept with the men voluntarily. The Russian-German community took to the streets in protest, carrying signs saying "We're against the refugees" and "Lisa, we're with you." Even Russian Foreign Minister Sergei Lavrov got involved in the story of the girl he called "our Lisa," accusing Germany of "covering up reality in a politically correct manner for the sake of domestic politics" ("Berlin to Moscow").

By month's end, the entire case had unraveled. Lisa admitted that she had not been raped but had spent the night with a friend (a nineteen-year-old man who apparently did not have sex with her), because she was afraid to tell her parents about some trouble at school. Subsequently, Lisa underwent treatment in a psychiatric ward (Knight, "Teenage Girl").

Everything about this story is horrible, including its falsification: while the Russian and Russophone media were only too happy to believe the story of a rape committed by dark-skinned men (a phenomenon that should be familiar to Americans, whose historical record in this regard is atrocious), the general tendency in Russia, as in so much of the world, is to doubt women's rape claims.[25] Just as the Tawana Brawley and Duke lacrosse incidents undermine the cases of actual rape survivors, Lisa F.'s tale does women no favors.

Or it wouldn't, if her story's debunking had been treated as news. On February 1, just days after Lisa's confession, her mother was on TV repeating the initial allegations ("Vorwurf der Vergewaltigung"). More important, the Russian media treated the outcome of the Lisa F. case with skepticism before dropping it altogether.

Lisa F. is clearly a troubled girl, but her story's impact is not about her lived experience (or even the falsification of her lived experience). Naming "Arabs" as her rapists may well have been more a matter of cultural reflex than of intentional xenophobia. Like Susan Smith, the American woman who drowned her sons in 1994 after first claiming that they had disappeared when her car was stolen by a black man, Lisa F. concocted a story that fit what her audience was ready to believe. After all, her disappearance occurred only weeks after the notorious wave of sexual assaults in Cologne on New Year's Eve, in which most of the suspects were not of German origin.

But if Lisa F. was ever in control of her own story, she lost that authority once the Russian media got involved. On January 6, the Saturday edition of Channel One's *Vremia* broadcast a ten-minute report on Lisa ("Iznasilovanie"). After presenting Lisa's tale, the reporters moved to an odd video allegedly uploaded by Anonymous, showing a group of young migrant men bragging to each other about the gang rapes they'd committed. Meduza subsequently reported that the video was not, in fact, the product of Anonymous, but of a German pseudo-Anonymous collective specializing in Islamophobia and antisemitism. Moreover, the video had been online for close to seven years, rendering any connection to Lisa's case highly dubious.

At the risk of sounding heartless, I would point out that women and girls throughout the world are raped every day. The elevation of Lisa's case was an obvious political move, one that looks calculated to incite hostility and perhaps even violence against migrants, not unlike Donald Trump's repeated invocations of Kathryn Steinle's murder by an undocumented immigrant in San Francisco in 2015 (Stahl). Moreover, the fact that Russian speakers in Germany, as elsewhere in Europe, watch Russia's Channel One means that the network was creating a feedback loop, further angering an already riled community of Russian speakers and then reporting on their outrage back home (and back to the diaspora community yet again). But setting aside the fact that Lisa speaks Russian, what could possibly be the benefit in playing up this story to the point where Meduza, among others, compared it to the notorious case of the "crucified boy" in Ukraine, which will be discussed in the final chapter (Kuz'menkova)?

Just as Channel One has two audiences (domestic and diaspora), the Russian media's coverage of migration in Europe has a dual agenda. First, the Russian Federation has its own problems surrounding migration; applying the lessons of Europe to Russia is a simple matter.

But it is the second goal that fits the overall shift in Russia's coverage of Western Europe. Gayropa, after all, isn't just about gays anymore; it is an effete, dying civilization whose idiotic liberalism makes it vulnerable to rapacious outside forces. REN TV's Igor Prokopenko, host of *Military Secrets* (Voennaia taina) and *Fallacy Territory* (Territoriia zabluzhdenii) has been playing up the dangers of migrants in Europe for years now. On October 12, 2015, *Military Secrets*, Episode 729, featured an extended report on violent attacks by migrants.

The entire story is stunning in its undisguised orientalism, not to mention racism: we are told that the "Eastern mentality" is such that the only way to resolve conflicts is by beating people up. But Europe, which is wallowing in multiculturalism and tolerance, cannot defend itself against migrant assault. Tolerance, one "expert" tells us, is a "terrible evil." Prokopenko ends his report with a diagnosis: Europe is dying out, and so it needs migrants to maintain the population. They could just have "more white Christian European babies," but instead they have chosen a more dangerous path.

The February 6, 2016, broadcast of *Fallacy Territory* is even more appalling. Men from Arab countries are natural rapists who assume that "European girls" are "sluts." What these "girls" need is for their men to defend them, but the men are so effeminate (cue footage of spas that cater exclusively to a male clientele) that many European women are looking to ISIS for a strong male shoulder to lean on. After all, how can they expect to find male "ruggedness" (*brutal'nost'*) when every other bar is covered in gay rainbows? And perhaps, Prokopenko tells us, the European women who put on hijab and marry jihadists are on to something: perhaps the only way traditional values will return to Europe is if migrants force it on them. Migration, then, is not merely a blight on Europe: it is a decidedly sexual menace that meets little resistance in countries that have succumbed to androgyny. Gayropa not only is raped but exists only to be raped: as a civilization it is, as the saying goes, asking for it.

Lisa F. was a perfect poster child for the evils of Gayropan migration: both Russian and German, she was an innocent Europe with which the Russian viewer was invited to identify. As a mere child, she represented that lost innocence that the entire edifice of the new Russian social conservatism uses to justify its existence: children must be protected at all costs.

The only thing that the Russian media love more than migrants attacking white women is the PC nightmare of Europe's educational and family bureaucracy. These are the front lines of the culture war, where children are indoctrinated by "gender fascism."

For the sake of brevity, I'm going to concentrate initially on my favorite whack job media figure: Igor Prokopenko. It's a tough call: Arkady

Mamontov and Dmitry Kiselyov are equally reliable sources of outrage and, since they are on Channel One and Rossiia, respectively, guaranteed a larger audience. But the sheer scope of Prokopenko's paranoid sensationalism is unrivaled. As a top figure at REN TV (technically not state-owned) and the host of two weekly broadcasts devoted to the military and conspiracy, he has to be hungry for content. He is also a transmedia success story, drawing on his broadcasts to produce more than twenty books to date, with such titles as *Conspiracy Theory: Who Runs the World?*, *Space Aliens of National Importance*, *The Whole Truth about Ukraine*, and *Great Mysteries of the Universe* (I have read or skimmed twenty-two of them so far). And one of his favorite themes is the "perversion" of childhood in Europe.

Sometimes his focus on Europe has an obvious domestic connection. In the June 25, 2016, broadcast of *Military Secrets*, he speaks briefly about the scandal that would eventually bring down Child Ombudsman Pavel Astakhov, only to say, "But the West is no better," and move on to European and American scandals.[26] Prokopenko's staff cherry-picks the most outrageous-looking examples and reports on them with expressions of shock and concern. On January 1, 2016, *Military Secrets* devoted fifteen minutes to scenes from European and American playgrounds and amusement parks featuring sexually suggestive equipment, as well as various niche toys and dolls whose anatomical correctness or morbid humor would, according to "experts," traumatize children.

On *Fallacy Territory* the following month (February 6, 2016), Prokopenko shows clips from a Swiss children's education program narrated by animated sex organs and talks about a kindergarten in Norway that avoids using gendered pronouns. Children are also taught that gays are the same as other people and should be accepted as they are. We are also informed that children are taught the alphabet with a book made up entirely of drawings of naked people.

All of this is part of a general push to show Europe as a land that rejects not only "traditional" sexual norms but gender itself, a land whose future is a posthuman nightmare. Of all the myths that continue to circulate throughout the Russian media and Internet, there is one that exemplifies both this information policy and the extent to which the truth is distorted: the myth that the West has banned the words "mother" and "father."

Initially attributed to the Council of Europe, this ban has somehow migrated to the United States and the United Kingdom. Nikolai Vinnik has traced the origins of this story, which began to circulate in Russia in 2010, to a July 25, 2010, resolution by the Council of Europe. This resolution was a recommendation only and concerned gendered stereotypes in government publications and broadcasts (the words "mother" and "father" don't even appear in the text). But the story was picked up by the German tabloid *Bild*, which mocked the idea of avoiding sexless language. Since the resolution contained few examples, the authors of the story instead cited a Swiss practice of replacing the words "mother" and "father" on official documents with "Parent #1" and "Parent #2." As Vinnik points out, such a reform looks particularly ludicrous in German, which lacks a gender-neutral equivalent to "parent," at least in the singular.

That this story would be picked up by the Russian media is no surprise; broadcasters such as Prokopenko (not to mention the RT network) routinely rely on highly partisan Western sources while presenting them as neutral (Breitbart is a particular favorite). It also fits the overall message about European decline: Europe is dying because it has turned away from traditional values. The focus on the (mis)education of children is a perfect fit. Not only does it exemplify Europe's insistence on gender-based self-sabotage, it points back to the leitmotif of media coverage of migrants: how can an effete, antifamily, antireproductive Old Europe possibly withstand the onslaught of the rugged, patriarchal, aggressive dark-skinned foreigners who, despite their existential threat to Christianity, exude the heterosexual vitality rejected by liberal Europe? Once again, Russia provides a third way: an Orthodox, profamily civilization that has taken on the mantle of what the Victorians called muscular Christianity.

The Passion of Irina Bergseth

Europe's role in Russia's discourse of sex, gender, and the family over the last quarter-century is conveniently bracketed by two famous Russian women and their unsuccessful romances in and with Scandinavia. In Pyotr Todorovsky's scandalous hit film of 1989, *Intergirl* (adapted from Vladimir Kunin's novella of the previous year), Tanya Zaitseva is a nurse by day and hard-currency hooker by night who escapes from the Soviet daily grind by marrying a client from Sweden. But her newfound Scandinavian paradise confounds her with its boredom and pushes her toward her inevitable demise.

Fast forward two decades to a woman who, unlike Tanya, is a real person, even if it seems as though she has been trying her hardest to turn her life into lurid fiction. In 2005, Irina Frolova and her small child move to Norway, where Frolova marries Kurt Bergseth and adopts his last name. Three years later (coincidentally the exact amount of time necessary for Mrs. Bergseth to gain permanent residency status), Irina leaves her husband. And this is where her story begins in earnest.

I'll let Irina Bergseth describe her travails in her own words. What follows is an excerpt from a speech she gave in her capacity as coordinator of the Russian Mothers movement and organizer of the March 2, 2013, March in Defense of Children, an event whose main focus was the plight of Russian children adopted and allegedly abused by American parents:

> My name is Irina Bergseth. I'm a simple Russian mother who was victimized [*postradala*] abroad. I was victimized in Norway. Norway considers itself the USA's 51st State. All the laws are copied entirely from American laws. So the tragedy that happened to me, it is reminiscent of the tragedy that happened to the children who died as orphans in adoptive families. Two police officers knocked on my door and two social workers, and they said that my children belong to the state, and not to me. They were taken away without any paperwork and put in an orphanage. My older son, who was 13, fled Norway to Russia. To the land, the last island where you can live with your biological parents [*s rodnymi roditeliami*]. My younger son was given to his pedophile father. The Norwegian system denied a Russian mother all contact [with her children]. I'm not allowed to talk to my children on Skype. I'm not allowed to call, I'm not allowed to see my child, because I'm Russian, and because the 51st American state thinks I might kidnap my own child and take him to Russia. I don't want to kidnap him. I want to live with my children here on the last island of parenthood. Today, when this tragedy occurs, when boys and girls die in the USA at the hands of barbarians and sadists, I cannot remain silent. If we parents don't stand up for the orphans, who will? Children are separated from their parents everywhere but in Russia. (*Irina Bergset marsh*)

At this point, Bergseth is trying to Americanize her Norwegian tale of woe, linking it to the then-current transnational adoption controversy.

The connection does not stand up to the slightest scrutiny; in fact, Norway's laws regarding the treatment of children go far beyond anything seen even on the local level in the United States. The common framework Bergseth is invoking here is *iuvenal'naia iustitsiia*. Sometimes rendered into English by the false cognate "juvenile justice," the term as it is used in Russia is less about a separate court system for offending minors than it is the network of laws and institutions regarding child welfare or child protection. As such, it is usually painted in the Russian media as an unmitigated evil, a system designed to destroy biological families in favor of an overreaching state.

To the uninitiated, Norway might seem an unlikely heir to Sodom and Gomorrah, but for years it has been mired in controversy about children, child welfare, and foreign residents. The strictness of Norwegian child abuse laws (which include a ban on spanking) makes conflicts with residents from different cultural traditions inevitable (Berglund, "Minister Defends 'Barnevernet'"). In addition, confidentiality laws forbid Barnevernet, Norway's child protective service agency, from commenting on a case, thereby ceding control of the narrative to the parents who see themselves as victims. Media coverage of Barnevernet in India, Poland, Lithuania, and Russia makes Norway look like a terrifying place to bring one's children, oversimplifying the process by which a child can be removed from the home even while exposing what looks to be, at the very least, overzealousness on Barnevernet's part (Idicula; Parry; "Swedish Paper"). This coverage often moves beyond the facts of the cases at hand, fitting Norway into a preexisting narrative of a rapacious, underpopulated West: reports on Lithuanian television, for example, assert that Norway suffers from extreme inbreeding, which Barnevernet combats by seizing East European children in order to improve the gene pool (Parry), and Arkady Mamontov devoted a segment of *Special Correspondent* to Barnevernet's "antifamily" policies and their connection to a general Western effort to destroy the traditional family (*Spetsial'nyi korrespondent*, November 28, 2014).

In Russia, Bergseth became the face of such arguments. Although her views are clearly useful for propaganda purposes, they are, sadly, not unusual enough to account for her ubiquity. Rather, her authority comes from her story of privation and abuse at the hands of an aggressive, totalitarian social service system. More than simply espousing the ideology condemning Europe as a liberal dystopia, she is dystopia's poster child.

She was something of a fixture on state television in 2013–2014, and her claims were taken seriously (indeed, championed) by none other than Pavel Astakhov, the children's ombudsman associated with the ban on American adoption. Bergseth contributes to a narrative that should already be familiar by now; in a 2014 column for the extremist newspaper *Zavtra*, she casually asserts that Europe is suffering at the hands of a "gay dictatorship, a homo-dictatorship, a sodomite dictatorship" whose main instrument is "tolerance" ("Protiv sodomskoi chumy"). Among its crimes are a ban on the words "boys" and "girls" in schools, and an intensive program to turn children gay. Even worse, she claims that Europe encourages pedophilia and guarantees sexual access to children.

After initiating divorce proceedings, Bergseth alleged that her husband had sexually abused their son. When officials from Barnevernet investigated, doctors found no evidence of physical abuse, and social workers determined that the boy's story was a text he had memorized in advance. Instead, it was Bergseth's mental health that was called into question, and she was denied custody and contact with her son.

Here commences a long, international saga involving Bergseth's flight to the Russian border with her older child, and Pavel Astakhov's intervention to get the two of them back into Russia. In part thanks to Astakhov, and in part owing to her friendship with an editor at pravda.ru, Bergseth became a media sensation. Her assertions are presented on broadcasts such as Mamontov's *Special Correspondent* and in Astkahov's book *Our Children* (Nashi deti) as incontrovertible fact, even if she is frequently ridiculed on the Internet and in liberal publications.

Bergseth would be more believable if she knew where to stop, but instead, she keeps spinning one absurd story after another. It turns out that zoophilia has been legal in Europe since 1969, and Germany, Denmark, and Norway have a hundred thousand zoophiles each (all of whom have access to Europe's numerous "zoo-bordellos"). At the March in Defense of Children, Bergseth explained:

> I'm a simple person. But I was stupid enough, dumb enough, I don't know the right word for it, to give birth to a child not in Russia, but in this terrifying land of Vikings, in this white Africa, where children are treated like merchandise. They dress my son in a Putin costume and people line up to rape my four-year-old boy. And here I'm supposed to keep quiet and not go to demonstrations, because if I talk about it, they'll declare me insane, and

I'll never see him again. And maybe I'll lose him. But I survive only by help-ing other people. As of today, dozens of children and families have fled from the West to Russia because they've seen my story, because they've heard my words, and people are learning what Norwegian and Finnish "juvenile jus-tice" really are.

The comments on YouTube are, naturally, merciless: "I'm all aquiver: where can I find a 'Putin costume'?" "Hello! I've just moved to Norway, and I want to rape a four-year-old boy. Can anyone tell me where I can buy a Putin costume?" But setting aside for the moment the implausi-bility of her claims, it is worth noting her engagement in orientalizing geopolitics whenever she compares Russia to the West: the supposedly civilized Norway is equated with its Viking ancestors, while the racism of the phrase "white Africa" speaks for itself. Bergseth handily condenses the discourse of Gayropa and American PC insanity, rendering the clash of civilizations a struggle between morality and vice.

And this is where, once again, Bergseth's story converges with Tanya's from *Intergirl*. In each case, the decision to leave Russia/the USSR for Scandinavia is a terrible mistake that amounts to more than simple home-sickness. The Russian heroine is an openhearted, inherently good woman lured by material wealth and luxury, recognizing the soullessness of her adopted homeland after it is already too late. The differences between their two stories only emphasizes how much the narrative of Europe has changed. Tanya fled a Scandinavia whose triviality threatened the soul, while Bergseth's Norway is aggressively evil. Norway is what happens when "tolerance" runs wild.

Tolerance as a Social Disease

How can anyone be against tolerance? To English speakers, "tolerance" is not, first and foremost, a political idea; to the contrary, its political usage is an extension of its function as an everyday virtue. Thus translating Rus-sian screeds against "tolerance" can look a bit like an article from *The Onion*.

Such a caricature would be unfair. Though the Russian language does have its own word for tolerance (*terpimost'*, along the lines of "patience" or "putting up with something"), this term is rarely invoked in discussions about racial, ethnic, or sexual difference. Why this word was rejected is not entirely clear; perhaps it still conjures up connotations with brothels due to the antiquated term *dom terpimosti* (literally, "house of tolerance," borrowed from the French "maison de tolerance").

Instead, acceptance of difference was saddled with yet another imported world (*tolerantnost'*), as if to emphasize that tolerance is not a local virtue. This is a shame, because it foreclosed any attempt to mythologize tolerance as a Russian trait by rendering the attempt linguistically laughable. Any discussion of the *tolerantnost'* of, say, the nineteenth-century Russian peasantry would be almost as jarring as wondering about their access to Wi-Fi.

An English- or French-speaking country can be full of intolerant people, but not people explicitly crusading against tolerance. This is not the case in Russia, where tolerance joins liberalism and political correctness as terms whose ideas are framed to be as alien as their morphology. Just as liberals are routinely called *liberasty* (libfags), the proponents of tolerance are dismissed as *tolerasty* (tolerance faggots). The reliably outspoken Archpriest Vsevolod Chaplin declared in 2012 that tolerance "is the death of freedom of speech, freedom of thought, and the transformation of a person into a mechanism with Western functions."

The film director Nikita Mikhalkov, a longtime Putin supporter and advocate of "traditional values," takes issue with tolerance in his *Besogon*.[27] Most of his discussion is based on an October 23, 2013, blog post by "family values" activist Mariia Mamikonian. Mamikonian's initial target is the Soros Foundation, whose Open Society Institute she accuses of trying to destroy traditional Russian values through subversive grants and textbooks, and its Tolerance Center in her home city of Ulyanovsk. From there she moves to Lyudmila Ulitskaya's series of children's books about "difference" (The Other. Others. About Others.), which she and other local parents consider gay and pedophile propaganda.

Mamikonian decides to investigate the origins of this strange word *tolerantnost'*, a word she first heard during perestroika. She discovers that it is a medical term referring to the decrease in immunological reaction to foreign stimuli. While she is right that "tolerance" has a medical meaning, she either deliberately or accidentally elevates its immunological connotation to the status of primary definition (a move that would be impossible in a language to which "tolerance" is native). Thus "tolerance" is a plot by foreigners and liberals to weaken the Russian cultural immune system, rendering it susceptible to foreign moral infection.

This is an old idea, of course: it recalls Nazi social hygiene and at the same time works well with the notion of Russian Orthodoxy as a cultural shield. And it's an idea that Mikhalkov clearly loves:

> It turns out that the concept of tolerance is very closely linked to immunity— rather, to the lack of an immune response.
>
> Immunity! National immunity!
>
> What is national immunity? It's the possibility of resisting anything that could destroy you, your family, your society, and your state.

Mikhalkov works himself up into a righteous frenzy, warning that tolerance will somehow lead children to the unthinkable: the rejection of Pushkin. He closes on a warning: "It seems to me that the question of national immunity is a question of national security because if a people has been without immunity since childhood, has its system of roots undercut and its genetic code broken, you can do anything you want with it!"

As a threat to social hygiene, tolerance is thus inherently dystopian, a nightmare future being built in the West and slowly exported eastward. In Russia, it has even become the key feature in a brand new subgenre of right-wing science fiction designed to scare and amuse its readers onto the path of righteousness: liberpunk.

Smug New World

In 2005, the evils of political correctness, liberalism, and tolerance found an official literary home with the declaration of a new form of science fiction called "liberpunk" [*liberpank*]. Authorship of the term is commonly credited to the online game producer Vyacheslav Makarov, whose participation in a series of online exchanges about the phenomenon culminated in "The Definitions of Liberpunk" (Opredeleniia liberpunka), posted on February 7, 2005. The liberpunk enthusiast Artyom Gularian cites Vladislav Goloshchov as the creator of this particular neologism (Gularian).

As with most such manifestos of a new literary movement (including most notably Zhdanov's declaration of Socialist Realism), the participants in the liberpunk discussion codified the genre in part by continually invoking a common set of exemplars: the oldest, Konstantin Krylov's "New World Order" (Novyi mirovoi poriadok), a mock dictionary, dates back to 1997. More recent examples include Arseny Mironov's *The Dead End of Humanism* (Tupik gumanizma), numerous stories by Mikhail Kharitonov, Kirill Benediktov's *The War for Asgard* (Voina za "Asgard"), and Vyacheslav Rybakov's *Next Year in Moscow* (Na budushchii god v Mosvke).

The list was quickly expanded to include the work of Yuri Burnosov, as well as many of the works of Dmitri Volodikhin, who, as both a scholar and practitioner of science fiction, would soon become the movement's primary polemicist. Later that year, the annual Bastion science fiction conference (Bastion-2005) would be dedicated to liberpunk, resulting in a collection of essays whose print run of two thousand copies has so far rendered it impossible for me to find (Levenchuk; Sobolev). If none of these names mean anything to my readers, whose collective knowledge of Russian literature exceeds the norm by several orders of magnitude, this is a testament to the power and limits of literary subcultures. Many of these writers were established SF authors whose works were, if not bestsellers, familiar to any hardcore reader of Russian science fiction.

Moreover, several of them have reached a broader audience than they could ever have dreamed of by joining in the Internet media producer and United Russia Duma Deputy Konstantin Rykov's gargantuan transmedia project *Ethnogenesis* (Etnogenez), a series of novels and online games that create a fictional history of the universe, from millions of years BCE to the Russian-dominated far future. The books, which fall into several different generic categories, follow the exploits of people who gain access to mysterious objects (*predmety*) that grant their bearers superpowers but also entangle them in time-traveling interstellar conspiracies involving more groups than could be fit on a single scorecard.[28]

Most of the protagonists are the descendants of Lev Gumilev, and his theory of ethnogenesis is soft-pedaled and fictionalized as part of the series backdrop. I mention this not only because I have read or skimmed nearly seventy of these books and need something to show for it, but also because their explicit patriotic pedigree and vague Eurasianism could be seen as an ideal setting for a kind of liberpunk-lite, facilitated by the fact that both Burnosov and Benediktov were key figures in the Ethnogenesis collective.

Benediktov, who apparently had an editorial role in the group, has authored or co-authored seven Ethnogenesis books to Burnosov's eight.

All of this begs the question: what, exactly, is liberpunk? The name was developed by analogy to cyberpunk, the subgenre that reinvigorated Anglo-American science fiction in the 1980s. Most closely associated with the early works of William Gibson, Bruce Sterling, and Neal Stephenson (and Ridley Scott's reinterpretation of Phillip K. Dick in *Bladerunner*), cyberpunk typically takes place in a near future in which information technology dominates a postindustrial world run by corporations and all but abandoned by weak governments. Virtual reality, body modification, and a quasi-libertarian ethos set the stage for the adventures of misfit, outcast heroes whose closest literary ancestors are found in noir detective fiction.

The "punk" suffix soon became linguistically productive, leading most notably to steampunk (Victorian-styled alternate history emphasizing steam or analog technology) and, more recently, silkpunk (Misra). "Liberpunk" is relatively euphonious in Russian, since it rhymes with *kiberpank*. When translated back into English, the word is far clunkier, sounding more like a dubious cut of meat than a literary genre (virtually nothing in English rhymes with "cyber"). If cyberpunk was noted for its focus on "high tech, low life," liberpunk, according to its advocates, would create a world of "high law, low life" (Makarov).

Liberpunk posits a dystopian world (usually the near future) in which the ideals of liberalism have triumphed, resulting in a rigid, stultifying, and soulless society fought against by only an enlightened few. Liberalism might seem like an odd template for an oppressive regime, since, by definition, liberalism is supposed to be anti-oppressive. In the Russian context, however, dystopian liberalism makes a certain amount of sense. First, because whatever one might think of the Yeltsin years, what happened in the country in the 1990s was understood as part of a new liberal regime; the chaos of these years is already not far from dystopia. By the Putin era, the excesses and disorder of the 1990s were being officially and unofficially associated with liberalism, and the number of politicians willing to call themselves "liberal" was rapidly dwindling. And whether or not liberal ideals and liberal programs are to blame for the 1990s, the identification of the one with the other allows antiliberals to demonize not only liberals but the very tenets of liberalism themselves.

For liberpunk authors, if liberalism is the ideology, then political correctness is the implementation and enforcement. One of the most frequent tropes in liberpunk fiction is the transformation of a liberal or PC ideal into a draconian law whose violation incurs penalties from forced reeducation to the death penalty.

Thus in "Big Dog: A Liberpunk Parable" (Bol'shaia sobaka: liberpankpritcha) Volodikhin details the negotiations of a committee trying to make sure it has representatives from all the required groups—which representative is legally recognized as a feminist? Without a feminist, the group cannot continue to exist. In Yuliya Ryzhenkova's "Demkontrol," heterosexuality has been all but eradicated, replaced by single-sex families with children raised by the "aunties" and "uncles" who adopted them together. These children are the result of an enforced breeding program that functions like a Russian military draft: on coming of age, young adults without the necessary connections will have to undergo the humiliating experience of sexual intercourse for the sake of procreation (artificial insemination isn't an option, because if it were, the author wouldn't have a story). Naturally, the heroine refuses to part with her baby, and her liberationist struggle against the system begins.

In Leonid Kaganov's "Over the Gay Rainbow Parade" (Dalekaia geiParaduga), an inspector comes to a school to make sure that tolerance and multiculturalism are being taught correctly (if not, teachers could be fired); when the inspector attends a physics class, she is appalled to discover that "male" and "female" are being used as metaphors for the poles of a magnet, thereby insidiously instilling heterosexism in children's impressionable minds.

If my capsule summaries of these stories sound tendentious, it is because these texts are so explicitly satirical and ideological. Theoretically, the tropes involved could be employed by non-liberpunk writers to make the exact opposite points. For example, one of the things that liberpunk shares with cyberpunk is the prevalence of gender modification and polymorphous eroticism. For cyberpunk these are libertarian technological virtues, while for liberpunk they are signs of moral corruption.

Even some of the basic scenarios I've described could be used as calls for tolerance rather than "traditional values." One can imagine describing a society based on compulsory homosexuality as the means to get straight readers to identify with the plight of an oppressed sexual minority, just as writers in the United States have used the science fiction toolkit to estrange the experience of racism for a white audience (Thomas M. Disch and John Sladek's *Black Alice*, John Hersey's *White Lotus*; almost any given episode of the original *Star Trek*). For Western liberalism, victimhood is an essentially fungible experience; it can happen to anyone, and therefore it should happen to no one. Liberpunk does not recognize victimhood as a universal; rather, discrimination can be either just or unjust, and the victims of just discrimination should accept their lot. Liberpunk thus accepts the problematic hierarchy implicit in such phrases as "reverse discrimination" or "white slavery," each of which seem to suggest something particularly improper about the suffering of a majority or dominant group.

Though liberpunk's most obvious targets occupy roughly the same territory as Garner's *Politically Correct Bedtime Stories*, the critique of liberalism goes far deeper. Particularly odious to liberpunk writers is the procedural legalism that classical liberal structures require. Here liberpunk reveals its Slavophile roots, sharing a Russian conservative disdain for systems based on equal recourse to identical legal procedures rather than on a more "organic" emphasis on achieving the proper moral result—the idea of a criminal going free on a technicality, for example, is antithetical to such an "organic" approach. Once again, the distinctions between different usages of the word "liberal" vanish: what starts as a screed against liberal immorality morphs into an indictment of the procedural liberalism that has little to do with contemporary Western political debates. Thus liberpunk creates dystopias with hideously complex and invasive bureaucracies that exemplify a liberal preoccupation with the letter of the law.

Ironically, such dystopias are made worse by reflecting the excesses of Russian bureaucracies as well as their Western counterrparts. For example, in the story I mentioned above, at issue is not just the definition of a feminist, but the all-important registration of the official feminist with the proper governmental authority. This emphasis on registration is alien to the American model that haunts so much of liberpunk fiction; the United States doesn't even have a national ID system, let alone the multiple registration regimes that make Russian bureaucracy so daunting.

Liberpunk can also be seen as a critique of not just the substance but the pace of change. Burnosov's story "Moscow, Year 22" (Moskva, dvadtsat' vtoroi) does this by borrowing from the Rip Van Winkle scenario used so effectively by Edward Bellamy in his utopian *Looking Backward* and by H. G. Wells in his dystopian *When the Sleeper Wakes*, a story to which Burnosov's protagonist directly refers.

In Burnosov's tale, the main character awakens from an eight-year-long coma to discover that the LGBT agenda has transformed Russia. For daring to express disgust at a gay pride parade, a favorite liberpunk symbol of liberal decadence, and using the slur *pidor* (faggot), he narrowly escapes arrest, only to find that his best friend, who now makes a living rewriting classics for the school curriculum as gay love stories, has divorced his wife and married a man.

Joe Haldeman used a similar scenario as an allegory for the alienation of returning Vietnam veterans in his SF classic *The Forever War*, although even with the help of Einsteinian relativity effects, the rapidity of this social transformation defied credibility. But credibility is clearly not part of Burnosov's agenda, as his story fails several basic tests of plausibility that most self-respecting science fiction stories could be expected to meet, not the least of which is the protagonist's perfect physical health after eight years of immobility. Burnosov's story suggests one of the reasons that a liberpunk critique could resonate in postsocialist Russia: a country that has already undergone radical transformation from 1986 to 1991 might not be willing to remake itself so quickly again to meet any agenda, liberal or otherwise.

"Moscow, Year 22" also draws our attention to the conceptual slippage inherent to liberpunk: liberalism and America are presented as virtually the same thing. In Burnosov's story, the triumph of liberal PC ideology (which legalizes zoophilia and pedophilia, proposes a ban on gendered pronouns, and links homosexuality to career advancement) is perfectly consistent with the fact that Leninsky prospekt is now known as "George Bush Avenue" (Prospekt Dzhordzha Busha). The conflation of political liberalism with American hegemony is realized to perfection in Mikhail Kharitonov's "Always Coca-Cola" (Vsegda Koka-kola). Here the United States is virtually undisputed in its mastery of the world, in part because it has made sure that no other countries can make scientific advancements and has required the teaching of American culture in schools across the globe. The allegedly freedom-loving Americans are entertained every Saturday with a beloved game show about bombing uncooperative countries around the world ("Today we're going to bomb . . . Rwanda!").

In liberpunk, liberalism, tolerance, and US policy exist in a sphere beyond transactional politics. Rather, they form a monolithic evil ideology that must be resisted, and that is best opposed by Russia, with its traditions of "spiritual values." Indeed, in its messianism, confidence, and Russophobia, American liberalism is essentially the "anti-Russian idea," a satanic inversion of everything that Russians hold dear.

American Horror Story

After years on the margins, liberpunk has gained more mainstream attention through a clever repackaging that fits seamlessly with current ideological debates. Since 2011, the liberpunk brain trust has released four thematic anthologies, edited by S. V. Chekmaev, that call attention to specific hot-button issues rather than to Liberpunk per se: *Antiterror 2020* (Antiterror 2020, 2011), *Liberal Apocalypse* (Liberal'nyi apokalipsis, 2013), *No Family* (Sem'i.net, 2014) and *Relentless Tolerance* (Besposhchadnaia tolerantnost', 2012).[29] It is last of these four (the first one published) that represents the perfect synthesis of liberpunk ideologies with neo-Putinist values: the title (*Relentless Tolerance*) zeroes in on the idea that tolerance itself is the enemy.

Tolerance, liberalism, and political correctness do not present a clear and present danger to Russia today—on the contrary, liberals in Russia are looking more and more like an endangered species. Then how does liberalism play such a productive role in the Russian dystopian imagination? Why does the Russian hell look so much like Berkeley? And what does this all tell us about the evolution of dystopian thought?

The political content of liberpunk is understandable for the reasons I've already laid out; it is part and parcel of the general antiliberal trends that have animated public discourse in the Putin era, and that threaten to become something of a state ideology in the aftermath of the Crimean annexation. It is the elaboration of this ideology through the generic framework of science fiction that makes liberpunk so noteworthy.

Prose fantasy and science fiction (F&SF) are complex genres whose variety and depth belie the common association between SF and escapist melodrama such as *Star Wars*. F&SF offers a multitude of benefits to the close reader, most notably in the realm of ideology: the ideological scaffolding of F&SF cannot be hidden as easily as it can in mainstream fiction. The act of imagining a world different from our own lays bare the political and sociological assumptions on which the fantasy is based.

For example, the feminist SF writer and critic Joanna Russ finds fault with a great deal of Golden Age (the 1940s) American science fiction in that it assumes that gender and family relations are a constant not worthy of even elementary extrapolation; she calls the settings of these stories "galactic suburbia" (Russ, 206). This should not be surprising. Much of F&SF can be considered a part of popular culture, and a popular fantasy world can reasonably be expected to reflect and reinforce popular ideology. This, by the way, is one reason liberpunk would be unlikely to achieve popularity were anyone to translate it into English. Explicitly antiliberal tales can be found largely in the subgenre of military science fiction (something of a self-selecting audience); the excesses of something like liberalism may be lightly satirized in Dave Eggers's *The Circle*, but his is more of an insider critique than a hostile polemic.[30]

It is precisely the political components of F&SF that traditionally attract mainstream writers who wish to go slumming in these degraded genres before returning to more conventional realism or modernism (Aldous Huxley, Chang-Rae Lee, Cormac McCarthy, George Orwell). This is also the reason that one of the subgenres of SF that is most congenial to such authors, and most acceptable to mainstream readers and critics, is dystopia. Liberpunk writers see themselves as the next step in a dystopian tradition whose focus on language may suggest *1984*, but whose ideological orientation is presented as the heir to Huxley's *Brave New World*. Huxley and Orwell were the twin idols of twentieth-century dystopia, establishing apparently opposite views of the road to hell. Orwell gave us our classic image of totalitarian control, while Huxley described a world in which all meaning was lost to the pursuit of pleasure.

Liberpunk revives Huxley through a creative misreading. Huxley's bête noire was the trivialization brought on by a hedonistic mass culture, but this critique is not, at heart, moralistic: the polymorphous sexuality of the World State is an obstacle to the depth of feeling rather than being a carnal sin. Huxley's novel lacks an explicit moral framework in large part because it doesn't need one. Liberpunk blames the excesses of World State society not just on mass consumer culture but on the soulless moral relativism it finds at the heart of liberalism.

Liberpunk is a truly American horror story. Huxley and Orwell were two British men whose nightmare futures were modeled on the superpowers that would emerge in the twentieth century: Russia/the Soviet Union for Orwell, America for Huxley. We have long understood the role of a Soviet totalitarian model in the American cultural imagination, but with liberpunk, we are witnessing a kind of transcultural symmetry. Finally, America takes its rightful place as the model for Russian ideological nightmares.

The Tyranny of the Minority

If migrants, political correctness, and the LGBT community are all objects of Russian right-wing scorn, the surprise is not that they are met with disapproval; rather, the question is: why are these the issues that have risen to such prominence?

Migrants are a predictable folk devil, given the number of people from former Soviet republics who have sought work or shelter in Russia, but the focus on migrants in Europe is not a reaction to the world outside Russians' windows. The LGBT community, while never beloved by the population at large, managed to get through the first fifteen years of post-Soviet Russia without being demonized. And if political correctness is a real phenomenon in twenty-first-century Russia, it's fighting for closet space with most of the country's lesbians and gays.

The rhetorical fight against a PC straw man is the key, since political correctness is framed as an odious attempt to respond to the needs or demands of minority and/or oppressed groups. Just as American conservatives have tried to recast gay rights as "special" rights or privileges, today's "traditional values" movement in Russia sees minority and majority rights as a zero sum game. As liberpunk shows, the imaginative leap from minority rights to minority dominance is close to reflexive. If the majority does not defend itself, minorities will overwhelm it.

Majority status has its privileges, and chief among them is the right to reject the very idea of majority accommodation to the minority. At this point, any explanation I might provide for the discursive construction of the "majority under siege" can only be speculative. Certainly, it resonates with the xenophobia of the European Far Right, but the idea of a fragile Russian majority is an unlikely Western import. Instead, three particular frameworks come to mind.

The first is postcolonial, a holdover from the Soviet era, when Russian language and culture dominated de facto, but had little status de jure. Even as the Soviet government continued a decades-long policy that highlighted the cultural and ethnic specificity of the USSR's constituent republics, any similar overemphasis on "Russianness" as connected to ethnic Russians looked reactionary. The balance between a Russian national (ethnic) consciousness and an imperial (multiethnic) consciousness has always been delicate.

The second framework is more complicated. It would be a gross overgeneralization to say that Russia and the Soviet Union historically rejected all forms of pluralism; the mere fact of a multiethnic empire that was not based on all-out Russification necessitates the recognition of diversity. Instead, I would argue that pluralism and diversity have traditionally existed as phenomena that, while accepted, must also be carefully managed.

Certainly, this is the case currently when it comes to questions of faith. The 1997 Law on Freedom of Conscience and Religious Associations granted a higher, protected status to "religious organizations" (Orthodoxy, Islam, Buddhism, and Judaism) than to "religious groups" such as Mormons, Baptists, and Lutherans. The law's concern is less for individual freedom of confession than it is for the categorization and limitation of religious bodies. Like a car or a gun, a religion must be registered.

Finally, late and post-Soviet Russia have provided an uncomfortable home to subcultures. In the 1960s and 1970s, the United States and Western Europe witnessed a subcultural boom, particularly in the counterculture. The Soviet authorities, while encouraging hobbyist "circles" and interest groups that worked through the existing structures, such as Palaces of Culture, looked on independent subcultural movements with great suspicion, an attitude that has not entirely vanished since the Soviet Union's collapse. Even fans of *The Lord of the Rings* are frequently discussed in the same terms applied to cults.

These frameworks help us see how the minority enemy is constructed, but they go only so far. Minority enemies are an extension of the same discursive problem that the rhetoric of Russophobia helps to solve, providing a scapegoat so useful to the Russia narratives I discussed in the introduction. Late Putinism desperately needs to project Russian unity (look no further than the name of the ruling party, United Russia), at the same time that it must acknowledge and fight internal dissent. The fight against LGBT "propaganda," like the construction of the migrant "threat" and the PC ideology that allegedly facilitates all these phenomena, turns dissent and difference into an assault on the body politic while rendering border-crossers akin to vectors of infection. Labeling all dissent and difference as foreign-inspired sets the United Russian body politic against contaminants that want to weaken and even usurp it. It would certainly be possible to see sexual minorities, migrants, and liberals as a set of unrelated phenomena, social ills that arise independent of one another. But then they would be no one's fault and might not be subject to a coordinated counterattack. It would also be the equivalent to seeing the economic devastation and crime of the 1990s as mere chaos, rather than having the strange but real comfort of knowing that it's all part of hidden manipulators' master plan. Weaving the social ills of liberalism together into a nefarious plot sponsored by the ever ill-intentioned West reminds the United Russian body politic of the importance of unity while emphasizing Russia's crucial role as the guardian of "traditional values" that, like Russia itself, are under attack. Liberalism and related phenomena are not simply wrong; they are the latest manifestation of the ideological attacks posited by the Dulles, Harvard, and Houston plans, not to mention *The Protocols of the Elders of Zion*. Against such a determined assault, a united Russia must clearly fight back.

5

The Talking Dead

Articulating the Zombified Subject under Putin

"What does it matter who is speaking," someone said, "what does it matter who is speaking."

—Samuel Beckett, as quoted by Michel Foucault

"We've been hearing for over a decade now that we're being zombified by propaganda" (*O tom, chto nas vsekh zombiruet propagandoi, my chitaem i slyshim vot uzhe vtoroe desiatiletie*)

—Quoted by Michelle Berdy, "The Zombies Are Coming"

Zombie Nations

Our world has been overrun by zombies. This, at least, is the conclusion we may draw from our mass culture, and the border between our mass culture and our world is a sketchy one. The blurriness of this boundary immediately points to one of the main purposes to which zombies have been used in American culture (though not, as we shall see, in Russia). After all, one of the logical reactions to the breakdown of civilization prompted by a zombie uprising would be hoarding, the frantic accumulation of consumer goods. But zombie critique reminds us that this is what we already do with our lives: George W. Bush told a traumatized United States after 9/11 that it should go shopping. Slow-moving zombies simply make us pick up the pace of our own consumption as we try desperately to avoid being consumed.

The American zombie is, of course, a Haitian import that has been transformed almost beyond recognition. Like most products of black culture in the United States, it has been whitewashed, only this time to an extreme, deathly pallor. The zombie of voodoo is, we should recall, an individual; it took George Romero and his disciples to make us see zombies in the plural. Thus zombies have become the United States' go-to metaphor for the problem of mass culture. We may lament a face-to-face world, but we don't want to replace it with a face-eat-face world. Zombies are pure bodies—small wonder that, in so many versions, they crave brains.

Yet zombies are also very much about knowledge and subjectivity (brains again), even if they function so effectively as a symbol of a total lack of selfhood. As a shorthand, we can understand the zombie and the ghost as polar opposites: the ghost is the self without a body, and the zombie is the body without a self. Rarely do we ask ourselves what mindless zombies are thinking about, with Hugh Howey's *I, Zombie* as a disturbing exception.[1] Yet the figure of the zombie demands that we reconsider questions of knowledge and selfhood. The philosopher David Chalmers has quite productively addressed the "philosophical zombie" as a way to think about the possibility of living without consciousness.

Indeed, the prevalence of zombies as a media phenomenon turns them into bodies of knowledge, figuratively for those watching, and literally for those who used to watch but now find themselves in their own terrible zombie stories. Zombies are the nothing we know everything about. In Mira Grant's Newsflesh series about bloggers two decades after a zombie uprising, an inordinate number of characters are named "George" or "Georgia," out of gratitude to George Romero for inadvertently training the population through films that now look like zombie-preparation public service announcements. By contrast, the television version of *The Walking Dead*, unlike the comic, is set in a world that never had zombie movies, depriving the show of the multiple levels of self-consciousness available to other zombie entertainments (Newton). Thus zombies both embody the danger of the mass media and the need to pay attention to the mass media. The life saved by a zombie film could be your own.

Moreover, the fight against zombies is often not just existential (as a matter of survival) but ontological. In a world where basic survival is the sole preoccupation, "I" am the subject of the sentence "fights zombies." In the television version of *The Walking Dead*, when Michonne is left to wander a desolate landscape in the company of a zombie herd, she is in danger of mentally becoming a zombie herself. Rick famously says, in both the show and the comic, "We are the walking dead" (Kirkman and Adlard; Ramsay). But the fight against mindlessness can also reawaken a sense of self.

This is one of the themes of the novel, if not the movie, *World War Z*. An oral history of the zombie war, it cannot work without the almost palpable subjectivity of its subjects, many of whom live unsatisfying, automatic lives before the disaster strikes. The threat of the zombies prompts a similar coming-to-consciousness of those who fight them. A rising tide of zombies lifts all biped boats.

The Zombies of Postsocialism

If zombies are such a powerful locus for anxieties about subjectivity and selfhood in the mass-culture, consumer-fixated landscape of postmodern late capitalism, itself an apocalyptic term, what do we make of the post-socialist zombie? The zombie metaphor is alive and shambling in Russia as well, though one could argue it comes to the former Soviet Union second- or thirdhand. Thirdhand, in that it comes from American movies, which themselves are a transformation of the voodoo zombie. Secondhand, in that the myth is somewhat more directly refreshed with references to Haitian practices (as in Victor Pelevin's essay "Zombification").

The postsocialist zombie is harder to pin down with our assorted discursive pitchforks, because the postsocialist zombie does not exist. Obviously, the zombies of contemporary Western entertainment are not real either, but they are fully imagined and imaginable. In the Russian Federation, only since 2013 do we see an increasing number of zombie stories that are not simply a translation or adaptation. Among them, my particular favorite is an anthology by Vladimir Vasilyev, *The Zombies Here Are Quiet* (A zombi zdes' tikhie . . . , an allusion to the popular war film *The Dawns Here Are Quiet*), also the title of a much-maligned web series produced by regional Russian television (L'vov). In 2016, Sergei Lukianenko, best known for his hit Night Watch series of novels and films, tried his hand at the zombie genre with a novel called *Quasi* (Kvazi, with Valerii Kukhareshin), a twist on the "buddy cop" trope pairing up a human police officer with a sentient zombie colleague. The next year, the Latvian-based Russian news outlet Meduza featured the work of Max Degtyarev, who had spent more than three years illustrating possible uses of the Moscow subway as a refuge during a zombie attack ("Surrounded by the Undead").

The most sustained attempt at imagining the postsocialist zombie in Russia today might best be understood as precommunist (and preapocalyptic): the philosopher Oksana Timofeeva's publications, lectures, and performances about zombies and revolution. Timofeeva's approach is outlined in her 2015 English-language "Manifesto for Zombie Communism," as well as a 2017 Russian-language lecture posted to the Vimeo Channel of Chto delat, a leftist intellectual and artistic collective that has been active since 2003. In commemoration of the hundredth anniversary of the October Revolution, Chto delat produced a short film narrated by and starring Timofeeva, set in St. Petersburg: *Palace Square, One Hundred Years After: A Film—Lecture "Four Seasons of the Zombie."* In all of these works, Timofeeva explores the revolutionary potential of the zombie. While admitting the standard conception of the modern zombie as the embodiment of capitalist consumption, she finds several Marxist contexts for understanding the walking dead. Noting that Marx, without actually using the word "zombie" (which he could not have known), at times describes the proletariat in terms of an unconscious body living on the border of life and death, she goes several steps further. In the film she describes a dream in which she is a zombie with two arms but no legs, while her comrade has two legs but no arms. To save each other, they share limbs, suggesting the maximum solidarity afforded by an infinitely decomposing, divisible body. She then explains, in both the film and her manifesto, the power inherent in the zombie's impersonal hopelessness:

> Zombie is the one who is dead, who therefore does not have any hope, but still has a desire, and consciousness, or bodily feeling, or even a kind of instinct or inertia related to the fact that an extreme injustice of his situation

cannot be tolerated—this is an ultimate despair. As already dead, he just cannot live, and that's what, paradoxically, makes him an undead, or a living dead. His decomposing body is not individual any more, it does not belong to any person. A zombie does not have individual life, nothing to take care about, and yet he does not agree to rest, he still desires, and his impersonal body acts.

When we think about zombie apocalypse, we tend to identify ourselves with those who will survive (forgetting, for example, that in capitalism one survives at the expense of the other—isn't this fact already absolutely unbearable?), but what if we are not among those happy survivors? What if we are already on the other side? Forget the hope: revolution starts in the hell. (Timofeeva, "Manifesto")

Timofeeva's zombie is a feat of politically engaged intellectual imagination; it is also a utopian interpretation of total apocalypse that resonates with the Marxist notion that communism is likely to be preceded by (productive) catastrophe. But, like Timofeeva's politics, her zombie is something of a niche phenomenon, deliberately diverging from the Russian mainstream. By and large, the postsocialist zombie is less an imaginary creature than it is a state of mind. This, too, would sound paradoxical, particularly given our earlier distinction between the ghost as a self without a body and the zombie as a body without a self. As it turns out, the zombie metaphor in contemporary Russian discourse is deployed quite differently. As in the West, zombies are the product of contagion, but along a completely different disease vector. Russian discourse is less concerned with zombie as thing than it is with zombie as process: not zombies but zombification.

Western zombies are the threat of the Other, even if one might see oneself reflected in the Other's empty eye sockets. These zombies will destroy you. In Russia, the anxiety is different: the zombie will become you. Russian zombification is not about the perils of commodity capitalism, even after commodity capitalism becomes imaginable as part of Russian everyday experience.[2] Rather, Russian zombification is primarily about the relationship between the mass media and their audience: zombification occurs when the viewer's or consumer's consciousness becomes colonized or hijacked thanks to media input.

Zombification (*zombirovanie*) is almost always a metaphor when deployed in contemporary Russian cultural and political debates, but it is a metaphor that reveals a great deal about the crisis of selfhood in the post-Soviet space; we might call it the "undeath of the subject." To invoke zombification is to posit a particular anthropology, based on largely unspoken but also widely shared conceptions of the boundaries of selfhood and the power of media and propaganda. Zombification posits both the self and culture memetically as information moving from brain to brain, taking hold and never letting go. Both in fiction and in the media, individual Russians—particularly the young, who are the perennial focus of societal fears—are portrayed as defenseless against the onslaught of outside (foreign) influence: popular music, consumer culture, nontraditional religions, and even seemingly innocuous children's fare such as the Teletubbies.[3]

Zombification makes sense, even as a shorthand, only if one is willing to believe in the overwhelming power of media input and the helpless passivity of the media consumer. In turn, invoking zombification is inevitably a political gesture, a statement about the relationship between the governing and the governed. A reification of the Russian governmental power vertical, zombification dooms the Russian audience to an inner life impoverished by constant manipulation that brooks little resistance. And, as Russian-language discussions of the events in Ukraine show, the willingness to invoke zombification as an explanation is a sign that nearly all sides in Russia's political debates are speaking a common language when it comes to politics and subjectivity: no one has any faith in the population's ability to evaluate media messages.

Zombification is the culmination of years of pseudoscientific discussion of mind control and conspiratorial manipulation, whose roots go back ironically to the Cold War and to American anxieties that imported and distorted proclamations of Soviet subjectivity and reforging as a myth of mind control: the brainwashing debate.

Russia imports the idea of brainwashing in the early 1990s, initially as both *zombirovanie* and *kodirovanie* (coding), when activists associated with the Russian Orthodox Church appropriate the scholarship of the Western anticult movement in their fight against so-called totalitarian sects. As the culprits behind zombification proliferate and return to their association with governmental and national actors, the notion that people can be easily brainwashed ultimately renders the concept of free speech moot. Speak all you want; virtually no one is capable of listening.

The metaphor of zombification reinforces one of the points made at the beginning of this book: living in a paranoid or conspiratorial world is tantamount to being a character in a work of fantasy or science fiction. On a broader scale, the national conspiratorial narrative (i.e., malign internal and external forces have never ceased to plot the nation's downfall) erodes the distinction between geopolitics and epic fantasy. Zombification joins trolls, bots, avatars, and daemons in describing a media ecosystem that seems designed to produce agency panic. The networked self, rather than taking constructive advantage of the flows of information that it navigates daily, might prove to be nothing more than a dumb terminal. Even Nietzsche's master and slave paradigm starts to look like a matter for cybernetics rather than ethics.

Zombification also completes the cycle of F&SF metaphors by turning anxiety over subjectivity into the stuff of horror. What starts as an external threat ends by transforming the subject into the embodiment of that very menace. Zombification is teratogenic: if we consume the wrong thing, we become the monster. This is a paranoid scenario that depends on the subject's vulnerability to either corruption or supplantation by outside forces—including mind control, body snatching, and possession—but F&SF also provides lesser-known models where the forces of paranoia move in the opposite direction, from the inside out. Rather than agency panic, the F&SF that Frederic Jameson describes as preoccupied with subjectivity is able to posit a process of self-zombification or self-deception (*Archaeologies of the Future*, 92–99). Here I turn to that most paranoid of American science fiction writers, Philip K. Dick.

In one of his earliest novels, *Eye in the Sky* (1957), after a vague, 1950s-style accident involving a particle accelerator, a seemingly random group of people loses consciousness, only to awaken in a world that is not exactly the one in which they started. Rather, it is an externalized version of the world as understood by the first person to wake up. That person has to be knocked out in order for the group to wake up in the "reality" of the next person to regain consciousness.

Thus in one version of the world, insects sting anyone who blasphemes; in another, communist spies are literally hiding everywhere, while in a third, the sun revolves around the earth due to an old man's insistence that heliocentrism is a fraud. *Eye in the Sky* suggests the primacy of a self that is wedded to errant beliefs and will selectively sort through all inputs to maintain a worldview virtually impervious to critique. In each version of reality, there is only one character who is unable to see that there is anything wrong—the one for whom reality has always been this way.

Eye in the Sky indirectly highlights one of the main problems with the zombification metaphor: that is, the assumption that a worldview divergent from reality is entirely the result of false, invasive information. If I am infected with a zombie virus, I have no choice about becoming a zombie; I was bitten that way. Eat brains though they might, zombies do not have an eating disorder; instead, they are following all the rules of a healthy zombie diet.

But perhaps what gets identified as "zombification" is multicausal, like a weight problem: the food industry should not be pushing junk food on us, but we would like to think we know better than to eat it. Or rather, the food conglomerates are not trying to make us like sugar where we didn't like it before; they've researched what we already like and are tempting us further down a dangerously non-nutritious path.

Like it or not, the simplistic idea of zombification has become the master metaphor for the Russian subject's relationship to mass media. But where does it come from?

Engineers of Hearts, Minds, and Human Souls

Why should people in Russia—or, more precisely, the media narrative about people in Russia—lend credence to models of mind control, and to what extent is such a belief particular to Russia? Why so much mentalizing about the mental incapacity to resist outside influence? Theories of the vulnerable mind appear accurate to the extent that they spread and are repeated: the more verbiage there is about mind control, and the more the "mind control" meme gets assimilated by the broader public, the more minds are actually influenced by a set of verbal inputs. Which leads to a somewhat paradoxical formulation: one does not have to believe in brainwashing to believe that people are being "brainwashed" into believing in brainwashing, "zombified" into believers in zombification.

The brainwashing/zombification narrative works because it posits the vulnerability of *others* while reinforcing a sense of one's own strong, inviolate self: I am not zombified, because I can see how zombification has worked on other people. The reader who comes to believe in zombification has undergone the sort of conversion experience demanded by tendentious fictions, particularly by utopias: they believe themselves to have forsaken the darkness of Plato's cave for the light of truth. But as the idea of zombification becomes normalized, and therefore an almost universally available weapon in everyone's rhetorical arsenal, the resulting allegory of the cave begins to resemble Escher's famous drawing of the hands drawing themselves: in this instance, no one can agree as to which side is the cave and which side is the light.

The brainwashing/zombification paradigm, though developed in the West, has long had a strong connection to Russia, starting with Marxist-Leninist thought and ending with a Putinist absence of thought. Marxism shares a belief in the malleability of human nature in general, and the individual human subject in particular, with the broader utopian tradition. The New World must be inhabited by New People who will be formed by the social processes of developing socialism. Moreover, Marx famously transforms the idea of "coming to consciousness" into something on the order of a law of history: changing the world starts with changing people's minds. This is a proposition that Bolshevism would reverse: first socialist conditions must be established by a vanguard party on behalf of the people, and then the people will, by living in these conditions and being brought to class consciousness, turn their own minds into the proper subjects of a new socialist order.

The Marxist subject is not a closed-off, integral self. Nor are the Leninist and Stalinist selves, despite their roots in Marxist heresies. Thus we see the emphasis on education, reeducation, reforging, and education through labor that starts in the 1920s and takes on its most famous form in the works of the Soviet education theorist Anton Makarenko. The post-Soviet scholarship on Soviet subjectivity, while overturning so many key elements of Cold War historiography, only reinforces this sense of the malleable subject, albeit a subject who might actively choose to appropriate the dominant discourses in order to create a better self.

By the time the term "brainwashing" comes into currency in the West in the aftermath of the Korean War, it is not only a response to Chinese "thought reform" and the experience of prisoners in communist Asia; it is an idea that appropriates the Marxist malleable self for decidedly un-Marxist purposes.[4] What if the Communists really can change people's minds? What if they are trying to change our minds right now? If the Soviet leadership views artistic production as a way of creating better citizens of communism (here we recall Stalin's famous description of writers as "engineers of human souls"), then perhaps our own cultural productions have been coopted by propaganda meant to subvert and transform us. The brainwashing narrative is the demonic inversion of Marxism's optimistic take on human malleability; this essential ingredient of utopian thought becomes the foundation for a dystopian nightmare.

In the West, anxieties over "brainwashing" expressed themselves directly in *The Manchurian Candidate* (1962), and obliquely in *Invasion of the Body Snatchers* (1956). Even Czeslaw Milosz gets into the act: his 1953 book *The Captive Mind,* which was hugely influential on Western Cold War thought, borrows from Ignacy Witkiewicz's dypstopian novel *Insatiabilty* in using mind control as one of its basic metaphors. By the time George Romero unearthed the zombie legend in *Night of the Living Dead* (1968), brainwashing had become a familiar trope of thrillers and horror, with no need of undead corpses to supply it with metaphorical power. Brainwashing was a nightmare of communist indoctrination, not (like the zombie) an allegory of the perils of capitalist consumption.

The actual mechanics of brainwashing were unimportant and varied from narrative to narrative, much like the mechanics of time travel in the sort of low-rent science fiction that would eventually inform the brainwashing narrative. Throw in the numerous "exposés" of top secret Soviet parapsychological research, nearly always about some form of mind control, and the Soviet Union becomes ground zero for a wide variety of mind control fears.[5]

But the brainwashing meme would follow a familiar epidemiological pattern, making a critical species jump in the 1970s. The menace would no longer be communism, foreign or domestic, but the new religious movements (NRMs) that sprang up so frequently in the wake of Sixties counterculture. Castigated as "cults" by their detractors, these movements had leaders or founders who were ascribed quasi-mystical, pseudoscientific powers. Innocent victims allegedly found themselves brainwashed, with the only hope of their rescue in the hands of a new profession: the deprogrammers.

The result is a controversy that continues to generate a great deal of literature, scholarly and otherwise. On one side is the anticult movement, whose faith in brainwashing is used to dismiss the faith of new religious converts, and on the other, the NRM scholarly community, whose approach to its object of study is more ethnographic and anthropological, and which has developed an alternative set of paradigms for explaining NRMs' appeal.[6]

In this new incarnation, brainwashing steps away from pure, unadulterated paranoia, for it has now been dragooned into the service of postcounterculture moral panic. Cold War brainwashing fears were about subversion and treason, but they were in the service of something understandable (communism and its allegorical instantiations), but the "cult" narrative uses brainwashing to explain the inexplicable: how could a seemingly ordinary person start believing in things that, from the outside, look like patent nonsense? Communist brainwashing weakened the nation from without, while cult brainwashing transformed it from within.

How to Win Friends and Zombify People

When brainwashing finds its way into Russian discourse as "zombification" after 1991, it is defined largely by the cult context. Its roots in Cold War anticommunism all but ignored, the discourse of zombification is one of many cases in which what is essentially an ongoing debate in the West is imported as one-sided received wisdom in the Russian Federation ("political correctness" being an even more important example). Thanks to the tireless work of the Russian Orthodox anti-cult crusader Alexander Dvorkin, new religious movements are routinely termed "totalitarian sects" and treated as zombification factories. In an ironic and indirect fashion, Russian anxieties about cult zombification look to the same culprit as did cold warriors in their warnings about brainwashing: the KGB. When the first major cult panic hit the former USSR in 1992–1993, it centered on the Great White Brotherhood of Maria Devi Khristos (discussed earlier in this book). Maria Devi and her husband, Yuri Krivonogov, were routinely accused of manipulating their impressionable followers. But it was Krivonogov who became the main object of suspicion. His prior work in a KGB "post office box" (that is, a secret research facility whose name is always hidden) is assumed to have provided him with state-of-the-art mind control techniques. Even worse, he apparently worked in artificial intelligence, leading one commentator to speculate that his actual project had been "the transformation of natural, human intelligence into artificial intelligence" (Lapikura).

Maria Devi Khristos brought zombification into the mainstream. First, because her followers hijacked long-standing means of spreading information in urban centers, plastering her image all over subway cars and trams. That is, at a time when Western-style advertising was both particularly novel and particularly annoying (television news announcers would inform viewers that there would be ads from, say, 17:40 to 17:43), when such advertising had already taken over the very same public physical and virtual spaces previously reserved for overt propaganda—signs, billboards, airtime—Maria Devi's ubiquity highlighted the very idea of message as contagion. Second, the bizarre garb and behavior of her followers, their willingness to leave their homes and their families, became legible only within the context of zombification (see Kathleen Taylor's discussion of brainwashing as a default explanation for inexplicable fringe behavior).

The portrayal of the cultists as "zombies" was also one of the few points of commonality with Western capitalist zombie tropes, since the Brotherhood was terrifying precisely because they were alleged to be so numerous; the media took at face value their claims to 144,000 followers, a figure whose biblical provenance should have led to skepticism about its accuracy as census data. By 1993, when the movement was disbanded and its leaders arrested, the population had, for all intents and purposes, survived a postsocialist zombie uprising. And, like all survivors, they were wary of repeat attacks.

Zombification in Russia is an idea based on an outdated understanding of the media. When cultural and media elites express anxiety over the presumably pernicious effects of a given mass media phenomenon, they rely on an implicit anthropology of the people on whom the media acts. In the early days of both media panics and media studies in the West, this imagined viewer, reader, or listener was assumed to be impressionable and unsophisticated, an entirely passive vessel for the media's messages.

Consider the Media Effects School, which dominated the Western study of mass media in the first half of the twentieth century: closely associated with moral panics about the dangers of comic books in the 1950s, this model assumes the utter helplessness of media consumers in the face of new technologies that render them passive. To borrow a metaphor from popular biology, a given media risk group (usually children or teens) lacks the immune system necessary to fight off an invasive media attack. Among scholars, the Media Effects School is now largely dismissed, though it survives on daytime talk shows and the local nightly news. Instead, critics now focus on the ways in which audiences wrest and create possibly unintended meanings from the media they consume. Zombification in Russia combines a belief in sinister manipulation with the naïveté of the Media Effects School to create a passive, vulnerable subject that is always ready to be duped.

The 1990s, by spreading the zombification meme far and wide, effectively domesticated the postsocialist metaphorical zombie. The media disseminated a wide variety of messages, as one would expect from any developed media culture, but one of the main metamessages was about the porousness and vulnerability of the self to external influence.

We see this metamessage in the rise of imported advice and lifestyle tracts; indeed, in this context, Dale Carnegie's seminal *How to Win Friends and Influence People* (a post-perestroika runaway bestseller) takes on a slightly sinister ring. Mind control (often KGB-derived) was also a recurring trope across the spectrum of crime and adventure fiction in Alexander Bushkov's *That's Why They're Called Wolves* (Na to i volki): the addled Children of the Galaxy who follow the teachings of their Astral Mother look no more crazed than the clearly brainwashed defenders of the White House (in both their 1991 and 1993 iterations), although some do believe that the Astral Mother gains followers by exposing them to a virus (96–97). The heroine of Alexandra Marinina's *Death for Death's Sake: The Infinity of Evil* (Smert' radi smerti: beskonechnost' zla) discovers that an ex-KGB research facility is using electromagnetic waves to turn the inhabitants of one Moscow neighborhood into bloodthirsty killers. The leaders of a pernicious cult in Polina Dashkova's *Gold Dust* (Zolotoi pesok, 2002) use inverted pentagrams, high-frequency radiation, and vegetarian food to zombify their victims. Arkady Rasskazov, a former KGB general whose repeated attempts at world domination are foiled only by the heroic Savely Govorkov, nicknamed "Mad Dog" (*Beshenyi*), creates a "biorobot" using scientific methods developed by one of the FSB's "main architects of the development of biosensory influence on the human brain (Dotsenko, *Vozvrashchenie*). A group of Satanic sex fiends tries to brainwash the heroine of Bushkov's *Madwoman* (Beshennaia, 1998). Episode 1 of the television series *National Security Agent* (Agent national'noi bezopasnosti), "The Light of Truth" (1998) pits the hero against a sect that uses a "powerful psychotropic drug" to turn hapless dupes into zombies.

The Red/Brown conspiratorial novel, whose roots go back to both the Dulles Plan and Klimov's homophobic and antisemitic ravings, took zombification as an article of faith—for example, in Norka's *Inquisitor* trilogy. In *Mister Hexogen* (2002), Alexander Prokhanov places the blame for the collapse of Russian morals and the brainwashing of the population squarely on the shoulders of the (Jewish) oligarchs who, he claims, control the mass media: the Ostankino television tower is a notorious "center of evil," so virulent that any psychics who employ their abilities within its vicinity collapse from heart attacks and strokes. Inside, specialists in computer science and mind control use their "anthropological laboratory" to develop television shows that model the new reality, teaching Russians to hate themselves and admire Jews (Prokhanov, 165–69). Sergei Kara-Murza would produce three gargantuan tracts about the role of "the manipulation of consciousness" in postsocialist Russia. But the bard of zombification was the novelist Victor Pelevin.

Pelevin introduces the topic in a 1994 essay titled "Zombifikatsiia," a term that would quickly be supplanted by *zombirovanie*. After a rather lengthy overview of voodoo tradition, Pelevin makes the rather easy argument that everyday life in the Soviet Union was, in itself, an ongoing zombification project. Pelevin, however, would quickly adapt zombification to post-Soviet reality (or, at least, for what passes as reality in Pelevin's deliberately elusive fiction). Mind control through media manipulation is a recurring motif in Pelevin's novels, achieving its ideal form in his 1999 novel *Homo Zapiens*: Pelevin's hero discovers that the post-Soviet mass media are part of a political and mystical conspiracy to rule (and dupe) the country's population (even Yeltsin turns out to be nothing more than a hologram). Tellingly, the hero's journey to consciousness (imagine the Allegory of the Cave + Photoshop and holograms) starts with Dale Carnegie, moves through the basics of Western advertising, and culminates in his understanding of the deceptive unreality of the mediated world that he himself has helped maintain. The computer programmers in *Homo Zapiens* who produce a simulacrum of a Russian government for mass consumption (257–62) are not that different from the Svengalis who run Prokhanov's "anthropological laboratory" in the Ostankino television tower. One of Prokhanov's characters notes that the satirical *Puppets* (Kukly) program is actually an exercise in sympathetic magic, using ESP and electromagnetic waves to control viewers' perceptions of the world (171), while the protagonist of Pelevin's *DPP(nn)* creates his own puppet show (starring caricatures of then-current Russian political figures) to strengthen his own program (in this case, a metaphysical agenda involving the numbers he believes play a positive role in his life). Though Pelevin's work shares many tropes with other post-Soviet conspiratorial novels, it differs radically in tone. Norka and Prokhanov are sounding the alarm, while Pelevin is registering a mixture of admiration, amusement, and disdain.

Instead, Pelevin is taking part the corrosive cynicism of the post-Soviet era, tacitly encouraging his readers to assume all speech, particularly political speech, is suspect precisely because it is trying to be persuasive. The rhetoric of mind control is a powerful persuasive weapon that devalues the persuasive political speech and ideals of one's opponent, consigning all those who believe what they are told (by people one abhors) to the realm of the zombified.

Everybody's Talking (And Nobody Says a Word)

Accusations of zombification are a useful tactic in the general undermining of all political discourse, in that they serve as a substitute for actual evaluation. The very question of free speech is thus rendered moot: rather than *evaluating* speech according to its worth, its sincerity, and its effects, speech can be entirely dismissed. Speech becomes excess (either as the flood of verbiage that zombifies its audience or as the meaningless sounds uttered by the zombified subject). The zombie who repeats what he or she has been told is something of a hybrid (a zombie/parrot); the classic zombie does not speak at all.

The dismissal of so much speech as nonsense is a powerful idea (rooted in Orthodox hesychasm, if one wants to bother to go that far). It suggests that perhaps the discourse would be more productive if more people would choose to be silent. The political advantage that such silence might hold for powerful elites is clear, but it also parallels an aesthetic judgment that partakes of a different kind of elitism. Recall Anna Akhmatova's lament that, through her example, she encouraged women (poets) to speak, and now she only wishes they would shut up.

Decades later, Milan Kundera mounts a sustained critique of a vapidly confessional culture in *The Book of Laughter and Forgetting*, populating his novel with graphomaniacs who labor under the illusion that their inner lives are worth expressing. Kundera captures this idea in one of the novel's most powerful images, that of six apparently anxious ostriches on display in a zoo: "The ostriches were like messengers who had learned an important message by heart but whose vocal cords had been cut by the enemy on the way; so that when they reached their destination, they could do no more than move their voiceless mouths" (129).

Written in 1979, *The Book of Laughter and Forgetting* targets a capitalist commercial culture that is still largely analog, and that still finds its abject Other in the world of "developed socialism." Yet in the decades that have seen both the digital revolution and the collapse of communism, Kundera's skepticism about the proliferation of words seems prescient. The intelligentsia's handwringing about the market's vulgarization of culture would be quickly superseded by the occasionally disturbing democratization of discourse online.

Returning to Putin's Russia, this is where the regime and the opposition come together: the regime apparently assumes that people are idiots easily duped by what they see on television, but their message is coated in populist invocations of the common people's values. The opposition finds itself falling into the trap of agreeing with the regime's attitude toward the population; hence the repeated, disdainful use of the word *bydlo* to describe them. An obsolete word for cattle, *bydlo* as a collective noun describing stupid, lumpen masses is separated from the zombified only by species.

Can the Zombie Subaltern Speak?

Critics of the media scene during Putin's third term, a time when the state's grip on the largest media outlet grew stronger and more obvious, posit an imaginary Russian media consumer, a post-Soviet couch potato whose gullibility helps the regime ruin the country. Hence the frequent accusation that so-called patriots and the majority of the population that allegedly supports Putin are victims of zombification, as the opposition leader Boris Nemtsov asserted only two months before his assassination: "Zombifying people is the main attribute of Putin's regime." Putinists, in turn, hurl the same accusation at the supporters of Maidan, essentially conflating crowds at a street protest with the proverbial zombie hordes. In both cases, the primary tool for zombification is said to be television, the "zombie box" (*zomboiashcik*), which is the Russian equivalent of the boob tube.

The critique of the zombified television audience is a revolution that will, in fact, be televised. In 2015, the science fiction writer Yuri Khor exploited the "zombie box" metaphor with a twist in his novella *Zombie TVN* (Zombi TVN). The novella's capsule description puts it more clearly than the actual novella: "The ancient magic of necromancy has been forgotten . . . But modern technology is our daily reality. A reality filled with the so-called information field created by all the various broadcasting media, from newspaper to radio, from television to the Internet. The latest innovation in broadcast formatting has led to an unexpected effect, creating actual zombies."

When television journalists using the new TVN format point their cameras at a dead body, that body rises up and becomes a zombie. In Khor's story, zombification is not what the television does to the viewer, but rather what the television does to the viewed. *Zombie TVN*, perhaps inadvertently, highlights the multidirectional nature of accusations of zombification. It is not simply that the viewer is being zombified by television, but that television is offering its viewers images of others who are framed as zombified. Any consideration of the current zombification paradigm must take into account the manner in which people on the screen can be used to support the notion that people are being zombified *by* the screen.

The material produced on state television (whether in Russia or Ukraine) is not the sole justification of the zombification paradigm; it is the videos that viewers make of themselves for YouTube that are invoked as evidence of the zombie box's power. Not long before Putin began his third term, the zombified viewer took on a specific face: the video blogger turned cult figure who refers to himself as "Astakhov Sergii."

Astakhov Sergii was a Muscovite in his early thirties who started post-ing videos to his YouTube Channel in July 2010 (he died in early 2017). Though his video archive is an object lesson in the perils of bad labeling (six videos in a row bear the title "My New Russian Orthodox video"), by 2013, he was accumulating viewers through both YouTube and the popu-lar social media site Vkontakte (VK), becoming one of the Russian Inter-net's most famous *friki* (freaks). That same year, Anatoly Ulyanov related a twenty-minute documentary compiled from Astakhov's clips, under the inevitable name "My New Russian Orthodox Video." Whatever else one might think of Ulyanov's work, this distillation of more than two hundred videos is something of a service to viewers, in that it functions as a "great-est hits" reel.

Astakhov described himself as an "invalid," referring casually to his "many physical and psychiatric diagnoses" (most of which remained un-named). Kinder viewers have speculated that he might have been schizo-phrenic, or that he fell somewhere on the autism spectrum (less charitable commentators choose from a variety of insulting epithets).

Ulyanov's video—as well as a more recent documentary called *No Country for Fools* (Durakam zdes' ne mesto) by Oleg Mavromatti—are careful to show some of Astakhov's more amusing and idiosyncratic be-haviors (dancing nearly naked, kissing the computer screen, talking about his favorite foods ad nauseam), many of which would be familiar or at least legible to people who have watched some of the many autobiograph-ical videos of neurodiversity that YouTube facilitates.

But both Ulyanov and Mavromatti are particularly taken by Astak-hov's discussion of religion, politics, patriotism, and sexuality, which vary from the oddly profound to a confusing word salad in the course of under a minute. In one breath, Astakhov will refer to himself as a "Russian Or-thodox patriot" who demands the elimination of "sodomy" and "gays" from his motherland, yet who refers to his own sexuality by explaining that he understands men because he herself is a man (*potomu chto ia sama muzhchina*).

As a documentary subject, Astakhov appeals to both his directors as an embodiment of everything that is wrong with the Russian media in general, and the Russian media consumer in particular. In the description of his film on YouTube, Ulyanov writes: "Sergii Astakhov is contemporary Russia, gripped by patriotism and Russian orthodoxy. Here, against the backdrop of endless Olivier salads while watching television, the 'very biggest' shopping centers are being built and laws against 'homosexual propaganda' are being passed. Living on the outskirts of Moscow, in a labyrinth of faceless gray high-rises, Astakhov absorbs this caricatured 'Russian World' and expresses it in his very sincere YouTube videos."

Neither director is at all interested in considering the ethical dimensions of using Astakhov as a subject, since Astakhov himself made these videos public. Nor do they seem particularly concerned with the ramifications of their work for the disability community, though Ulyanov is quick to point out that the new media have given shut-ins an unprecedented opportunity for public self-expression. Yet Astakhov's apparent disability, whether defined neurologically or psychiatrically, is part of their overall point: his cognitive differences are what allow the directors to critique the current Russian media/political environment.

For each of them, Astakhov is something of a limit case that clarifies the condition of a notional average Russian media consumer: one of the first things Astakhov says in Ulyanov's film is "I like to watch Channel One." His blind faith in Russian state television and his ability to hold multiple, seemingly irreconcilable beliefs at once are set up for the viewer as the proverbial mirror of satire—Gogol's famous "Don't blame the mirror if your mug's on crooked." Viewers are meant to recognize themselves—or, more likely, the neighbors they disdain—in Astakhov's image. Mavromatti is usually less explicit on the matter than Ulyanov, but the fact that Mavromatti's film debuted in a festival titled "Signals: Everyday Propaganda" speaks volumes. These films attempt to expose the weakness and gullibility of the Russian viewing subject by suggesting that said subject is, by definition, an idiot. Ulyanov and Mavromatti assault the imagined Russian viewer through identification with a person who no one, presumably, would want to be.

Ulyanov calls Astakhov "defenseless" in the face of the media onslaught to which he willingly exposes himself everyday, thereby offering him up in support of the most simplistic model of propaganda: "[W]e can look at [Astakhov] as, for example, a portrait of Russia that, due to his psychological particularities he soaks up all this media landscape of our country. . . . In a sense, he is a kind of sponge in which that whole 'Russian world' and Russian culture in its current state has been absorbed, along with that out-of-control Orthodoxy and patriotism and all those messages . . . he expresses them straightforwardly." In one interview, Olga Riabukhina asks Mavromatti point blank: "So you're equating Astakhov and the new Russia that is being born right before our eyes?" It should come as no surprise that Mavromatti answers in the affirmative.

Ulyanov and Mavromatti juxtapose Astakhov with the imagined television viewer in a manner that insults them both: Astakhov, in that every simile and metaphor used here completely deprives him of agency (when even Ulyanov had also recognized the power of YouTube precisely for self-expression), and the Russian "patriotic" viewer, who, in addition to his presumed passivity, is also implicitly being called an idiot. By denying viewers agency, Ulyanov and Mavromatti fall into the very trap that they imagine awaits the Russian media consumer: if there are messages in the media, their content is irrelevant and unworthy of evaluation. Instead, we pay attention only to the manner of presentation. It is the metadata, rather than the medium, that are the message.

Speaking Putinist

The use of Astakhov Sergii as a symbol for the Putinist audience results in a particularly damning view of the population. Framed as mentally defective, Astakhov is essentially always already zombified. He is also the ideal subject for the outmoded Media Effects model and an ironic inversion of Stephen Kotkin's notion of "speaking Bolshevik," in that, as he tries to "speak Putinist," he is dealing with a language that he has not mastered. Whether or not he is on the autism spectrum, he does belong on a spectrum with his fellow viral video star Sveta from Ivanova, the naive, cow-eyed young woman whose tongue-tied attempts to explain her support for Putin's United Russia made her an Internet sensation:

> My name is Svetlana, from the city of Ivanovo. United Russia [Putin's party] had made very many accomplishments: they've raised put the econo . . . economy, we've started to . . . dress more better, and there wasn't what there is now—these are very big accomplishments! In agriculture everything's good. . . . There's more . . . land . . . more, well, . . . I don't know how to say it . . . more land sown . . . and, yeah, vegetables, rye—all of that. What else . . . Since our country is multinational, we have lots of people in Moscow who help us a lot . . . from other cities. . . . Yes, it's a big

accomplishment! Very good, even! See, well . . . see, back in Ivanovo medicine has gotten good . . . uh, what else . . . the cities are well-maintained . . . housing . . . no problems with that. People are helping very well.

It is telling that her signature phrase shows her to be inarticulate: that, under Putin, things have gotten "more better" (*bolee luchshee*). In Sveta's case, her video fame also led to a career in reality TV, a career that could not have been successful if her fan base were limited only to those who appreciated her as kitsch or camp ("'Nashistka'").

Sveta and Astakhov indirectly point to one of the political inadequacies of the zombification model: both speech and the reception of speech are assessed entirely according to the standards of rational, intellectual discourse. When individual subjects—or, worse, large segments of the population—produce speech that is logically and ideologically incoherent, it is easy to dismiss the speakers for their presumably faulty standards of judgment. Both Astakhov and Sveta remind us of the extent to which political beliefs and their expressions are not the products of an idealized Cartesian subjectivity. More often than not, such pronouncements are the product of emotional rather than intellectual reasoning: Do you have a reflexive sympathy for the underdog, for the oppressed? Do you find group solidarity of paramount importance? Zombification is not just based on false psychological and informational premises; it is based on the belief that politics are the product of rational thought and that intolerable political beliefs are founded in faulty rationality. Zombification looks plausible in a conflict between competing affects, devaluing not only the content of the speech but the feelings that supply the content. Those feelings are the metamessage, and we belittle them at our own peril.

Stop Making Sense

A world in which one's ideological opponents are, a priori, zombified—or, in the American case, duped by "fake news"—is a world in which words are no longer trusted. More specifically, words are taken to be purely performative, their constative value (assessed according to truth or falsehood) becoming less a matter of cognition than of affect and allegiance. Engaging *with* the demonized discourse—whether dubbed zombification, propaganda, or fake news—starts to look suspiciously like engaging *in* it.

This is the logic (or, perhaps, antilogic) that animated the protest movement of 2012, when Russians in the two capitals of Moscow and St. Petersburg took to the streets in response to rigged elections, another phrase that now carries more venom than it does meaning. Protesters carried signs with playful slogans that resembled clever status updates on Facebook taken to the streets. The protests combined two important features: the sheer fact of bodies on the streets and an absurdist refusal to engage with official rhetoric on its own terms.

The protests and the actionist art that grew out of them refused to fall into the trap of the articulate. This is the essence of Pussy Riot's Punk Prayer—the scandalous, guerrilla anti-Putinist performance in Moscow's Church of Christ the Savior that led to the arrest of three of the participants. Pussy Riot set aside all notions of reasoned argument in order to make a set of emotional, deliberately shocking performative statements. Pussy Riot did not *argue* with the regime (at least, not before their trial, at which point they pulled off a stunning code switch and assumed the roles of articulate intellectual dissidents); they yelled at it.

The denial of discourse is an even more prominent feature in the work of Pyotr Pavlensky, who first came to fame for literally sewing his lips shut in response to the persecution of Pussy Riot—a stance that night have availed him better than his verbal statements in response to the recent rape accusations against him. His subsequent abuse of his own body (nailing his scrotum to Red Square, cutting off part of his ear on the roof of the Serbsky psychiatric institute) appropriates, as Anastasia Kayiatos so deftly argues, the nonverbal language of defiance practiced by Gulag inmates in Soviet times.

The rhetoric of zombification, like the zombie plagues of film and fiction, spreads inexorably through contact and engagement. The main difference is that the heroes of zombie tales know that they can't stop zombies through argument, nor do they think their opponents are dupes of a Machiavellian power. The response to zombies and zombification cannot depend on words. It is not that words fail us, but that words have already failed us before we even began to fight.

6

WORDS OF WARCRAFT

Manufacturing Dissent in Russia and Ukraine

Marina's neighbors from the Palisades assumed
Ukraine was full of Mexicans, asking Marina
what language Mexicans spoke in Donetsk.

—ANYA ULINICH, "PETROPOLIS"

A War with No Name

While it would be difficult to decide which of the many statements
made by the brilliant French theorist Jean Baudrillard is the most profound, there is little question as to which is the most obnoxious: look
no further than the title of his 1991 collection, *The Gulf War Did Not
Take Place*.

Baudrillard's point was not to dispute the human cost of what sadly
came to be called the First Gulf War; quite to the contrary, he argued
that the extensive media manipulation and stylized propaganda charac-
terizing the war's presentation to Western citizens rendered a bloodbath
available as a simulacrum while simultaneously reinforcing a postmodern
model of the citizenry as the state's audience. As the US military moved
from Operation Desert Shield to Operation Desert Storm, the American
public was treated to a carefully stage-managed presentation of an otherwise incomprehensible war, starting with falsified atrocity propaganda

in congressional testimony about Iraqi soldiers tearing Kuwaiti babies from their incubators and culminating in the repeated images of the same American "smart bomb" destroying the same Iraqi target.[1]

In a similar vein, the war in Ukraine is a highly mediated phenomenon, a conflict that most people in Russia and Ukraine are fortunate enough to experience only as audience. It is this virtual war that serves as my subject, a war that shares as much with fiction as it does with fact. This is not to cast doubt on the suffering of the dead and displaced citizens of Eastern Ukraine. Reliable statistics are difficult to obtain, but according to the UN Human Rights Monitoring Mission in Ukraine, the death toll surpassed 10,000 by June 2017, including the 304 passengers of Malaysian Flight MH-17; to these appalling figures we must add a refugee crisis, with 1.5 million people displaced by the fighting (AFP).

But the exploitation of this human misery for propaganda value itself operates as a kind of displacement of real pain into the realm of the political and the national. The bodies of the actors and acted upon are all too real, but their experience has been hijacked from what Lacan would call the Real with a capital "R" (prelinguistic, pre-Symbolic bodily experience that defies the power of language) and transfigured into the realm of the Imaginary (stock representations that short-circuit complex, discursive thought more often than they aid it).

The complexities extend to basic questions of language, indeed, of simple naming. Unlike the First Gulf War, which was branded and trademarked before it actually began (Desert Storm), the on-again, off-again fighting in Ukraine defies nomenclature. We often resort to a mealy-mouthed, anodyne locution: "the conflict in Ukraine," a bloodless and bureaucratic phrase with echoes of the "Korean conflict" of the 1950s. To call it a civil war would be to downplay the role of Russia's military, a role that the Russian government manages to confirm and deny almost in the same breath; to call it an invasion would ignore the internal dynamics of a long-troubled Ukrainian state while inflaming the rhetoric about an alleged Russian threat to world peace.

The framework for discussing the Ukrainian conflict is just as disputed in the West as it is in the former USSR: was the Euromaidan protest movement the expression of popular desire for European values and American-style democracy ("Truth, Justice, and the Ukrainian Way"), in opposition to crypto-Communists and would-be USSR revivalists, or was it yet another example of the fallout from the United States' overseas hegemonic blundering in general and failed Russia policy in particular (heedless NATO expansion, quasi-imperialist encouragement of "color revolutions," and a conditioned reflex to see in Vladimir Putin the second coming of Joseph Stalin)?

The lack of a conventional name for this particular war is offset by the plethora of new and revived toponyms for the area in which it is fought: "Donbass," itself a customary abbreviation based on the name of a Don River tributary, has yielded to the Donetsk People's Republic (DNR) and the Luhansk (or, if you're a Russian speaker, Lugansk) People's Republic (LPR), all subsumed into the fantasy known as "Novorossiya." To those in the separatist East, their enemies are not simply "Ukrainians" but "Banderites," "fascists," and "Galicians," while the Russian Federation forces whose presence was intermittently acknowledged by Putin's government were put forward as simply "polite people" and "little green men."[2] Once again, a Real military conflict approaches the world of high fantasy, populated by fantastic creatures. But the same dynamics that threaten to turn real events into a fantastic story are also behind the insistence on interpreting them as *plot*, both in a literary and conspiratorial sense. The violence in Ukraine, continually posed as a proxy war, would then be the work of malign forces pulling strings offstage (the State Department, Putin, NATO).

This Country Which Is Not One

When Alfred Jarry bid farewell to the nineteenth century with his delightfully baffling *Ubu Roi* (1896), he set the play in "Poland—that is to say, nowhere." Not content with simply denying an event, Jarry negated an entire country, thereby managing to outdo Baudrillard's polemical nihilism ninety years before the Gulf War did or did not take place. Partitioned and repartitioned within an inch of its life, Poland was a Real place for which there was no room on official Symbolic maps. Or perhaps one could say it survived as a literary and cultural phenomenon: simultaneously a touchstone for avant-garde pataphysicians (Jarry) and the source of fantastic modernist experimentation (such as Stanislav Wyspianski's *The Wedding*, written just five years after *Ubu*).

It is sadly appropriate, then, that a significant chunk of Polish (nonexistent) territory would eventually become part of Ukraine—nearly all of Ukraine's land is a geopolitical Trojan Horse, smuggling in its neighbors' territorial claims. The Russian literary tradition gives little comfort to participants in territorial disputes. In the title of one of his many didactic fables, Tolstoy would ask, "How Much Land Does a Man Need?" His story unfolds in the context of Russian colonialism, telling of a greedy Russian carpetbagger who covets Bashkir land. When the protagonist dies as a result of his overreach, we learn the answer to the title's question: a man needs just enough land to bury him in.

Closer to home, the title of a lesser-known story by the Russian (Ukrainian!) writer Nikolai Gogol might well apply to Ukraine: "A Bewitched Place" (Zakoldovannoe mesto) (1832). In Gogol's tale, the bewitched place alternates between immobilizing the feet of the person who stands on it, magically transporting him to a cemetery, and offering a treasure that turns out to be slops and waste. Read deliberately against the grain, "A Bewitched Place" is a cautionary tale against territorial attachment; soil (native or otherwise) is just another form of filth. In questioning the ontological stability of the ground beneath one's feet, Gogol's story can remind us that a land (here, Ukraine) is not just an exercise in magical thinking ("If we build it, they will come"), but magical realism.

This may be its true inheritance from Poland. At the beginning of the twenty-first century, Poland is definitely somewhere: its borders consistently delineated on most maps, the country has the reassuring object permanence that only NATO membership can bring. Meanwhile, Ukraine's status (both Symbolic and cartographic) has a tendency toward the blurry. Recognized internationally since 1991, Ukraine nonetheless finds its very existence as a real country constantly called into question, which only reinforces a reflexive nationalist desire to trumpet the nation's value. One side claps for the continued life of a Ukrainian Tinkerbell, while the other side would gladly see her fade away.

The most notorious dismissal of Ukraine's reality is an oft-cited quote attributed to Putin himself by an unnamed source in 2008. According to *Kommersant*, Putin told then-president Bush: "You don't understand, George, that Ukraine is not even a state. What is Ukraine? Part of its territories is Eastern Europe, but the greater part is a gift from us." (Allenova; Marson) Gordon M. Hahn argues that, in the absence of a named source, this quotation can only be taken seriously as a piece of anti-Putin propaganda. If so, it nicely bookends the fake Madeleine Albright quotation discussed earlier. Albright allegedly lamented that Russia's control of Siberia's natural resources is unfair. Putin's assessment of this fake quote could apply equally to the comments about Ukraine attributed to him ("I'm not familiar with this quote . . . , but I know that such thoughts wander through the minds of certain politicians"). Even if Putin never told W. that Ukraine wasn't a real country, the quotation itself represents a casual dismissiveness that should be familiar to anyone who has spent much time in Russia after 1991.

But what does it mean to be a "real" country? In relation to Ukraine, this question has nothing to do with international recognition, established currencies, or membership in the United Nations. Nor is it a matter of being a "failed state," a phrase that may have gained some currency in the aftermath of the Maidan but was rarely part of the dismissiveness toward Ukraine that preceded it (Dutsik). Certainly, there is the postcolonial assumption that the power to take a state seriously rests with those in charge of the Russian Federation. The country's juridical status as successor to the Soviet Union, which was crucial to questions of national debt, nuclear nonproliferation, and UN Security Council membership, structurally reinforces the identification of Russia with the authority that prevented the other Soviet republics from going their own way.

For those who grew up in the United States or Canada, countries whose histories are a mere blip in comparison to the far older lineages of the average European nation (let alone China), the casual dismissal of "younger" states may be hard to fathom. Russia in particular has a long cultural tradition of establishing the country's "greatness" firmly in the realm of historical *longue durée* and high cultural accomplishment (seen as contributions or gifts to world culture and civilization). Russia, a country whose lack of a national epic was so troubling to eighteenth century Neo-Classicists, has turned its history into the equivalent of that missing epic. For a country to be real, it must have something to offer that is in some way comparable. The end of the Cold War led to the establishment of twenty-five new states out of the ruins of three (the USSR, Czechoslovakia, and Yugoslavia). Some of these countries could lay claim to a long and storied history—after all, the Russian Federation is one of them. But even the Soviet recognition of "nationality" as a meaningful category was based on a clear hierarchy, a family of "little brothers" aligned with its eldest sibling, Russia.

The problem is further complicated by the rise of quack historiography and garbled metaphysical ethnography discussed in a previous chapter. Unsatisfied with Russia's already impressive lifespan, Fomenko's New Chronology is dedicated to the proposition that virtually every great accomplishment and event in the world's past can be understood as Russian or proto-Russian. Even more insidious is Gumilev's theory of ethnogenesis, which insists that nations are, rather than contingent historical constructs, virtually biological entities that result from understandable physical laws (based on astonishingly bad pseudoscience). Gumilev, whose ideas have become mainstream since the final days of the Soviet Union, transforms Romantic notions of nationhood into "scientific" fact, complete with "greatness" as an important historical force. Conveniently, he also put forward the "superethnos" as an ethnic group so great and so large as to encompass smaller, contiguous or overlapping ethnicities. Such as, for example, Ukrainians.

Sergei Belyakov ended his recent, prize-winning biography of Gumilev with a lament that Western "conformism" leaves no place for ethnogenesis: "Gumilev will be of interest to Western scholars only after the Western world itself changes to the point of being unrecognizable." This certainly holds true for the Western scholarly world. From the point of view most common in Western academia, all nations are consensual fantasies. The denial of Ukrainian sovereignty breaks the laws of the fantasy genre by refusing to suspend disbelief.

A doctrine of primordial nationhood implicitly disadvantages former imperial holdings, and even more so when the colonized resemble the colonizer. Once conflicts break out into the open, even foreign commentators (who presumably have less of an emotional investment) can find themselves trapped in an essentialist rhetoric of nationhood. Probably the best known post-Cold War examples would be Robert D. Kaplan's *Balkan Ghosts*, which, by advancing "ancient hatreds" as an explanation of the Yugoslav collapse, recapitulates the makeshift, opportunistic, and protofascist nationalisms of Slobodan Milošević (Serbia) and Franjo Tudjman (Croatia). In the case of Ukraine and Russia, even a scholar as eminent and well versed as Stephen F. Cohen repeatedly calls for understanding Ukraine as "two Ukraines," a formulation that implies permanent conflict and even rupture (even if rupture is not what he advocates). Tatiana Zhurzhenko, in response to an earlier articulation of the "Two Ukraines" thesis by Mykola Riabchuk, calls this approach the "Huntingtonization of the Ukrainian political discourse), referring to *The Clash of Civilization*.[3]

Ukraine's identity is a math problem based on dodgy accounting. Mathematically, identity means numerical equality ($1=1$); here it is denied by the assertion that $1=0$ (There is no real Ukraine) or that $1=2$ (There are two Ukraines). Accountants have a name for this sort of thing: cooking the books. If Ukraine itself is stuck in some fuzzy quantum state (both real and unreal until Schrödinger's box is opened), is it any wonder that the Ukrainian war defies categorization? With the benefit of hindsight, it is remarkable just how much the idea of Russia involved in a war with/in Ukraine had been absolutely unthinkable and thoroughly thought-through at the same time.

On the level of daily interactions and lived experience, Ukraine was an unlikely enemy. While history has provided any number of reasons for nationally minded ethnic Ukrainians to resent Russia, and perhaps Russians, the feeling was only intermittently mutual.[4] Grievances accrued primarily to one side, grievances that the other side could barely be bothered to acknowledge, let alone feel guilty about. Ukraine may not have been a "real" country, but Ukrainians, rather than being the enemy, were at worst a variety of Russian who talked funny.[5]

But the demonization of Ukraine was not simply cooked up by Surkov, Kiselyov, and the other Voldemorts of state propaganda. It reflects the attitude found for years in quasi-fascist newspapers such as *Zavtra*, or the many tracts about the Ukrainian falsification of history that have been written since 2003 but only later became bestsellers. Not long before the war broke out, the political consultant Anatoly Vassermann published a book whose title said it all: *Ukraine and the Rest of Russia* (Ukraina i ostal'naia Rossiia, 2013) The next year, Dmitry Kiselyov introduced his new Ukraina.ru news portal with the following words: "There is no Ukraine. Now there is only a virtual concept, a virtual country. If you want to live in a virtual world, go ahead. . . . But Ukraina.ru is a real portal. Not about the country but about that territory which was under the rule of that country. Now it is a failed state" (Shelepin; "failed state" is in English in the original).

For over a decade, however, Ukraine was painted as both a puppet in the hands of evil Western "Atlanticists" (read: NATO and the United States) and the likely stage of an upcoming apocalyptic conflict between Russian and the West. However, this portrait was restricted to two overlapping, but still marginal discursive communities: political tracts by Eurasianists such as Alexander Dugin or new imperialists along the lines of Mikhail Yuriev, and military science fiction. The Russian author and media persona Dmitry Bykov, who can always be relied on for a good turn of phrase, has called the battle for Ukraine a "writers' war" (Young). He is absolutely correct. It's worth adding, though, that it's a bad writers' war ("bad" modifying not just "war" but "writers"). In the Russian Federation, we have a largely unimaginative media apparatus that stirs up the public by invoking familiar clichés. In Eastern Ukraine, it's far worse.

The leaders of the anti-Kyiv faction included Igor Strelkov, previously known as an enthusiast for war reenactments. After years of playing soldier, he moved on to the real thing. He was joined by Fyodor Berezin, the author of military science fiction describing wars between Russia and Ukraine (and Russia and NATO over Ukraine) in several tedious books, including *War 2010: The Ukrainian Front*, published in 2009, and its follow-up, *War 2011: Against NATO,* published in 2010. Presumably the events that began in 2013 made further sequels unnecessary. Both of these novels treat an imagined war in Ukraine as a proxy for the United States' ongoing project aimed at Russia's destruction, with occasional references to the Golden Billion and supposedly nongovernmental Western organizations such as Greenpeace that are actually taking orders from the State Department.

Berezin was one of several writers working in this particular subgenre. In 2009, Georgy Savitskii, the pseudonym for a Donetsk-born science fiction writer, inaugurated a series called After the Battle (Posle boia) with a novel titled *After the Battle: Ukraine. The Broken Trident.* (Posle boia— Ukraina. Slomannyi trezubets). Compared to Savitsky, Berezin is a diplomat. One typical passage describes the conflict as follows:

Even after destroying everything, America was not satisfied. NATO's strategists decided to use the territory of Ukraine as a staging platform for its cruel, forceful pressure on Russia, in an attempt to weaken the only power in the world that still dared slap the hamburger-fed face of the "global he-gemon." Manipulating nationalist feelings in Ukrainian society, artificially fanning the flames of nationalist hostility, forcing its miserable "culture" on them, the USA wanted to destroy once and for all everything that reminded people of the brotherhood of the two Slavic peoples. And the well-bribed "Ukrainian elite" made every effort to distance itself from Russianness, from the centuries-old Slavic culture, from the Orthodox faith.

The novel even features a clear stand-in for the Cold War architect Zbigniew Brzezinski (Zbigniew Krzinski in the book), who, after the tri-umphant speech by the victorious Russian president, whispers the novel's last line: "Once again I underestimated the Russians . . ."

Both Berezin and Savitskii would later appear on a list of books banned for importation by the Ukrainian government ("Na Ukraine opublikovali . . ."), which must have been gratifying. Berezin, Savitskii, and their ilk would love to be considered prophetic, in the tradition of the common, naive understanding of what science fiction is for (predicting the future). And let's give credit where credit is due: they are prophetic, but not in the way it might seem. They predict not the war itself but the particular modes in which the Russian media would frame it to make it legible and palatable. The Russian media assaults Ukrainian statehood on three fronts: history, geography, and iconography.

Whom You Gonna Call?

On August 17, 1995, the Presidential Administration of the Russian Fed-eration issued Executive Order no. 1495, "On Writing the Names of the Former Republics of the USSR and Their Capitals" (Rasporiazhenie). In the scheme of things, this would be an easy executive order to miss. It is blessedly brief—probably two pages printed out, and one of them is a table of names. But it signaled an important shift in the Russian govern-ment's attitude toward its neighbors, or at least, it was a recognition of an attitude that may have prevailed but was left unspoken.

In the wake of the Soviet collapse, Russians had to adjust not only to new borders and new neighbors but also to novel, often unlovely names. On television, broadcasters dutifully began referring to four different former Soviet Republics according to the preferences of their government. Thus Moldavia became Moldova, Belorussia became Belarus, Turkmenia became Turkmenistan, and Kirghizia became Kyrgyzstan (breaking two fundamental rules of Russian spelling and pronunciation along the way). The rest of the world quickly followed suit, though not without confusion—I remember a lot of anxiety in the US Embassy in Moscow in 1992 over whether or not the former Belorussia's capital was now Mensk (with nary a Google or a Yahoo to consult).

Barely five years later, the novelty of the nomenclature must have worn off, and the Russian government reversed itself. The change fits into the evolving narrative of resistance to linguistic policing (the Orwellian PC menace discussed in the previous chapter), but there is much more at work here. One of the tenets of progressive attitudes toward language is that all groups have the right to determined how they should and should not be addressed—a power traditionally wielded by the majority is now yielded to the minority. In this case, Russia, the juridical heir to the Soviet Union, reclaims an imperial right to determine identity and to ignore the apparently trivial claims of its former subjects.

On the surface, Ukraine was a simpler case, since its name never changed, although many of its cities, such as Kyiv, are now called by their Ukrainian names in the West instead of their Russian ones. But the country's name can encode an attitude that Ukrainian patriots reject: its root *krai* suggests a region or an edge rather than a full-fledged country (like Krajina in Croatia). In English, this sense of Ukraine as a territory was facilitated by the use of the definite article, which is why Ukrainians and their allies have fought against calling the country "the Ukraine," an argument that must be easier to make in English, since Ukrainian doesn't even have definite articles.

In recent years, however, a comparable distinction in usage can suggest Russian speakers' attitudes toward their Western neighbor. Traditionally, being "in" or going "to" Ukraine required the preposition *na* (on), which is used for islands and territories rather than countries, but now Ukrainians and their supporters are more likely to say *v* (in), the same preposition used for most other countries. On Russian state television one hears *na*; on the liberal TV-Rain channel, the anchors say *v*. For the overwhelming majority of Russian speakers, usage is surely a question of habit; in journalism and diplomacy, it is a political choice.

At issue is not simply a denial of Ukrainian statehood but a denial of Ukrainian selfhood. And where poststructuralists dismiss the self as an illusion created by the confluence of various discourses, anti-Ukrainian propagandists lay the blame for Ukrainian selfhood on the usual suspects: the State Department, Russophobes, and Nazis.

The Russia/Ukraine identity question is a poor fit for the most common Western model of ethnic and international conflict, in which the enemy group is systematically portrayed as a dangerous Other. It might seem to resemble the suppression of Kurdish identity in Turkey or Turkish identity in communist Bulgaria, but these comparisons quickly fall apart. First of all, the official national/ethnic designation "Ukrainian," recognized by the Soviet Union, remains legitimate in the Russian Federation; and second, at issue is not so much an internal minority as a neighboring state.

The underlying psychodrama of Russian-Ukrainian relations rests on a frequent assertion that Ukraine is not at all Other but instead simply a variation on "Russia" that has no legitimate reason for existence. After all, both countries look to Kievan Rus' as their point of origin—can it really belong to each of them? This question, while much debated, is far too abstract to serve as a basis for Russian aggression. Though Kiev/Kyiv is claimed as the cradle of both Russian and Ukrainian civilization(s), it is not an East Slavic Jerusalem, at least not in the current political sense.[6] Russia does not need actual possession of Ukraine's capital city to bolster its own claims of legitimacy or selfhood. If Moscow is the Third Rome, Kyiv was never even Rome 2.5.

Fear-mongering to the contrary, the Russian Federation has not been pursuing a plan to conquer Ukraine as a sovereign state; even if it were possible, it would cause more trouble than it could be worth, and in any case, few of the military actions by Russia or by separatists would point to such a goal. What makes the endeavors of Russia-aligned interests in Ukraine legible, tolerable, and even desirable to a significant portion of the Russian population is a disbelief in Ukraine as a concept: as a sovereign entity, it has no place in the popular imagination or Symbolic geography. From this point of view, Ukraine is not simply a failed or failing state; it is a state whose very existence is something of a historical joke.

In the propaganda campaign against Ukraine, then, the Russian media have an unusually complex task: maintaining the sense of Ukraine as "self"—that is, not really different from Russia—while demonizing the opposition as "other." The conflict cannot be dismissed by an appeal to Freud's famous formulation of the "narcissism of small differences" or Jonathan Swift's sendup of rival Lilliputian factions who cannot agree on the proper ways to eat a boiled egg. Though one might argue that it is this very type of dismissal that characterizes the popular Russian disdain for Ukrainian sovereignty: any emphasis on "Ukrainianness" is simply magnifying a small distinction in order to drive a wedge between Ukrainians and Russians. On the Russian side, the underlying problem with Ukraine could be summed up as follows: "Who do you think you are? How can you say you are not us? You are us; we are the same." The assertion to the contrary is tantamount to betrayal. Clearly, the population of "Ukraine" is being duped by enemies both internal and external, hellbent on weakening Russia through the assertion of false nationalisms. Ukrainians have somehow been brainwashed into thinking they exist.

One consequence of this insistence that the Ukrainian Other is simply another variety of self is the automatic assumption that events in Ukraine are, first and foremost, about Russia. No doubt there are geographic, economic, and strategic reasons for Russia to be vigilant about the political development and international ties of its closest Western neighbor, but the intensity of the identification with Ukraine goes beyond political pragmatism.

Mama Dramas

Even some of the most incisive critics of Russia's actions in Crimea, Donets, and Luhansk tacitly accept Russia's precedence and priority. In July 2014, Vladimir Sorokin, one of the most critically acclaimed living Russian writers, published an essay in *The New York Review of Books* under the eye-catching title, "Russia Is Pregnant with Ukraine." According to Sorokin, the Euromaidan's "yellow and blue sperm . . . did its manly job under the colorful fireworks of granddads, the flares of Molotov cocktails, and the whistle of snipers' bullets." Russia, staring dumbly at its television set, found that a "new life stirred in her enormous womb: Free Ukraine."

The object of Sorokin's satire is the Russian state (along with its media apparatus), so perhaps he should be forgiven for looking at Ukrainian political life entirely through the lens of Russian interests (a forgiveness that I am asking on my own behalf as well). His pregnancy metaphor could hardly surprise those familiar with his fiction; after the infamous anal sex scene involving clones of Khrushchev and Stalin in *Blue Lard* (*Goluboe salo*), a couch potato Mother Russia knocked up by her neighbor with possibly premature patriotic exuberance looks positively tame. Sorokin dispenses with the illusions of the primordial state in an efficient flattening of the Oedipal romance. Ukraine is both inseminator and offspring; the child truly is father to the man.

Claude Lévi-Strauss argues that the varieties of the Oedipus myth, Freud's included, play out the tension between sexual reproduction (an uncomfortable reminder of one's parents having sex) and autochthony (self-generation from the soil itself, free of parents but always yielding monsters) (206–31). The theory of ethnogenesis—which, given Gumilev's complicated relationship with both his famous parents, begs for a psychoanalytic reading—has a strong autochthonous component, but Sorokin refuses to allow for the birth of a nation that doesn't involve pain, bodily fluids, and inadmissible desire.

Sorokin's portrayal of Free Ukraine's birth is traumatic to the Russian maternal body. Craving meat, it gobbles up Crimea, while all its population can seem to talk about is its neighbor/fetus. His essay ends:

> Russia is pregnant with Ukraine. Birth is inevitable. There is more to come: the intensifying labor pains, the tearing of the umbilical cord, the newborn's first cries . . . The infant's name will be beautiful: Farewell to Empire. Will it have a happy childhood? We don't know yet. Many people sincerely hope it will grow up strong and healthy. But what of the mother? The coming labor will be difficult, and there will certainly be complications. Will she survive? And what about the rest of the world? ("Russia Is Pregnant with Ukraine")

Sorokin transforms the problem of Russian and Ukrainian identity into a more familiar biological drama of nurturing and separation. Make no mistake: nothing about this metaphor suggests an actual Ukrainian perspective, but it does posit a future in which such a perspective is inevitable. Given the bizarre temporal mechanics of Ukraine as both father and child, a "future" Ukrainian perspective is not proleptic. On its own terms, it

already exists, having impregnated Russia with the seed of her own transformation or imperial demise.

Undead Ukrainian Nazis (and the
Americans Who Love Them)

When it comes to the status of Ukraine as "self" or "other," Russian state
propaganda manages to have it both ways. One aspect of the strategy is
familiar from the Russian media's demonization of domestic opposition:
discrediting any expression of dissatisfaction with Russian policies as the
work of secret puppetmasters who stir up dissent either through brainwashing ("Western" style innovations in pedagogy, the pernicious influence of the Western media, and, of course, the public menace known as
"grants") or bribery (the reflexive accusation that protesters are paid by
enemies was a feature of Russian political culture long before Donald
Trump brought it to the American mainstream). The conflict in Ukraine
fits nicely with one of the master narratives of post-Soviet conspiracy theory: not satisfied with destroying the USSR, the Americans are busily dismantling Russia both as a world power and a sovereign state.

With NATO at its borders and a portion of the population looking
west rather than east, Ukraine becomes the logical site for a proxy battle
between Russia and the United States. Intentionally or not, successive US
governments have encouraged this sort of thinking by approving NATO
expansion right up to Russia's borders and shamelessly taking public sides
in Ukrainian internal political conflicts. Whatever principles have guided
US foreign policy since the end of the Soviet Union, discouraging Russian
paranoia does not appear to be among them.

To make matters worse, this is by no means the first time that Ukraine
has served as either buffer or battleground in a conflict between Russia and the West: invading Russia from the west without going through
Ukraine is theoretically possible but inefficient. For a recent precedent that
is never far from the popular consciousness, we need look no further than
World War II.

World War II is widely recognized as the touchstone for Soviet national
pride and the source of a national myth that supersedes even the October
Revolution. Setting aside the complex questions of Stalin's leadership, not

to mention the Molotov-Ribbentrop Pact with Hitler, the centrality of the Great Patriotic War for Russian political and public culture has only become more obvious in the Putin years. It also serves as something of a "get out of jail free" card for any Russian accused of supporting a policy that might be considered fascist ("I can't be a fascist; my grandfather saved Europe from Hitler").

Theoretically, the Soviet triumph could be claimed by all the former Soviet republics, since they all were once part of the victorious Soviet state. But just as the Russian Federation assumed the entirety of the Soviet debt along with the nuclear arsenal, it has also assumed the lion's share of pride in the defeat of Nazi Germany. In particular, Ukraine is in no position—political, geographic, or otherwise—to make an uncomplicated claim on the Soviet Union's victory. Like so many countries in Eastern Europe once occupied by the Nazis, Ukraine has a checkered history of resistance and collaboration that haunts public expressions of national pride.

At issue is probably the second most sensitive topic in Russian-Ukrainian relations in Soviet times (after the Holodomor): the participation of Stepan Bandera's Ukrainian Liberation Army in World War II on the side of the Nazi invaders. Viewed as a traitor in Russia, Bandera and his insurgency against Soviet power have been coopted by a narrative of Ukrainian national struggle, his alliance with the Nazis largely whitewashed when it isn't being actively championed by extremist, far-right forces.[7] Many Russians find the current appropriation of Banderovite images and slogans—such as "Glory to Ukraine," which would sound innocuous if it weren't for its history—disturbing, but the exploitation of this phenomenon is depressingly familiar: the Russian media are borrowing from the Serbian scriptbook of the early 1990s, when a similar revival of Nazi-era Croatian symbols allowed Milošević's men to label their Croat enemies as Ustaše (World War II-era fascists). Thus where a naive American media paints the post-Maidan Ukrainian government as a pro-Western, democratic bulwark against Russian imperialism, the preferred term in the Russian media is "fascist junta."

The fighting in Ukraine gets recast as a long-delayed sequel to World War II, with cryptofascists emerging from their bunkers after seven decades of presumably cryogenic suspension. It's like the scenario for Captain America, only with the Nazis on ice instead of the antifascist superhero. If this sounds flip or, because of the American reference, irrelevant, it is anything but. The miraculous return of Nazis thanks to the miracles of mad science is a cliché of adventure fiction around the world (*The Boys from Brazil*, *Hellboy*), and Russia is no exception. One of the key players in the Ethnogenesis cycle, a sprawling, four-dozen-plus series of novels spanning continents and millennia, is the Fourth Reich, complete with a frozen Hitler in its Antarctic Ultima Thule base.

Ethnogenesis is an odd bird; in the attempt by the pro-Kremlin media ideologue Konstantin Rykov to integrate Gumilev's theories into popular entertainment, the authors inadvertently consign these widely accepted but profoundly crackpot ideas to what should be their natural habitat: low-rent science fiction. Yet the conflict in Ukraine seems tailormade for an Ethnogenesis novel. The backward-looking, black-and-white morality of official Russian propaganda transforms all of Russia's international conflicts into a retread of World War II. And, thanks to the United States' own checkered history of harboring Nazi scientists to help with the postwar arms race, the Nazi narrative does not contradict the portrayal of the United States as anti-Russian masterminds.

The equation of Ukrainian nationalists with fascists serves at least two functions. For one, it allows critics to refrain from calling them "Ukrainian" at all, in part to avoid legitimizing them, and in part to maintain the appearance that it is not Ukraine itself that is the enemy. This allows Ukrainians to continue to function as both "self" and "other": the "bad" Ukrainians are essentially Nazis and traitors and can be named as such, while the broader masses of "good" Ukrainians are simply another variety of Russians, who one hopes will soon cast off this Ukrainian nonsense and rejoin the fold. Meanwhile, Russian propaganda fulfills the classic psychoanalytic function of displacement: fostering an intolerant climate for minority populations and adopting repressive legislation is a Ukrainian problem, not a Russian one.

More Wrongs about Buildings and Food

Ukraine's role in Russian paranoid fantasy proves a cornucopia of Freudian delights. One of them is present in both the previous discussion of foreign invasion and Sorokin's outrageous declaration that Russia has been impregnated with (and by) Ukraine. Rather than the "window to the

West" opened by Peter the Great in the city that shares his name, Ukraine is Russia's poorly guarded back door, an orifice that renders Russia vulnerable to all manner of unwanted penetration. The rhetoric of Ukrainian "fascism" has formed a discursive, if not domestic, partnership with the moral panic over "gay propaganda": the Ukrainian *svidomii* (conscious, self-aware), used as a descriptor of Ukrainian national consciousness, is combined in Russian with the slur "sodomites" (*sodomity*) to form *svidomity*, a term of abuse for Ukrainians who do not want a tight connection with Russia.

Ukraine-centered Russian conspiracy theory is preoccupied with boundaries and their violation, with bodily integrity and the dangers of improper consumption. This is conditioned not only by Ukraine's function as a border but also by its traditional role as the provider of Russia's food: once the breadbasket of the Russian Empire, the Ukrainian Soviet Socialist Republic maintained that role for the Soviet Union, though in a manner that was far more fraught with tension and tragedy. Thus it makes sense that the post-Soviet Russia-Ukraine drama would so often play itself out in alimentary terms. It is a drama that parallels our earlier discussion of television, propaganda, and zombification, in that it is about not just food but *feeding*: what might Ukraine be sneaking into Russia's political diet?

While one could choose to look at this problem in terms of the metaphor of disease—"color" revolutions and Maidan are repeatedly castigated in the Russian media as a virus—food is still central. All of twentieth-century Russian-Ukrainian relations fall under the shadow of the Holodomor, the human-made famine that officially killed anywhere from seven to ten million people in Ukraine (with unofficial estimates going as high as twelve million). The causes were multiple and still the subject of scholarly disputes, but they clearly include the criminal excesses and incompetence of Soviet collectivization, the state's refusal to provide famine relief, and, according to most scholars (most famously Timothy Snyder in *Bloodlands* and Anne Applebaum's *Red Famine*), the deliberate targeting of Ukraine. Recognized by the United Nations as genocide, the Holodomor was denied by the Soviet state, while the post-Soviet government of Russia refuses to see the famine as anything other than a tragedy that afflicted the Soviet Union as a whole.

Decades later, the Soviet Union would still have difficulty feeding itself, being reduced to importing grain before President Jimmy Carter declared an embargo in response to the 1979 invasion of Afghanistan. Through no fault of its own, the Ukrainian SSR found itself (along with Belorussia) embroiled in another food drama in the aftermath of the Chernobyl nuclear accident: if Ukrainian crops were irradiated, could the rest of the Soviet Union be expected to consume them? (The answer, it turned out, was "yes.")

After the Soviet collapse, the United States managed to pay sustained attention to the former Soviet Union for at least four years straight—a post-Soviet record that will be beaten only if Donald Trump is elected to a second presidential term. In 1992, out of concern that newly impoverished citizens might be tasting "freedom" only to starve for food, the Bush administration inaugurated a program to airlift food and medical supplies to dozens of cities in the Commonwealth of Independent States under the name Operation Provide Hope (Friedman).

If the phrase sounds vaguely familiar, there's a good reason: the project used the same naming conventions that became famous during the First Gulf War, when Operation Desert Shield gave way to Operation Desert Storm. Thus what was most likely an earnest attempt at humanitarian aid did little to alleviate the sense that the victors were showing self-satisfied noblesse to the benighted residents of the countries they had conquered.

To make matters worse, the food, which was distributed primarily for the consumption of the elderly, was not simply culturally inappropriate: a large portion of it consisted of MREs (Meals Ready to Eat) left over when the Gulf War proved to be a much shorter conflict than anticipated. In Moscow, I worked briefly for the program and found myself in the absurd position of explaining to the local *babushki* the finer points of vacuum-packed chili. Given that the average Russian senior citizen recoils from any hint of spice like vampires exposed to garlic, this was a losing proposition.

Operation Provide Hope followed on the heels of the infamous "Bush legs," the frozen chicken quarters supplied to post-Soviet countries as part of a 1990 Soviet-US trade agreement (Schwirtz). The popular press repeatedly published stories about the hidden dangers of US chicken, from antibiotics and hormones to possible allergic reactions to chlorine. Meanwhile, stores and stands were inundated with US products, including fast food and junk food. Snickers bars quickly became a symbol of this phenomenon: the advertising for them was pervasive and catchy, the claims that they provided "energy" were puzzling, their ubiquity was annoying, and their taste was foreign and odd while also being immediately popular.

These new, imported foods were themselves advertisements for a longed-for prosperity, and their sheer variety could only be confusing. In "A Real Man's Drink," the third episode of the hit television series *Cops* (*Menty*) (1995/1997), a team of police officers arrives at the scene of a murder in a communal apartment. A nosy old lady provides commentary while snooping around the apartment of her now deceased neighbor. Attracted by a colorful bag, she reaches in to sample a snack, eats several pieces, only to exclaim "Ugh!! This Kitty-Kat stuff is crap!" (*T'fu! Griaz' zhe etot kiti-kat!!*).

Tabloids went beyond simply decrying foreign imports as unnatural or unhealthy, because their threat lay on the cusp of nutrition and information. Not only were the products themselves new, but the means by which they entered popular consciousness were a shock to the (post-)Soviet informational ecosystem: bodies were polluted with chemicals and empty calories while minds were hijacked by jingles and catchphrases.

In 1994, *Komsomol'skaia pravda* published an article on the mind-altering effects of advertising, including a reference to the "Uncle Ben Effect," which caused children to vomit after repeated exposure to the US rice company's commercials (Agentstvo). The metaphor of mental and physical consumption becomes literal, with the body in revolt expelling harmful informational input as poorly digested physical output.

America, then, tempts the former Soviet Union with tasty ideological poisons. Which brings us back to Ukraine. And to the Notorious Victoria Nuland.

Cookies from Hell

Any consideration of culinary diplomacy must reserve a special place for former US Assistant Secretary of State for European and Eurasian Affairs Victoria Nuland, whose world-famous cookies were either a colossal PR miscalculation or an inept show of soft power strength to observers in the Kremlin.

Nuland was one of the many Obama administration figures the Russian media loved to hate. Her leaked January 2014 telephone call, in which she and a colleague discussed their preferences for positions in the post-Maidan Ukrainian government, only reinforced her image as the face of US imperialist overreach (her casual dismissal of Europe—"Fuck the EU"—did not help matters) ("Ukraine Crisis"). But what she is best remembered for in Russia is her goodie bag.

On December 11, 2013, three weeks into Euromaidan, Nuland is filmed making her way to Maidan, accompanied by her staff. Initially she has the look of someone about to go on a dreary shopping trip, carrying a plastic bag filled with food and wearing a look of grim determination. After a cut in the video, she is smiling at the camera, walking up to protesters to shake their hands and talk to them (in English): "We're here from America. Would you like some bread? Take something. Please. Take something. Guys, are you hungry? No? Take something. Take some stuff." Nuland hands out the food with all the grace of a Soviet shopkeeper ("Kak Nuland").

It is a bizarrely staged event: Nuland holds out her overflowing bag to everyone she meets (culminating in an offer to the Berkut officers on duty), as though she were on some sort of reverse trick-or-treating expedition. The Russian media and Internet loved it, but not in the way Nuland must have intended. "Nuland's cookies" became a persistent meme, with headlines referring to "Nuland's poisoned cookies" and one blogger referring to "Victoria Nuland, with her cookies laced with hallucinogenic drugs in order to subvert Ukraine" (Iablokov; Ray).

The entire situation is thoroughly gendered, playing into the anti-Nuland diatribes. Sexism may not have been why Nuland was so disliked (it would be hard for any Obama official to hear a kind word in the Russian media), but it certainly colored the *way* in which she was disliked (see under Hillary Clinton). She was performing a traditionally feminine task (feeding people), and she was terrible at it. Nuland soon found herself disputing the characterization of her Maidan expedition: "First of all, to correct some disinformaciya, they were sandwiches, they were not cookies" (Sandwiches). As I watch the video, I would split the difference and call them crackers, but it is hard to see how this distinction would help.

Nuland explained her actions by appealing to her own Slavic roots (her father apparently has relatives in Ukraine): "I couldn't just leave, so in keeping with Slavic traditions, I handed out sandwiches to hungry people but they were meant not just for the demonstrators, but for the Berkut soldiers as well" ("Nuland: Ia razdavala").[8] Nuland's appeal to "Slavic tradition" to justify a media event that looked very much like American partisanship in an internal Ukrainian dispute is rather odd, especially since there are no sandwich-distributing rites in the Primary Chronicle. What, then, could she have had in mind? Probably the traditional greeting of guests with an offering of bread and salt, a ritual played and replayed in countless Soviet broadcasts of leaders being received in towns throughout the USSR. Nuland's actions were in fact an inversion of hospitality, the assumption of local prerogative: the assistant secretary of state was the guest, not the host.

Cloudy with a Chance of Meatheads

On July 29, 2015, in response to US and European sanctions against the Russian Federation for its actions in Ukraine, President Putin signed a decree calling for the public execution of contraband meat, cheese, and vegetables, to take effect on August 6. The next weeks saw the ongoing spectacle of the crushing and burning of hapless dairy products and lush vegetables that were too ripe to meet such a terrible fate.

Meanwhile, Sputnik International, part of the Russian Federation's "news" services aimed at a foreign audience, responded to the events in a truly bizarre fashion: with an extended article denying the reality of the Holodomor, the 1932–1933 Ukrainian famine engineered by the Soviet leadership (Blinova).

That was on August 9. The next day, Sputnik did cover the destruction of the imported food, in an opinion piece titled "Why Russia Is Not Rising up against the Destruction of Parmesan." Sputnik chides the Western media for whipping up nonexistent outrage, noting that "the reaction in Russia has been considerably more mixed. In a country where 90 percent never tried jamon serrano, arguably the most famous sanctioned product because of its association with the high wealth of its consumers, the biggest issue has become one of efficiency." Giving away the food to the poor or to orphanages would be impractical, and in any case the food no longer had any health certification. The biggest concern, apparently, was how to burn the food in an environmentally friendly fashion.

Four days later, Sputnik gives us an amusing human interest story: "Millionaire Son Burns $245k Ferrari to Make Dad Buy New One." An unnamed nineteen-year-old Italian rich boy, who "reportedly has 'no less' than fifteen other luxury vehicles and receives an allowance of 5,000–10,000 dollars a month from his father," was not satisfied with this "obscene excess," and torched a three-year-old car that simply wasn't good enough anymore.

So in the course of one food-burning week, Sputnik moves from Holodomor denial to downplaying the burning to a story about a burning Italian car. What is going on here? To be clear: I am not arguing that this sequence of articles was deliberate, or that the editors of Sputnik saw any connection between the Ferrari story and the banned cheeses. This is not the work of some ladder-day Dr. Goebbels; instead, it cries out for help from Dr. Freud. Most likely, what Sputnik is doing is entirely unconscious. The mass destruction of food is too unsettling to be ignored, leaving a discomfort that must express itself indirectly through hysterical media symptoms. So Sputnik speaks of a long-ago famine (in Ukraine, of all places), denying that it was the work of the state. And rather than deal with the "obscene excess" of burning food, let's talk about a spoiled rich European guy burning a luxury car.

Sputnik is responding to an event that is profoundly troubling, but for reasons that are not easy to pin down. In a rare moment of candor, Putin's press secretary, Dmitry Peskov, admitted that the destruction of the imported food might be a "visually disturbing spectacle." Why, though, is it so disturbing? If we follow Sputnik's logic of class warfare, part of the problem is the stark, visceral rebuke to the values that made Putin's first two terms so successful. Russia in the early 2000s functioned under a tacit compact between the rulers and the ruled: leave the politics to us, and we will let you live comfortably. Buy whatever you want to buy; watch whatever you want to watch. All talk of ideals and greatness aside, consumption was not the enemy. Consumption was the Putinist success story.

Yet this only scratches the surface. Many have noted the oddness of the mass destruction of food in a country with a long memory of famine (and particularly during the Siege of Leningrad, Putin's home town), suggesting that we look further back in Russian history for an explanation. But the cheese burning evokes multiple historical time frames at once, accruing an uncanny power from all of them.

It was, after all, August, not long before harvest time. For decades, Soviet television celebrated the country's bumper crops, treating its viewers to scenes of boundless wheat. Indeed, Soviet TV offered up "food porn" long before it became popular in the West, focusing not on an individual sumptuous meal but on the sheer quantity of edibles that may or may not reach a store near you. The food destruction spectacle was a bizarre parody—Soviet agricultural footage crossed with slasher films ("I Know What You Ate Last Summer"). Moreover, there is something profoundly human about food, rendering its destruction inhuman. It is not just that the mass crushing and burning of food might recall the mechanized mass slaughter of humans that defined the twentieth century. The sheer wrongness of destroying food is directly linked to the rightness of eating it.

What, after all, is food for? It may be beautiful, it may be the result of hours of labor, but our response to it is to tear it apart with our teeth, let our body break it down with a variety of unpleasant acids, and excrete it as something generally considered disgusting. To destroy food is to acknowledge its eventual fate. It is the ultimate expression of the desire to cut to the chase. Taking a wonderful meal and flushing it down the toilet is simply eliminating the middle man. This is the same logic that the Soviet writer Andrei Platonov so brilliantly exposed in *Chevengur* and *The Foundation Pit*: if the final fate of all people is to become corpses, Stalinism will eliminate decades of human life in order to overfulfill the plan in corpse production.

Yet there is also something telling about the way in which the food is being destroyed. Crushing and burning food is a grotesque parody of consumption and digestion. As such, it becomes a perfect symbol of an overreaching state, arrogating the most basic human processes to a vast, inhuman mechanism. It is Stalinism as eating disorder, binging and purging on camera. And all in response to sanctions over conflict with a country for whom a Soviet human-made famine serves as a foundational national trauma. But it is also the apotheosis of the Putinist obsession with sovereignty: borders must be policed; state power must be exerted at all cost. If the state, rather than the citizen, is the most important subject, then the state can take on the job of eating and excreting.

Monumental Trolling

Ukraine's response to the tide of Russian propaganda, while initially puzzling, turns out to be quite appropriate and clever. In 2016, Kyiv embarked on a rather untimely de-Sovietization campaign, in an attempt to remove all symbolic vestiges of Soviet power. Parts of this process surely had unintended irony: "Soviet" champagne was renamed "sovetovskoe" earlier in January of the same year. "Sovetovskoe" doesn't actually mean anything, but really, "Soviet" was an empty signifier when the Bolsheviks seized on it after the February Revolution. More to the point, Soviet Champagne lost the right to call itself "Champagne" decades ago (the French protested), so now Ukraine is selling non-Soviet non-Champagne.

The most visible side of this campaign is not (un)Champagne but statuary. In late September 2014, protesters in Kharkiv pulled down an enormous monument to Vladimir Ilich Lenin, part of a nationwide campaign to de-Sovietize the country. While this was supposed to represent a step forward, there was something quaintly retro about the whole affair: wasn't Western Ukraine partying like it's 1989?

The campaign's brilliance revealed itself in the reaction in the Russian media, which consistently took affront at the whole de-Sovietization process. And it is here that, if subtly, Ukraine beat the Russian state media at their own game. The Russian government has refused to take any blame for anything done to Ukraine and Ukrainians under Soviet power, since that was the Soviet Union, not Russia. The media refuse any narrative that casts Russia in the role of the colonizer. Yet by taking offense, the Russian media are implicitly accepting the equation of the Soviet Union with Russia itself, taking on a historical mantle that is attached to a wide range of problems. Russia casts Kyiv as a band of Banderite fascists but at the same time finds itself stuck in the role of Soviet colonizer. When it comes to facile historical analogies as a shortcut to rational thought, anyone can play that game. This isn't propaganda, mobilization, or psychological warfare: it's just a very successful example of trolling.

Indeed, perhaps the most honest reappropration of familiar ideological symbols for current propaganda is the "Darth Vader" meme that swept the Ukrainian Internet. While most of the Vadermania looks to be nothing but pure absurdism (such as the man who instagrams himself every day performing ordinary tasks while dressed as the Sith Lord, or the appearance of Vader's name sixteen times on the ballot for the Odessa mayoral elections in 2015), the transformation of a Lenin statue into a monument to Darth Vader really says it all. An inadvertent echo of a scene in a 1990 film called *Sideburns*, in which a sculptor shows that he can turn a Lenin statue into a Pushkin statue faster than you can smoke a cigarette, Darth Lenin ironically points to the real truth behind the memory wars and fixation on history as a way to explain the everyday. In the post-Soviet world, history is not a long time ago, in a galaxy far, far away, and both Kyiv and Moscow are desperate to show their adversaries to be the real post-Soviet Evil Empire.

The War at Home

All this psychodrama over food and misfeeding, over Soviet and post-Soviet identity, points to something fundamental: modern Russia has never had an enemy quite like Ukraine. As we have seen, the country is not just on the border: etymologically and culturally, it is the border. And the border is a conceptual challenge. As the limit case to national geography, it is both of the land and outside it. When we consider what is involved in making an enemy of Ukraine, with historical, cultural, and familial ties as well as recent historical wounds, the animosity seems both unlikely and overdetermined. The fundamental obstacle in the Russian media and government is the refusal to see Ukraine as entirely separate and other, hence the continual, dismissive use of the Ukrainian term *nezalezhnii* (independent) to mock rather than reaffirm the country's autonomous status.

Instead of simply criticizing this attitude, let us follow where it leads. After all, one of the questions hanging over Russia's Ukrainian adventure concerns strategy: what is the Russian government's endgame here? Certainly, grabbing Crimea responded to a decades-long sense that the region's assimilation to Ukraine was an injustice to Russians, and Crimea also has strategic military value. But how do we explain the inconsistent commitment to the rebels in Donetsk and Luhansk? The denial of Ukrainian selfhood leads to a conclusion that was already easy to make. A domestic drama, the war in Ukraine has been invaluable to the Russian government as a matter of domestic politics. Civil war in Ukraine is a reminder of the eternal boogeyman of post-Soviet Russia: civil war in the Russian Federation. This is why the Russian media have been so intent on linking Maidan to any manifestation of dissent at home, as well as the logic behind the anti-Maidan movement built in Russia in the months following the events in Kyiv.

The war in Ukraine is a proxy war, but not, as Russian conspirologists would have it, between Russia and the United States or Russia and Europe. It is a proxy for a war between Russia and itself. So far, it is also a war that the regime has clearly won. Before Maidan, Putin's third term looked like it was going to be the story of popular protest and government concession. Instead, we have the state's consolidation of power in the media, culture, and popular opinion.

Infowars

There are few terms that smack more of propaganda than "information war"—with "propaganda" itself being one of them. Like most modern violent conflicts, information wars are not formally declared. Instead, they are called into existence through a variety of performative incantations: not a declaration of information war but a declaration that the "other side" is *already engaging* in an information war and that it is incumbent on our side to fight back. Thus the entire Putinist media apparatus constantly tells its audience that the West, in "slandering" Russia, is conducting an information war. Meanwhile, in Germany, Great Britain, and the United States, neo-Cold War hawks demand the revival of mid-twentieth-century soft power strategies—and, more important, soft power budgets—to combat the trumped-up threat of the Russian Federation's hilariously entertaining foreign television service, RT (formerly Russia Today) (Sanger).

The advocates of information war are happily ensconced in their own informational feedback loop: RT's director, Margarita Simonyan, shamelessly inflates the stats showing her network's effective reach, and Euro-American hawks are only too willing to believe her. The growing allegations of Russian interference in the 2016 US presidential election have only added fuel to the fire, despite the obvious fact that RT itself, with its relatively small reach and constant pandering to the lunatic fringe, could not have played a significant role in the outcome. Simonyan herself flatly denies accusations of interference and propaganda, but, like the Internet trolls who retweet her network's stories, she clearly enjoys the attention.[9] The sky is falling, and everyone under it couldn't be happier.

The one thing that would-be information warriors do get right, however inadvertently, is their proposition that the news media, rather than being transparent conduits for some kind of Platonic unadulterated truth, are engaging in the creation of fantasy. This is a proposition that is at once obvious and treacherous. The science fiction writer Nancy Kress has a trilogy of novels (*Probability Moon*, *Probability Sun*, *Probability Space*) positing an alien race that functions entirely according to "shared reality"—anyone or anything that contradicts it is declared "unreal" and possibly eradicated. By contrast, the global media, both old and new, have cobbled together a "shared unreality," or perhaps multiple "unshared realities."

There is a continuum here, starting from the simple fact that the news is reported by individuals and groups whose perspectives and biases can shape a story despite the best journalistic intentions, and ending with a model in which the news media as a whole take their marching orders from Svengalis in the central government. Certainly, there is ample testimony to the fact that Russian central television does, in fact, respond to very specific Kremlin directives, a phenomenon that is often displaced onto the North American media landscape, such as casual assertions on Russia Today that a particular negative televised report about Russia appeared at the behest of Barack Obama, never mind that the report aired on Fox News. But even this is not the entire story.

Rather, let us assume that neutrality is, at best, a goal the news media can strive toward rather than an actually achievable state. Further, I'm quite content to assume that the Russian news media are operating with an obvious mandate to tell their stories with a particular slant. This is, in fact, so obvious that it almost amounts to transparency. The "information war" paradigm is problematic because it is implicitly based on a naive, outdated model of media consumption that has not been taken seriously in the world of media studies for decades: this propaganda model, sometimes called the hypodermic model, assumes that an immensely powerful propaganda apparatus essentially reprograms the minds of hapless viewers and readers. We are back to the "consumer as orifice": passive, open, and vulnerable to all kinds of insertions.

Contemporary media scholars prefer to focus on media consumption as a process of negotiation, recoding, and even appropriation: there is never a guarantee that the message transmitted is the same as the message received. Such misprision was obviously an important strategy for media consumers in Soviet times, when there was no pretense of either a lack of censorship or the free market of ideas. Savvy Soviets habitually read between the lines, intuiting or simply creating meanings in the gaps and contradictions of official pronouncements. This, in turn, suggests an obvious problem with the hypodermic model in the case of contemporary Russia: how are we to understand the transformation of a media-consuming culture from the habitual distrust in the Soviet era (when Soviet viewers were arguably much smarter media mavens than their Western counterparts) to the more open mediascape of the 1990s to an era in which the entire population has been suddenly hypnotized into believing everything said on TV? But what does a more skeptical approach to propaganda look like? How can we understand the Russian public's apparent support for the government's program, particularly in Ukraine, without simply writing them off as brainwashed? And what happened to the Soviet skepticism of yore?

First, we should keep in mind the fundamental differences between Soviet and post-Soviet propaganda. One of the main flaws of Soviet propaganda was its vulnerability to immediate, empirical verification. That is, Soviet television painted a picture of Soviet reality that could be debunked simply by walking out on the street and into a store. Russian state television, rather than asking that viewers not believe their own eyes, assembles a model of reality that is already congruent with popular views, and whose distortions center largely on the outside world rather than on life in Russia. In comparison to Soviet news, Russian television looks almost like the result of focus groups and market research; if it trades in resentment, self-aggrandizement, and paranoia, it is responding to two decades of frustration with what is often mistakenly labeled "liberalism" and a pent-up desire to see, as Donald Trump might put it, the country "start winning again." And, as with Trump, this desire is inextricably bound up with hostility toward the entities whose alleged animus and bad faith have been keeping the country down.

In this sense, the Russian state media are, in the broadest strokes, giving their customers what they want. This does not mean that there have not been campaigns to drum up anger over issues that were probably not at the forefront of viewers' minds before the campaigns began, but rather that the campaigns themselves are much more consistent with a broad spectrum of popular, illiberal, nationalist, and xenophobic views that were less welcome on Yeltsin-era television. In this regard, Russian state television behaves more like US niche cable television than like CBS or ABC. Fox News can drum up resentment over Benghazi because its reporters know their audience; replicating the campaign on the *Rachel Maddow Show* and the liberal-leaning MSNBC would be pointless.

Stations of the Double-Crossed

Russian state television has entertained all these various fantasies to varying degrees in the Putin years, and they have served as the discursive backdrop for specific instances of reporting. Certainly, the Bandera meme looks unstoppable; before Russia joined the fighting in Syria, scarcely a day went by without some television report linking Kyiv to fascism. Even in this propaganda maelstrom, one story stood out, both for its intensity and its near-immediate debunking: the story of the crucified boy.

On Saturday, July 12, 2014, Russia's Channel One aired a report by Yulia Chumakova featuring eyewitness testimony from a woman named Galina Pyshniak, who claimed she saw Ukrainian troops commit an unspeakable atrocity on Lenin Square in the city of Slovyansk (Slavyansk in Russian):

Pyshniak: They took a three-year-old boy in his underwear and a t-shirt and they nailed him like Jesus to a bulletin board. One of them hammered, two others held him. And this was all in front of his mama. They held the mama back. And the mama watched as her child bled out. Screams. Shrieks. And then they made cuts on his body so he would suffer. It was impossible. People fainted. And then, after the child suffered for an hour and a half and died, they took the unconscious mama and tied her to a tank, which dragged her in circles around the square three times. And that square covers a square kilometer.

Chumakova: After this interview, you're in real danger. Do I under-
            stand this correctly?

Pyshniak: As a traitor to the Motherland, because I'm from Za-
            karpatskaya Oblast. My mother told me herself: if you
            come back, I'll shoot you myself. And the national guard
            will shoot you. I've committed two offenses punishable
            by firing squad. I'm not afraid for myself. I feel sorry for
            the children. If it weren't for the children, I would take
            arms and join the militia [*opolchenie*]. They're not the
            Ukrainian army, they're not liberators—they're mon-
            sters. When they came to town, there wasn't a single
            rebel [*opolchenets*]. They fired shots at the city. They
            looted. The old grandmas told us that even the fascists
            didn't do that. This is the Galicia SS group. They were
            locals. They brutalized the locals. They raped wives and
            killed children. And now their grandchildren have risen
            up. It's all started again. ("Siuzhet")

The fact that there were no other witnesses, that Slovyansk has no
Lenin Square, and that the story resembled a Facebook post by Alexander
Dugin from a few days before (about a child three years older in a different location) did not initially bother Channel One (Kashin). Scarcely was
the story broadcast before it started to unravel, but its author remained
at Channel One at least a year later. Pyshniak turned out to be the wife of
a Berkut officer turned rebel separatist. On December 18, 2014, Ksenia
Sobchak asked Putin about this incident during a live press conference but
got no response (Musafirova).

As atrocity propaganda, the crucified boy, is, of course, brilliant. By offering up a child victim, this story intensifies the family metaphor usually
reserved for civil wars. Now the Ukrainian conflict isn't just fratricidal;
murdering children is an assault on the future itself. Christlike innocence
and martyrdom are claimed by Russia, despite the fact that both countries
are traditionally Christian and have traditionally availed themselves of a
common Slavic myth of victimhood, as the Christ of Nations. Not only
that, but the means of the boy's alleged execution—making cuts on his
body "so the child would suffer"—echoes the old blood libel against the
Jews, most famously the subject of a trial in the last years of the Russian
Empire (a trial that took place in Kyiv).

The Soviet past is also implicitly cited here, reviving the previously un-expressed Christological roots of the 1932 story of Pavlik Morozov, the boy who allegedly turned in his own father for plotting against the state only to be brutally murdered by the rest of his family. As always, though, the most important context is World War II. Here we go beyond the typi-cal fascist characterization (even the fascists didn't do this): the enemy is the great-grandchildren of the local SS. Here, therefore, we face a different kind of blood libel: hereditary fascism. Even "fascist" is too mild a term for them, as the enemy is downright satanic. Can a Ukrainian-born anti-christ be far behind?

To the extent that this bit of "fake news" worked at all as propaganda, its success was based on the state media's main strategy in demonizing Ukraine: prioritizing gut feelings over rational discourse. As one former state television employee told Colta.ru, reporters and producers working on Ukrainian subjects were told to "make it more hellish" (*delaite bol'she ada*). It is absolutely crucial that all the news from the Ukrainian war be not just bad but a slow-motion catalogue of human misery that can only be the work of monsters. Even when the raw facts are so horrible that they need no embellishment (such as footage of crying old women stand-ing outside their bombed-out homes), the suffering is emphasized though seemingly unnecessary production touches (repeating the same footage again, but in slow motion accompanied by mournful music).

Russian state television may have been unable to prove the story, but it did not have to. Nor did it have to retract it. The story was a useful component to the overarching narrative pushed in the media: the nation's enemies, from America to the born-again Nazis, are hellbent on Russia's destruction. It is a narrative that would face an enormous challenge only five days after the "crucified boy" story was broadcast. On July 17, 2014, Malaysia Airlines Flight 17 was shot down over Eastern Ukraine, killing all 298 people on board. This terrible disaster set the Russian media on the path of nonstop paranoid fabrication.

Flights of Fancy

When Malaysian Airlines Flight MH17 was shot down over Donetsk Oblast, the Ukrainian conflict went global. True, the fighting had already dominated several news cycles in Europe and North America, but the death of 298 people with no connection to either Ukraine or Russia was a reminder to the rest of the world that that this local conflict could have wide-ranging repercussions.

In the Russian media, this conflict had been global from the start, a staging area for the struggle between Russia, as the hedge against imperialist liberalism and guarantor of conservative civilization, and a globalist, Atlanticist, expansive, Russophobic West. The fighting in Ukraine was inherently meaningful, a part of the narrative that the Russian media were in the process of consolidating during Putin's third term. How, then, could the MH17 disaster be assimilated to this geopolitical melodrama? The answer was conspiracy.

As a reminder, here is what happened. On July 17, 2014, Flight MH17 left Amsterdam for Kuala Lumpur, carrying mostly Dutch passengers, including seven AIDS researchers on their way to the Twentieth International AIDS Conference in Melbourne (a detail that will prove relevant later). At least twenty families were on the plane, including eighty people under eighteen. Early in the afternoon, the plane crashed outside Hrabove, spreading debris over fifty square kilometers. The recovery, marked by accusations of looting and disrespect to the bodies of the dead, would take over a month.

The human tragedy here is undeniable, but the downing of MH17 is also one of those events whose international media coverage directs the audience's attention to aspects of contemporary Russia that were previously unfamiliar. The Russian response to the MH17 disaster offered the Western media endless insight and black humor, drawn from the seemingly inexhaustible well of conspiracy theories spun in the aftermath of the crash.[10] These include:

(1) False flag (Ukraine). The Ukrainian government shot down the plane (possibly via jet) and framed the Donetsk separatists to make them look bad.

(2) Failed assassination attempt. Putin was flying nearby at the same time. The Ukrainians aimed at Putin, hit MH17, and then covered it up (see no. 1).

(3) The Illuminati did it. Because they always do.

(4) The Zionists did it. See no. 3.

(5) The CIA did it. See no. 3.

(6) The HIV Conspiracy. The plane was shot down to stop the researchers on board from either (a) revealing that AIDS is a manufactured disease, possibly having nothing to do with HIV and/or (b) sharing their newfound AIDS cure with the world.

(7) MH17 was actually the missing Malaysian flight 370, and all the people on board were already corpses. The corpse-filled plane also features in some of the other theories, though the provenance of the dead may vary.

With the Russian and North American media framing this story in entirely contradictory fashion, MH17 becomes a test of faith. The Dutch Safety Board's report confirmed what most Western experts and analysts had long claimed: the plane was downed by a Russian-made BUK surface-to-air missile shot from rebel-held territory. The Russian government has been at great pains to debunk this report and to demonize Bellingcat, the investigative journalism site that spent months posting evidence—or "evidence"—to support this explanation. The average media consumer (myself included) cannot be expected to read through all of these reports, let alone understand them at the level of detail and expertise to evaluate their truth or falsehood. Instead, we do what we usually do: respond based on our trust in the sources and institutions making the case.

The Donetsk BUK explanation has the virtue of simplicity, as well as consistency with the first bits of prespin information to come out of war-torn Ukraine. Before the identity of the plane was known, the Donetsk separatist leader Igor Girkin, whose nom de guerre is Streltsov (the shooter), bragged on VKontake that his forces had shot down a Ukrainian airliner, with Russia's LifeNews declaring "a new victory for the Donetsk militia" (Bugorkova). In other words, the rebels shot down the airplane by mistake.

This explanation was intolerable. While there are theoretically a number of different ways the rebels could have gotten their hands on a BUK, cooperation with the Russian military was the simplest and most obvious. Yet the same energy spent on devising ridiculous theories about the plane could have been expended on equally ridiculous theories about the BUK's origins. The proliferation of inconsistent stories fits the most popular paradigm of Putin-era propaganda—by drowning out the "truth" in a flood of contradictory "lies," the spinmasters cast doubt on every possible explanation.

But the response to MH17 shows something much more fundamental. In all likelihood, the downing of the Malaysian plane was a terrible mistake. We could call it an accident, except that this would obscure the fact that the rebels were, in fact, trying to shoot down a plane but hit the wrong target.

As horrible as it sounds, this is not unprecedented. In 1988, the United States shot down an Iranian passenger plane mistaken for a Tomcat fighter, killing all 290 on board. Though President George H. W. Bush expressed "regret" for the lives lost, he did not make a formal apology (during his election campaign he promised that he would "never apologize for the United States"). Eight years later, the United States agreed to pay Iran $131.8 million by way of a settlement. The parallels between Iran Air 655 and MH17 have been repeatedly noted online, with accusations of hypocrisy in US rhetoric about MH17 leveled by critics from Noam Chomsky to Samarth Gupta at the *Harvard Political Review* to Paul R. Pillar at *The National Interest*.

The key difference between Iran Air 655 and MH17, however, is the willingness to admit a mistake. Allowing for the possibility of random error is inconsistent with the conspiratorial mindset that has dominated Russia's coverage of the war in Ukraine. People do not spontaneously rise up to express their discontent; they are bought and paid for by the US State Department. Western Ukrainians could not possibly have legitimate reasons to want to keep Russia at a distance; they are being manipulated by the United States, the EU, and globalists of all stripes. And a missile-happy former war reenactor with surface-to-air missiles at his command could not have mistaken one target for another. The people who live and die in the course of this conflict are not nearly as important as the story that is told about them.

A World of Pure Imagination

The war in Ukraine is a triumph of the imagination and a failure of humanity. The Russia narratives discussed earlier in this book substitute often-paranoid fantasy for anything that might be called reality, but their geopolitical flights of fancy had yet to be played out in an extended, aggressive manner before Maidan. Where Russia is "imaginary" in contemporary discourse, Ukraine, thanks to habitual denialism, is doubly so: if Ukraine is not a real country, then its territory is a convenient screen onto which all manner of geopolitical phantasmagoria can be projected. Hence the repeated attempts to redefine Ukrainian territory by resurrecting tsarist-era nomenclature: Russian interests were not fighting against Ukraine, they were fighting for Novorossiya, a bureaucratic toponym that had been all but forgotten. Its newly formed constituent units, meanwhile, evoke a Soviet rather than imperial nostalgia: the Donetsk People's Republic and the Lugansk People's Republic. Life in Novorossiya has clearly been difficult, but it is discussed in terms of a regressive utopianism only made possible by the conflict. In November 2014, Alexander Mozgovoi, one of the Luhansk People's Republic's military leaders, announced plans to forbid women from entering bars, when they should be sitting at home practicing their cross-stitching ("It's time to remember that you're Russian! Remember your spirituality!") (Gumenyuk). Mozgovoi subsequently claimed that he was not really talking about policy: "It was just an attempt to get people to realize that it was time to think a little bit about morality" ("V LNR").

For all Mozgovoi's talk, Luhansk has yet to become the setting for an East Slavic retelling of *The Handmaid's Tale* (Mozgovoi himself was killed less than a year after the "cross-stitching" incident). But it makes sense that this sort of declaration was made in Luhansk rather than somewhere in the Russian heartland. The Russian Federation has laws, whatever one might think of their effectiveness or the consistency in their application, while the violence in Ukraine and the nebulous status of Novorossiya presented the possibility of acting on over a decade of right-wing fantasizing. This utopianism is the flip side of the war's apocalypticism. Ukraine can still be a latter-day Armageddon, the site of the final conflict between the power of Good (Russia) and the forces of imperialist decadence (the United States and NATO), with a Russian victory as the guarantor of a new conservative Slavic golden age. Perhaps the quotation ascribed to Putin about the nonexistence of Ukraine is accurate: for the purposes of these narratives, the country whose capital is in Kyiv is a land of Western-supported Nazis, the birthplace of a Russian revival, and the battleground between East and West. Expansive as these fantasies are, they have no room left for a Ukraine that would prefer to be the hero of its own story.

Conclusion

Making Russia Great Again

On November 9, 2016, Vyacheslav Nikonov, chair of the Russian Duma's Committee on Education and Science, told his fellow legislators that Hillary Clinton had been defeated, and that Donald Trump was the new president of the United States, finishing his remarks with the words "Congratulations to all of you!" Whereupon the Duma burst into applause (NewsFromUkraine).

To Americans who were already troubled by allegations that Trump's campaign colluded with Russia, this was high melodrama, the moment when the villain chortles in triumph while twirling his mustache. Trump himself had done little to reassure the suspicious; on the contrary, his July 27 press conference culminated in a direct if playful appeal to the leaders of the Russian Federation to shed light on Hillary Clinton's email scandal: "Russia, if you're listening, I hope you're able to find the 30,000 emails that are missing. I think you will probably be rewarded mightily by our press" (Harper).

Just halfway through Trump's second year in office, the story has only grown more complicated: former Trump campaign chair Paul Manafort stands accused of financial improprieties linked to Russia and Ukraine; Attorney General Jeff Sessions first denied, then admitted contact with Russian officials while serving as a Trump campaign surrogate; Trump's son-in-law, Jared Kushner, sought "back-channel" communications through the Russian Embassy, bypassing US intelligence services; Donald Trump, Jr. brought Manafort and Kushner to a meeting with a Russian (possibly Kremlin-connected) lawyer after she offered the campaign dirt on Clinton; and Trump business associate Felix Sater, who was trying to broker a deal for a Trump Tower in Moscow during the presidential election campaign, wrote to another Trump associate: "I will get Putin on this program and we will get Donald elected" (Apuzzo and Haberman). Not to mention the Steele dossier, best known for Trump's alleged water sports with prostitutes in a Moscow hotel.

Only a few years earlier, Mitt Romney was roundly mocked for declaring Russia his country's number one geopolitical adversary, while Barack Obama dismissed the Russian Federation as a regional power. On the face of things, Romney's declaration would fit best with Russian domestic narratives about Russophobia, but it was Obama whom the Russian media so openly loathed. Granted, Obama was actually president, so his policies and statements mattered more. But being discounted or ignored is conspiratorial kryptonite: all of the Russia narratives we've seen depend on the country's importance, if not centrality, to the fate of the world. Imagining oneself the victim of a conspiracy is a projection of self-love onto the persecutor. Victims of conspiracy *matter*.

This is not the place to adjudicate the fact and fiction of the Trump/ Russia story. Academic publishing that operates under peer review cannot keep pace with real-time scandal that evolves at the pace of late-night tweets, and the findings of the various investigations are bound to be rejected by certain constituencies (on many sides, to use one of Trump's notorious phrases). While the truth or falsehood of the accusations against Trump's team are of huge import to the political and civic life of the United States, it has little relevance to the focus of this book and its conclusion. For our purposes, what is significant is the structure of conspiracy, the prominence of the conspiratorial mode, and the way in which the scandal reinforces Russian conspiratorial rhetoric.

Conspiratorial Contagion?

Every Russianist today is expected to have an opinion about Trump's alleged ties to Putin, particularly since the meme of a Trump/Putin bromance became so ubiquitous in the 2016 presidential campaign. Does Trump in some way model himself after Putin? Does Putin's nearly two-decades-long primacy show us what to expect from a Trump presidency? And, more to the point, are Trump's flagrant disregard for the facts and constant complaints about "fake news" simply a variation on the propaganda techniques used in the Russian media? Is Putin somehow "to blame" for Trump?

While the slogan "Make America Great Again" is neither surprising nor particularly inventive, to Russianists it may resonate with the repeated refrain that Putin "raised Russia from her knees." In each case, the appeal to strength is framed as a remedy for the country's victimization, which is certainly a feature common to a range of populist, right-wing, and fascist movements. Any resemblance between Putin and Trump is less likely to be a matter of nefarious foreign manipulation (Putinism "infecting" the US body politic) than generic similarity. Like Putin, Trump is accustomed to a world in which he is largely immune to process and procedure, bending reality by sheer force of will ("I alone can fix it"); his admiration for strongmen is a displacement of his own self-regard.

Trump's many conflicting statements are examples of the conspiratorial stance at its purest: he asserts that the elections are "rigged" when it is to his advantage, steps back from this claim after winning the Electoral College, and then tries to have it both ways by claiming his loss in the popular vote was due to illegal aliens. If an assertion catches on with his audience, he repeats it; if it doesn't, he moves on. In this, his rhetorical style could not be more different from Putin's, whose statements tend to be deliberate and whose syntax is generally under his control. To put it simply: Putin does not tweet.

The role of conspiratorial discourse in the rise of Trump and the development of the Trump/Russia scandal has parallels in twenty-first-century Russia, but with a few important twists. As we have seen, Russia under Putin has brought the conspiratorial thought of the 1990s from the margins to the mainstream, but, compared to the Trump phenomenon, this has been a gradual process. Moreover, the mainstreaming of conspiracy in Russia owes a great deal to the evolving attitudes and needs of a strong central authority: the further Putin has moved toward reaction, the more the media have been turned into a platform for conspiratorial ideas. Conspiratorial thought did not give Putin power, but it has been instrumental in that power's maintenance and expansion. The forces associated with the term "alt-right" had also been around for many years before Trump, existing largely in their own self-contained media ecosystem, not unlike the previous marginalization of Alexander Prokhanov and his newspaper *Zavtra*. Trump's relationship with American fascism is much more symbiotic than Putin's connection to right-wing conspiracy mongers; Trump owes a significant portion of his platform and his rhetoric to the alt-right and the more extreme elements of Fox News.

Whatever changes in foreign policy might be instituted by a Trump presidency, the ascendancy of the United States' right-wing fringe groups suggests a rapprochement between American and Russia on the discursive level. Each country has an executive branch with little inclination to combat conspiracy mongering and every incentive to encourage it. Significant differences remain, most notably the fact that Trump does not—and, so far, cannot—control the media. Indeed, each country's path to the mainstreaming of conspiracy theory is exactly what one would expect, based on the respective countries' political systems, media structures, and economic base. Putin's regime holds sway over the commanding heights of mass media: television, from which the majority of Russian citizens still get most of their information, with largely marginalized pockets of free-thinking on the Internet, and, to a lesser extent, in print. In the absence of an equivalent monopoly on media in the United States, conspiratorial thought, now increasingly expressed through accusations of "fake news," arises out of a segmented, largely unregulated media market that, in theory, offers something for everyone. Guided by the heavy hands of social media gatekeepers and corporate media giants, consumers in the United States recreate for themselves the equivalent of an information monopoly by remaining within their own carefully walled gardens.

It turns out that information does not, as the cyberutopian dictum would have it, "want to be free." Freedom of information suggests that understanding of the truth depends primarily on access (the lack of suppression), but if information "wants" anything at all, it is simply to spread itself as far as possible by making itself attractive. We accept information when it creates or embeds itself within a compelling story. Russian state media have mastered a trick that its late Soviet predecessor had long forgotten: how to tell a story that the audience is ready to hear. The segmented US media markets have learned to appeal to their target audience and ignore the naysayers.

It is this segmentation that allowed traditional American elites to be blindsided by the rise of Trump and the prevalence of a conspiratorial mindset. Russian state television is difficult to ignore, but American liberals could, until 2016, go about their business while blithely unaware of a burgeoning, parallel right-wing media ecosystem. Caught unawares, liberals easily find themselves engaging in a compelling counterconspiracy theory of their own: the Russia scandal. Calling the Russia scandal a conspiracy theory is not meant to dismiss it; at this point, Trump/Russia, like Iran/Contra, could prove to be one of the rare conspiracy theories that turns out to be true. But it does mean that Russia, along with Trump himself and a few of his closest allies, is put in the position of conspiratorial mastermind.

If the collusion between Trump and Russia is proven, there is no reason to expect that the Russian government (and therefore the Russian media) will accept such a finding: it will never be true in Russia. In this scenario, Russia has been unjustly scapegoated by a Russophobic US establishment that has always seen Moscow as an enemy. Russia's renewed status as America's enemy both confirms and flatters: finally, as each side blames the other for all its woes, the two are once again engaged in an actual relationship. It is this very mutual antagonism that underscores the implicit rapprochement between the two political and media cultures. Plots against Russia find their reflections in plots against America, and everyone basks in the warm comfort of a good story well told.

NOTES

Epigraph to the book: This statement comes from the novel's preface but is omitted from the English translation.

Introduction

1. Under Putin, official attitudes toward Stalin and his legacy have been mixed. On one hand, Putin ordered the construction of a memorial to gulag victims in 2015 (Kishkovsky); on the other, the former prison camp Perm-36, which had been a monument to the victims of Stalinist repression, now focuses on labor history and the life of the guards (MacFahrquhar). This was after NTV broadcast a documentary alleging that the museum was "pro-fascist" (Cichowlas). In Oliver Stone's four-hour documentary consisting of interviews with the Russian president, Putin claimed that the "excessive demonization" of Stalin "is one of the ways to attack Russia and the Soviet Union, to show that the Russia of today has something originating in Stalinism" (Stone). On the politics of memory laws in post-Soviet Russia, see Koposov (*Pamiat'*), Koposov (*Memory Laws*), Laruelle ("Negotiating History"), Sherlock, and Torbakov.

2. In the introduction to *Reading for the Plot*, Peter Brooks discusses the multiple meanings of plot at some length: "I would suggest that in modern literature this sense of plot nearly always attaches itself to the others: the organizing line of plot is more often than not some scheme or machination, a concerted plan for the accomplishment of some purpose which goes against the ostensible and dominant legalities of the fictional world, the realization of a blocked and resisted desire."

3. Berdyaev's "Russian Idea" is both exceptionalist (in that it is Russian) and universal (in that it is hardly the only expression of one particular nation's exceptional virtues). For a polemical expansion of Berdyaev's notion to more than a century of Russian history and culture, see McDaniel.

4. I am persuaded by Emma A. Jane's argument in *Modern Conspiracy: The Importance of Being Paranoid*: "the investigative techniques and alarmism characteristic of conspiracist debunkers often bear a startling resemblance to the epistemological orientations and rhetorical armoury of those purportedly being critiqued. As we have seen in the case of Kay, critics of conspiracist thinking frequently condemn the catastrophic predictions of conspiracy theorists via equally catastrophic predictions of their own. This sort of mimetic 'doubling' is also evident in the way debunkers engage in paranoid hunts for hidden connections among ostensibly discrete conspiracist groups, in their infiltration of 'enemy' groups, and in their framing of the forces of conspiracist evil as unified, organized, personified, and driven by malevolent intent" (4).

5. Sergei Oushakine argues that *Living Souls* undermines rigid definitions of "national belonging" and the "predetermination of the national path" (64).

6. For more on alternate history as a genre, see Hellekson, Rosenfeld, and Schneider-Mayerson.

7. Bykov's novel has been discussed extensively by a number of critics, with particular focus on his approach to ideology. See Lipovetskii and Etkind, Lipovetsky, Minkova, and Oushakine Minkova connects the novel with Solzhenitsyn's controversial two-volume history of Jewish-Russian relations, *Two Hundred Years Together*.

8. Given the Putin regime's insistence on casting post-Maidan Ukraine as a Nazi revival show, these authors have clearly tapped into a powerful cultural script.

9. Here I am relying on Marlène Laruelle's blessedly compact summary of Fomenko's main ideas in her article "Conspiracy and Alternate History in Russia: A Nationalist Equation for Success?" I have thus far made it through only three volumes of Fomenko's collected works, with only limited motivation to forge ahead.

10. The publisher's description includes an unintentionally hilarious reassurance: "This book does not demand any special knowledge from its reader."

11. Both Fomenko's redefinition of nearly anything valuable as "Russian" and the old Soviet habit of claiming foreign inventions as their own reach their logical, if absurd conclusion in Mikhail Yuriev's (Iur'ev's) 2007 utopian novel, *The Third Empire: The Russia That Must Be*. After the entire world has been divided into spheres of influence (with a greatly expanded Russia as the primary superpower), foreign cultural imports have been drastically curtailed. Imported art is often passed off as Russian to avoid taxes or restrictions.

12. Here one might see Wimsatt and Beardsley's 1946 argument against the "intentional fallacy" as the struggle against the inherent conspiracism of the reader's belief in the author as master planner. But I'm sure such an interpretation was not their intent.

13. One of the challenges in dealing with this material is balancing a scholarly rejection of the very idea of "national character" or even "nationality" and "ethnicity" as anything but cultural constructs, but writing about a discursive and media environment that leaves primordialist assumptions unquestioned. In his magisterial study *Porog tolerantnosti: Ideologiia i praktika novogo rasizma*, Viktor Shnirel'man argues that, in the last decades of the Soviet Union, "ethnicities (*etnosy*) were understood as distinct and integral, not only with their own primordial cultures and languages, but with their own "psychological disposition" or 'national character.' They could be good or bad, show nobility and goodwill or, on the contrary, stand out for their vengefulness or treachery." Dale Pesmen explores contemporary Russian notions of "national character" in her ethnographical study, *Russia and Soul*.

14. See *The Jewish Century* for Yuri Slezkine's argument about the Jews' role in making modernity.

15. Pesmen notes that in discussing Russia, "people untiringly drew parallels between spiritual and physical geographies, material spaces and soulful values" (214), a trend that dates back at least as far as Berdyaev, who states on the first page of *The Russian Idea* that "There is that in the Russian soul which corresponds to the immensity, the vagueness, the infinitude of the Russian land, spiritual geography corresponds with physical" (1).

16. Piekalkiewicz defines "ideocracy" as "a political system whose activities are pursued in reference to the tenets of a monistic ideology" (25). Epstein's definition is more straightforward: he is concerned with the "dictatorship of ideas" ("Ideas")

17. Those looking for such an overview would be well served by Ilya Yablokov's 2018 study, *Fortress Russia*, which appeared while this book was going to press.

1. Conspiracy and Paranoia

1. Probably less than a day, considering the time difference; Kennedy was shot at 12:30 Central Time.

2. Though he fell out of fashion with scholars of conspiracy theories, Hofstadter has had a resurgence in the wake of the election of Donald Trump. See, for example, Edsall, Heer, Musgrave, Ribuffo, and Stephens.

3. This is a notion that *The X-Files* has occasionally flirted with, but as with everything else in that show, flirtation never translates into absolute commitment.

4. See Barkun's chapters on UFO conspiracies. In *The Dreams Our Stuff Is Made Of*, Thomas M. Disch traces the overlap between Whitley Strieber's work as a popularizer of allegedly nonfictional alien abduction accounts and his prior career as the author of science fiction about the same subject (21–27).

5. Or at least Season One Scully. By the time she's been kidnapped and impregnated by alien visitors, all bets are off.

2. Ruining Russia

1. The novel's Ukrainian setting hardly distances it from Russian reality, despite Mikhail Nazarenko's assertion that *Sweet Home Armageddon* is the Diachenkos' "most Ukrainian novel" (162–73). Certainly, the book makes clear references to Kyiv streets and landmarks, but the political and cultural systems imagined by the authors could be just as applicable to a fantasy version of a major Russian city. Roman Arbitman identifies the novel's "permanent apocalypticism" as a general post-Soviet idea, born "not only from the shaky, unstable, rocky post-Soviet reality—as in Ukraine, so in Russia!—but from the explosive atmosphere of hysterical eschatology that so recently gripped ancient Kiev, appearing out of nowhere along with the White Brotherhood and vanishing into oblivion." The White Brotherhood is discussed below.

2. For an overview of Russian apocalypticism, see Bethea (12–31).

3. See Borenstein, "Suspending Disbelief," "Articles of Faith," and "Maria Devi Khristos."

4. On *S.TA.L.K.E.R*, see Gambarato, and Sokolova, "Co-opting Transmedia Consumers," and Sokolova, "Eto vashe shou."

5. Prokhanov used the bombings as the basis for a major plot point in his novel *Gospodin Geksogen* (2002). Though Prokhanov refers to the various political figures involved by nicknames rather than identifying them explicitly, the novel clearly argues that patriotic forces within the FSB used the bombings to propel Putin into power. In her biography of Putin, Gessen presents the case against Putin as credible (*Man without a Face*, 37–40). See also Dunlop.

6. As Helena Goscilo notes, "the notorious binarism of Russian culture ideally conforms to the requisite conditions for the enactment of melodrama" ("Playing Dead" 287).

7. Cf. Gasparov: "It is far more important, in my opinion, to consider the theory's accuracy in re-creating the traditional outlook of Russian culture on the West through the language of semiotics" (27).

8. Again, Gasparov makes this very argument when introducing Lotman and Uspensky's work to the English-reading public: "Paradoxically, the very model they construct in the course of the analysis reflects a cultural bias no less than the material it seeks to explain. This binary model is in fact not so much a metatext—a description or interpretation—as it is a text of Russian culture; it does not interpret and explain so much as it spontaneously reflects the deep structure of the Russian cultural consciousness" (28).

9. By the last three seasons, the show seemed to be collapsing under the weight of its own inconsistent mythology, but the very omnivorousness of its explanatory mechanisms (alien plots are being faked by the US government; the aliens are making it look as though the government is falsifying alien activity; Mulder's sister was first kidnapped by aliens, murdered by a serial killer, and then transformed into an angel) was consistent with its source material. American UFOlogy has proven itself capable of incorporating virtually any conspiracy theory into its master narrative, going so far as to include subterranean lizard people and *The Protocols of the Elders of Zion* (Barkun, 141–46).

10. Gordon's critics observed that the show's primary aesthetic concern was to feature flattering shots of the author/director himself (Lesko, Munipov).

11. Igor Shafarevich's 1977 book *Socialism as a Phenomenon of World History* (Sotsializm kak iavlenie mirovoi istorii), argues not only that Jews are to blame for socialism, but that the movement's ultimate goal is the "death of humanity" (358). Shafarevich is discussed at greater length in the next chapter.

12. My copy of the 1997 Sovetskii Kuban' edition of *My Name Is Legion* is part of a "supplementary printing" of one thousand copies.

13. Klimov's works could be found not only on his own site but also on the largest Russian e-text server, Maxim Moshkov's library (www.lib.ru), as well as numerous sites offering e-books in formats more convenient for higher-end e-book reading software.

14. Mogutin himself has been identified with xenophobic Russian nationalism in his writings about Zhirinovsky and the war in Chechnya (Essig, *Queer in Russia*, 143–46; Gessen, *Dead Again*, 185–98), but even for him, Klimov's theories were too extreme to be taken seriously.

15. The brainwashing hypothesis would soon be adopted by the anticult movement, which alleged that nontraditional religious movements exert control over their members through psychologically complex techniques of indoctrination (Bromley, *Brainwashing/ Deprogramming Controversy*, 27). I have already discussed the ironic afterlife of this strange offshoot of the Cold War in post-Soviet Russia with the panic over "totalitarian sects" ("Suspending Disbelief," 453–55), and I will return to it in the chapter on zombification.

16. For example, Fidel Castro's brother is assumed to be gay because of his long hair (Klimov, *Kniaz' mira sego*, 280), while the red hair color of Lenin, Stalin's mother, and Alexander Solzhenitsyn shows that they are degenerates, and probably Jews (Klimov, *Imia moe—Legion*, 8).

17. According to the Norka website, the group consists of Evgeny Vladimirovich Myachin, Andrei Elin, Aleksandr Vasil'evich Orlov, Vladimir Alexandrovich Gorbunov, and Norka himself (www. norkag.ru/ru/about/).

18. Though Roth has never been one for allegorical readings, he did add fuel to the fire with his offhand criticism of the Bush administration in his *New York Times Book Review* essay about *The Plot against America* (Roth).

19. These plot twists make the show more politically palatable at the same time that they add to the suspense. In the first three seasons, a group of right-wing American terrorists turn out to be working for a Bosnian Serb, who in turn was apparently being manipulated by American oil interests. These same plutocrats (who inexplicably disappear from the scene almost as soon as they are revealed) were also the masterminds of a plot manipulating Islamic fundamentalists (one of whom is a blonde American woman who initially looked as though she were going to be the naive dupe of her swarthy foreign fiancé, when the situation was actually reversed). Subsequently a Mexican drug cartel trading in bioterrorist weapons was actually a front for a rogue British agent with an axe to grind. By the fourth season, the writers threw in the towels and simply made the villains Arabs.

20. One of the few exceptions is an almost offhand reference made by the Dark Horse in one of his first presidential speeches: "Everything has to be paid for. After crucifying Christ, the Jews ceased to exist as a nation and paid for their crime for two thousand years. In what way, and for how long, must Russians pay for this?" (Norka, *Inkvizitor*, 26). On the scale of Russian antisemitism, the "Christ killers" calumny is so mild as to be almost unworthy of notice; it is quite possible that the Norka group assumed it was appealing to unimpeachable historical fact rather than deliberately reinforcing an anti-Jewish canard.

21. Mikhalkov devoted the November 28, 2015, brodacast of his television show *Besogon* to the Dulles Plan (Mikhalkov).

22. Curiously, Dulles also actively denounced the *Protocols* as a forgery, trying to convince the State Department in 1921 to denounce them when he worked at the US Embassy in Istanbul.

23. Gábor Rittersporn provides a compelling overview of Stalin-era paranoia in chapters 1 and 2 of *Anguish, Anger, and Folkways in Soviet Russia.*

24. This is not to imply that the Russian government has endorsed the Dulles Plan. On the contrary, a regional court declared the Plan "extremist literature" in June 2015 ("Mificheskii plan Dallesa").

25. Here I am summarizing the first five chapters of Petrov's *Tainy upravleniia chelovechestva*, vol. 1.

26. The nationalist economist Sergei Glazev first popularized this idea in his 1998 book *Genocide: Russia and the New World Order.* The idea has taken on a life of its own, to the point where the pseudoscientist and TV commentator Irina Yermakova has asserted that GMOs are part of a plot to sterilize the Russian population as part of an overall program of genocide (Antonova).

3. Lost Horizons

1. I'm sticking to the masculine gender here out of linguistic rather than political concerns. I am trying my best to make this discussion understandable even to those who do not speak Russian, which is why the words are transliterated rather than rendered in Cyrillic. Non-Russian speakers are more likely to be familiar with *russkii* than the feminine *russkaia*.

2. Barry Adam points out that the term "homophobia" suggests both irrational fear and the possibility that its subject could overcome it, through therapy or education, as opposed to the more ideological "heterosexism" (388).

3. Andrei Tsygankov, the author of *Russophobia: Anti-Russian Lobby and American Foreign Policy*, would probably disagree. He argues that hostility to Russia has been at the heart of America's dealing with the rest of the world for decades, pointing at an "anti-Russian lobby." In any case, the ever-evolving scandal of possible collusion between Donald's Trump's presidential campaign and either the Russian government or particular Russian citizens (all covered by the shorthand "Russia") may prove to be a turning point in Russophobia's

development in the United States. The Trump phenomenon is treated in the conclusion of the present study.

4. A good starting point is Max Paul Friedman's *Rethinking Anti-Americanism*.

5. For example, in Viktor Dotsenko's *Mad Dog in Love* (Liubov' beshennogo, 1998), the eighth entry in his multivolume series of thrillers, the hero is surprised to learn that his American friend, the FBI "Lieutenant" (sic) Michael James, has two sons named Vasily and Viktor; it turns out that Michael's great-grandfather fled from Siberia to Alaska at the turn of the century. Michael's grandfather was forced to abandon his Russian last name because of the McCarthy witch hunts (*Liubov'*, 367). It's a small but telling mistake: American anti-communist hysteria in the 1950s becomes a case of ethnic discrimination.

6. Much of the anticult activity was spearheaded by Aleksandr Dvorkin, who began battling "sects" in 1992. His reasoning can be found in chapters 2 and 3 of *Sektovedenie*.

7. On the 1997 law, see Fagan (chap. 3); on its connection to sovereign democracy, see Anderson.

8. For more on sovereign democracy, see Casula, Makarych, and Petrov.

9. The history and context of Nashi is explained concisely in Hemment, and at much greater length and detail in Mijnssen and Perović.

10. It is easy to make too much of the power of "Kremlin propaganda." Peter Pomerantsev's lively and entertaining memoir of his work as a junior producer on Russian television has helped popularize the belief that Russian audiences are helpless before the onslaught of state television. As Ellen Mickiewicz points out, Pomerantsev's model of media consumption was debunked decades ago (Basulto). Nor does Pomerantsev make any bones about his own contribution to "information warfare"; he co-authored a highly partisan position paper, *The Menace of Unreality* (Pomerantsev and Weiss).

11. Putin's popularity confounds researchers and pundits in the West. In 2015, a team led by Timothy Frye managed to replicate the high approval ratings found by Russian pollsters within a ten-point margin (Frye).

12. The publisher Irina Prokhorova sees both the denial of Ukrainian identity and the overall jingoism of Putin's third term as symptoms of Russia's persistent "imperial vision" (Sokolov).

13. See Ilya Budraitskis's comparison of Putin's policies with Huntington's prophecies ("Putin Lives").

14. The term can be found in samizdat prior to Shafarevich's essay; as Robert Horvath notes, it had even been used by the perestroika architect Alexander Yakovlev. But the word's subsequent popularity is clearly because of Shafarevich.

15. Pages 167–92 of the June issue of *Nash sovremennik* contained the bulk of Shafarevich's essay. "A Painful Question," the section most directly dealing with Jews in Russia, was omitted, only to be published in the November issue (162–72), allegedly in response to readers' complaints about its absence. Krista Berglund notes that *Russophobia* had been circulating widely in samizdat by 1988. I am using the 2011 Algoritm electronic edition.

16. A more nuanced, fascinating, but still problematic, version of this argument is made by Daniel Rancour-Laferrière in *The Slave Soul of Russia*.

17. Building on Alexander Etkind's thesis about Russia's "internal colonization," Mark Lipovetsky argues that the "progressor," a late- and post-Soviet science fiction archetype, functions as an internal colonizer, usually allegorically through a displacement onto an imaginary, fantastic civilization (Lipovetskii and Etkind).

18. Shafarevich notes that he worked with many Jews throughout his career.

19. Horvath is unstinting in his condemnation of *Russophobia*, which he calls "the most original contribution to the literature of prejudice since The Protocols of the Elders of Zion" (174).

20. Berglund's defense of Shafarevich is so total that she finds the very question of his antisemitism offensive: "Having not lowered himself to directly answer in the negative to Bogert's earlier question 'Are you an anti-Semite?'—which of course was naively schematic to the point of being almost comically insulting—Shafarevich probably wanted to make it clear that of course he had Jewish friends and of course Jews enjoyed his full trust and respect just like any other people, and that this fact ought to be so evident that it would be merely embarrassing to everyone to state it any more directly" (324).

21. But it helps.

22. In addition, the name of the literally soulless Aranki, who have created a technocratic but uninspiring society, suggests a bilingual orthographic pun on "Yankee" (to English speakers, the Russian letter pronounced "ya" looks like a backward "R").

23. According to the Vagrius website, the first Mad Dog novel was published in 1989. http://vagrius.ru/authors/dotzenko.shtml.

24. Literally, the word would be rendered as "Kikemason." I have chosen "Jew" over "kike" for euphony and out of recognition of the vexed status of the English word "Jew" as both neutral and insulting.

25. The head of Russia's presidential administration in the thirteenth novel is a man named Levinson, who is connected to both the IMF and the Secret Order (*Kremlevskoe delo*, 26).

26. Like Rice, Gatti studied with Joseph Korbel, the father of "our beloved Madeline Albright." As Savely says on hearing this piece of information: "An interesting picture is being painted here!" (*Ostrov*, 104).

27. This is not unique to Russia; the American equivalent would be "anti-Americanism" or "They hate us for our freedom," a phrase used as an explanation independent of any actual information. The difference is that anti-Americanism is not central to American conspiracy theories, playing nothing like the unifying role that Russophobia plays in Russian conspiratorial thought.

28. Ironically, one of those theories could be the specific elaboration of Russophobia made by Shafarevich; more often than not, the word need not point back to Shafarevich and his book.

29. Again, one could make a similar but more limited argument for America: anti-Americanism as the abject Other of American exceptionalism. But, again, this is not a driving force for American conspiracy theorists.

4. One Hundred Years of Sodom

1. Alexander Dugin, who has made the fight against liberalism part of his life's mission, inadvertently highlights this confusion in a recent book, when he demonstrates the unpopularity of liberalism by noting how few people in Russia read "Hayek, Popper, Ayn Rand and [Richard] Rorty" (ebook).

2. Liberalism is the culprit in most of Starikov's monographs. For more efficient demonization, Starikov released a collection of his thought in Twitter-ready bite-sized chunks, with an entire section on liberalism. A typical example: "For the purposes of the decline and destruction of a rival country, liberal democracy was at some point created." Vladislav Inozemtsev notes that the politicians whom Russians consider to be "economic liberals" are better described as "libertarians."

3. There's an entire book called *Liberals about the People* (Liberaly o narode), composed entirely of quotes from Russian liberals about the backwardness of the Russian people (Garadzha)

4. Klimova published a revised edition called *Page Found* (Stranitsa naidena) in 2017 and intends to update the book every year.

5. One of Starikov's aphorisms about liberals: "Not every liberal is a homosexual, but every homosexual is a liberal."

6. Yet another irony: English, which does not recognize grammatical gender, has the word "gender"; Russian, in which every noun has to have one of three genders (including neuter), does not have a similar word that isn't bound up with categories that would conflict with feminist notions of what gender entails. The Russian word used for grammatical gender (*rod*) is far too rooted in concerns of family and clan to be available for a socially constructed category.

7. The exception here is the "born this way" mantra that has facilitated LGBT acceptance in the straight world. The insistence that sexual orientation both *is* innate and *must* be considered innate has been the subject of critique not only from opponents of gay rights but also from voices within the LGBT community (Khan; Ward).

8. Mikhail Zygar argues: "All decisions are indeed made by Putin, but Putin is not one person. He (or it) is a huge collective mind. Tens, perhaps hundreds of people every day try to divine what decisions Vladimir Putin needs to make. Vladimir Putin himself spends his time divining what decisions he needs to make to stay popular—to be understood and approved by the vast entity that is the collective Vladimir Putin."

9. Supporters also are quick to point out the existence of antigay laws on the books in several US states. Most of these laws, however, are old, and all of them, while potentially facilitating police harassment, are now unenforceable.

10. In January 2014, the editor-in-chief of *Molodoi dal'nevostochnik* was fined fifty thousand rubles for printing the words "being gay is normal" as part of a quotation from a schoolteacher who had been fired for his sexual orientation (Duffy).

11. And this is all without even addressing one of the major ill effects of the law: LGBT youth, who are at a higher risk of suicide, cannot be told that there is nothing wrong with them.

12. Alexander Kondakov and the Laboratory for Sexuality Studies have put together an online database demonstrating the sharp rise in homophobic violence. For an overview in English, see Kondakov. The Russian-language database is available at https://lgbtrightsinrussia. wordpress.com.

13. Not to be confused with the foreign-language television network RT, which used to be called "Russia Today."

14. On the history of homophobia in the Soviet Union and beyond, see Healey.

15. For more on the ties between North American and Russian antigay movements, see Levintova and Gessen, "Family Values."

16. In his unpublished article "Russia's Queer Science," Kevin Moss provides a detailed overview of the pseudoscience that currently passes for public scholarly discourse on homosexuality, with a particular attention to a distinction made between "genetic" homosexuality (a minuscule phenomenon) and "acquired" homosexuality caused by cultural and social forces.

17. See Human Rights Campaign, http://www.hrc.org/.

18. For more details on the antigay campaign, as well as a discussion of its effects on individual queer people in Russia, see Gessen, *The Future Is History*, chap. 19.

19. Actually, viewers of Igor Prokopenko's nonstop wing nut conspiracy mongering on RenTV's *Military Secrets* would know that Europe is obsessed with protecting the rights of pedophiles.

20. This remark should not be construed as an allegation that Steve Jobs actually had friends.

21. For what it's worth, Kristof's trilogy was quite popular in its Russian translation in the 1990s.

22. Nikolai Riabov and Tatiana Riabova have made a similar but much more detailed argument.

23. The homophobic framing here is intentional, as the Gayropa narrative assumes that a truly beautiful drag queen is impossible. Here we should recall the outrage on Russian social media over Conchita Wurst, the bearded, cross-dressing Austrian singer who won Eurovision in 2014.

24. Maria Engstrom argues that the theological concept of the Katechon (withholding), which in Russia dates back to the doctrine of the Third Rome, has been coopted by conservative Russian intellectuals and imported into the 2013 Foreign Policy Concept of the Russian Federation. The result is a synthesis of great power politics (Russia's crucial role in the world) and Christian messianism, with Russia's nuclear capacity forming not just a military, but a "spiritual" and "civilizational" shield (357–58; 368–70).

25. See, for example, the various reactions to the rape charges against a teacher at Moscow's prestigious School no. 57 (Litvinova).

26. After fourteen children died in a summer camp boating disaster that was apparently the result of neglect on the part of the sponsoring organization, Astakhov greeted the surviving children with the question, "So, how was your swim?"

27. The title of this book (and the TV series on which it is based) is supposed to link Mikhalkov to his namesake, Saint Nikita-Besogon—Nikita-who-drives-out-the-demons—but Mikhalkov seems unaware of the word's much more current meaning in criminal slang: liar, deceiver, bullshitter. I leave it up to my readers to decide which usage best applies.

28. For more details about the Ethnogenesis project, see Bassin and Kotkina.

29. This title "No Family" involves an untranslatable (and, frankly, uninteresting) wordplay. The last three letters of the title are in English, which makes it look like a URL (.net), but they are clearly meant to be read as the Russian word *net* (no).

30. More explicit antiliberal dystopias include Larry Niven's, Jerry Pournelle's, and Michael Flynn's *Fallen Angel* (1991), L. P. Hartley's *Facial Justice* (1960), Pete Hautman's young adult novel *Rash* (2006), Rob Grant's *Incompetence* (2003), and the 1993 film *Demolition Man*. Other works that might fit the bill include *Idiocracy* (2006), Ayn Rand's *Atlas Shrugged* (1957), and the entire Left Behind series. Even if we find more examples, they still are the product of isolated authors, and not a movement. The closest exception could be ENC Press, founded by the Russian émigré Olga Gardner Galvin (author of the 2003 antiliberal dystopia *The Alphabet Challenge*, also published by her press). My thanks to Lisa Howey for bringing this book to my attention.

5. The Talking Dead

1. Howey's scenario is that zombies look mindless from the outside, but they are actually still conscious. Unable to control their bodies, they exist in constant horror of their own actions.

2. John Powers goes against the long-established link between zombie plagues and capitalism, comparing the zombie hordes to the Occupy movement. Powers argues that zombies "represent an alternative to neoliberalism—an ideology that admits no alternatives."

3. Children's programming produced abroad is a common target for such fears. One commentator even goes as far as declaring that the Teletubbies are an "international conspiracy directed at Russia's younger generation" (Puzina). When the Teletubbies first began to appear on RTR, *Komsomol'skaia pravda* published an article about the show's hypnotic effect on children: some parents worry that the show is zombifying their children, while others compare the Teletubbies' dances to Buddhist meditation. Another suggests that even if

zombification is taking place, the Teletubbies message is benign: "But the children . . . now they get zombified, creating a new generation, with healthier brains! (*A deti . . . vot ikh i zombiruiut, sozdavaia novoe, bolee zdorovoe mozgami, pokolenie!*" (Shaidakova).

4. The link between "thought reform" and "cults" was facilitated by Robert Jay Lifton's 1961 *Thought Reform and the Psychology of Totalism: A Study of "Brainwashing" in China*, though Lifton himself only made the connection years later (vii–viii).

5. Among the many books written on the subject during the 1970s, Sheila Ostrander, Lynn Schroeder, and Ivan Sanderson's *Psychic Discoveries behind the Iron Curtain* (1970) was the most famous.

6. For more on this debate, see Bromley.

6. Words of Warcraft

1. The slaughter of the Kuwait babies was part of the infamous "Nayirah" testimony to the Congressional Human Rights Caucus on October 10, 1990, in the runup to Operation Desert Storm. It was debunked two years later (Knightley; Taylor, 228).

2. The Galicia region, previously controlled by Austria-Hungary and Poland, was a key site in the development of Ukrainian nationalism in the twentieth century (Plokhy, 240–41).

3. Riabchuk raised the question of "Two Ukraines" in 1992 ("Two Ukraines?"), just after the Soviet collapse. He has revisited and refined this formulation significantly on several occasions ("Ukraine: One State, Two Countries"; "'Two Ukraines' Reconsidered").

4. Ukrainians were a "problem" for the Russian elite in the nineteenth and twentieth centuries to the extent that they expressed an interest in national self-determination.

5. Nineteenth-century Russian ethnographers who worked in Ukraine tended to recapitulate pre-existing stereotypes about its people, portraying them as gloomy farmers with a tendency towards soulful lyricism (Beliakov, *Ten' Mazepy*, 29–30).

6. No matter how enamored seventeenth-century Ruthenians may have been of the idea that Kyiv was the "New Jerusalem," the idea did not gain a great deal of currency (Berezhnaya). Similarly, the Ukrainian Autocephalous Orthodox Church's declaration in July 2010 that the Ukrainian capital is the "New Jerusalem" has yet to make much of a ripple.

7. For a detailed discussion of Bandera's life and the controversies surrounding it, see Rossoliński-Liebe.

8. I have only found this quote in a Russian translation, which I have rendered back into English.

9. In response to the Office of the Director of National Intelligence's report, Simonyan tweeted: "Aaa, the CIA report is out! Laughter of the year! Intro to my show from 6 years ago is the main evidence of Russia's influence at US elections. This is not a joke!" (Goldman).

10. A helpful guide to these theories was compiled for Bellingcat by Aric Toler.

Works Cited

Adam, Barry D. "Theorizing Homophobia." *Sexualities* 1, no. 4 (1998): 387–404.

AFP. "Ukrainian Civilian Death Toll on the Rise in Rebel East: UN." *France 24*. June 13, 2017.

Agamben, Giorgio. *Homo Sacer: Sovereign Power and Bare Life*. Translated by Daniel Heller-Roazen. Stanford, CA: Stanford University Press, 1998.

——. *State of Exception*. Translated by Kevin Attell. Chicago: University of Chicago Press, 2008.

Agent natsional'nogo bezopasnosti. Season 1, Episode 1: "Svet istiny." Directed by Dmitrii Svetozarov. 1998.

Agenstvo Evropeisko-aziatskie novsot. "Lzhe-Golubkov popal v psikhushku na Urale, 14 September 1994." *Komsomol'skaia pravda*, September 14, 1994, 1.

Akunin, Boris. *FM*. 2010. Electronic ed.

——. *The Coronation*. Translated by Andrew Bromfield. London: Phoenix, 2010.

Alexievich, Svetlana. *Secondhand Time: The Last of the Soviets*. Translated by Bela Shayevich. Reprint. New York: Random House, 2017.

Allenova, Olga. "Blok NATO razoshelsia na blokpakety." *Kommersant"*, July 8, 2008, 9.

Anderson, John. "Religion, State, and 'Sovereign Democracy' in Putin's Russia." *Journal of Religious and Political Practice* 2, no. 2 (2016): 249–66.

Andreev, Daniel. *The Rose of the World*. Translated by Jordan Roberts. Herndon. VA: Lindisfarne Books, 1997.

Applebaum, Anne. *Red Famine: Stalin's War on Ukraine*. New York: Anchor, 2018.

Apuzzo, Matt, and Maggie Haberman. "Trump Associate Boasted That Moscow Business Deal 'Will Get Donald Elected.'" *The New York Times*, August 28, 2017.

Arbitman, Roman. "Konets sveta v kontse kvartala." *Knizhnoe obozrenie*, August 28, 2000, 16.

Associated Press. "Orthodox Jewish Paper Apologizes for Hillary Clinton Deletion." *The Guardian*, May 10, 2011.

Astakhov, Pavel Alekseevich. *Nashi deti: Ispoved' o samikh blizkikh i bezzashchitnykh*. Moscow: EKSMO, 2015. Electronic ed.

Astakhov, Sergii. YouTube Channel. https://www.youtube.com/channel/UCba4jRs0LIOk lXXd6ZayzNA.

Austin, J. L. *How to Do Things with Words*. Edited by J. O. Urmson and Marina Sbisà. 2nd ed. Cambridge, MA: Harvard University Press, 1975.

Avenue. "License to Harm." *Human Rights Watch*. December 15, 2014.

Bagdasarian, Vardan. *Antirossiiskie istoricheskie mify*. 2016. Electronic ed.

Barkun, Michael. *A Culture of Conspiracy: Apocalyptic Visions in Contemporary America*. 2nd ed. Berkeley: University of California Press, 2013.

Baron-Cohen, Simon, Leda Cosmides, and John Tooby. *Mindblindness: An Essay on Autism and Theory of Mind*. Revised ed. Cambridge, MA: MIT Press, 1997.

Bassin, Mark, and Irina Kotkina. "The Etnogenez Project: Ideology and Science Fiction in Putin's Russia." *Utopian Studies* 27, no. 1 (2016): 53–76.

Basulto, Dominic. "Nothing Is True and Everything Is Possible about Russian Propaganda." *Medium*. February 19, 2015.

Baudrillard, Jean. *The Gulf War Did Not Take Place*. Bloomington: Indiana University Press, 1995.

Begunov, Iurii. *Tainye sily v istorii Rossii*. Edited by Oleg Platonov. Moscow: Institut russkoi tsivilizatsii, 2016.

Beliaev, Dmitrii. "Propaganda LGBT detiam pod zapretom." November 18, 2011.

Beliakov, Sergei Stanislavovich. *Gumilev, syn Gumileva*. Moscow: AST, 2014.

——. *Ten' Mazepy: Ukrainskaia natsiia v epokhu Gogolia*. Moscow: AST, 2016.

Benediktov, Kirill. *Voina za "Asgard."* Moscow: EKSMO, 2003.

Berdiaev, Nikolai. *The Russian Idea*. New York: Macmillan, 1948.

Berezin, Fedor. *Voina 2010. Ukrainskii front*. Moscow: Eksmo, 2009.

——. *Voina 2011*. Moscow: Eksmo, 2010.

Berezhnaya, Lilya. "Topography of Salvation: 'Kyiv—the New Jerusalem' in the Ruthenian Literary Polemics (End of the 16th–Beginning of the 17th Century." In *Das Grossfürstentum Litauen und die östlichen Gebiete der polnischen Krone als interkulturelle Kommunikationsregion (15.–18. Jh.)*. Passau: Stefan Rohdewald, 2005.

Berglund, Krista. *The Vexing Case of Igor Shafarevich, a Russian Political Thinker*. Basel: Birkhäuser, 2012.

Berglund, Nina. "Minister Defends 'Barnevernet.'" June 12, 2015. http://www.news inenglish.no/2015/06/12/minister-defends-barnevernet/.

Bergset, Irina. "Protiv sodomskoi chumy." *Zavtra*. May 22, 2014. http://zavtra.ru/ blogs/protiv-sodomskoj-chumyi.

"Berlin to Moscow: Stop 'Exploiting' Girl's Case." *RadioFreeEurope/RadioLiberty*. January 27, 2016. https://www.rferl.org/a/lavrov-accuses-germany-covering-up-assault-on-russian-immigrant-girl/27513841.html.

Bethea, David M. *The Shape of the Apocalypse in Russian Fiction*. Princeton, NJ: Princeton University Press, 1991.

Beumers, Birgit. *Pop Culture Russia! Media, Arts, and Lifestyle*. Santa Barbara, CA: ABC-CLIO, 2005.

"Bezumie politkorrektnosti SShA." May 29, 2015. http://pravotnosheniya.info/Bezumie-Politkorrektnosti-SSHA-3069.html.

Birnbaum, Michael. "Russia Bans American Film 'Child 44' Because It Makes Stalin Look Bad." *The Washington Post*, April 15, 2015.

Blinova, Ekaterina. "Holodomor Hoax: Joseph Stalin's Crime That Never Took Place." *Sputnik*, August 9, 2015. https://sputniknews.com/politics/201508091025560345/.

Bohm. Michael. "My Clash with Homophobes on Russian TV." *The Moscow Times*, November 21, 2013. https://themoscowtimes.com/articles/my-clash-with-homophobes-on-russian-tv-29830.

Bondarenko, Vladimir. "Nash Grigorii Klimov." *Zavtra*, September 25, 1998.

Borenstein, Eliot. "Articles of Faith: The Media Response to Maria Devi Khristos." *Religion* 25, no. 3 (1995): 249–66.

——. "Defying Interpretation: Allegory and Ideology in Jurij Oleša's Envy." *Russian Literature* 49, no. 1: 25–42.

——. "Maria Devi Khristos: A Post-Soviet Cult without Personality." *Mind and Human Interaction* 5, no. 3 (1994): 110–22.

——. *Overkill: Sex and Violence in Contemporary Russian Popular Culture*. Ithaca, NY: Cornell University Press, 2007.

——. "Public Offerings: MMM and the Marketing of Melodrama." In *Consuming Russia: Popular Culture, Sex, and Society since Gorbachev*, edited by Adele Marie Barker, 49–75. Durham, NC: Duke University Press, 1999.

——. "Suspending Disbelief: Cults and Postmodernism in Contemporary Russia." In *Consuming Russia: Popular Culture, Sex, and Society since Gorbachev*, edited by Adele Marie Barker, 437–62. Durham, NC: Duke University Press, 1999.

Bradatan, Costica, and Serguei Oushakine, eds. *In Marx's Shadow: Knowledge, Power, and Intellectuals in Eastern Europe and Russia*. Lanham, MD: Lexington Books, 2010.

Bratich, Jack Z. *Conspiracy Panics: Political Rationality and Popular Culture*. Albany, NY: State University of New York Press, 2008.

"Britain Poisoned Double Agent Skripal to 'Nourish Russophobia'—Russian State Media." *The Moscow Times*. March 12, 2018. https://themoscowtimes.com/news/britain-poisoned-double-agent-skripal-to-nourish-russophobia-russian-state-media-60769.

Brodie, Richard. *Virus of the Mind: The New Science of the Meme*. Carlsbad, CA: Hay House, 2011.

Bromley, David G., ed. *Brainwashing Deprogramming Controversy: Sociological, Psychological, Legal, and Historical Perspectives*. Lewiston, NY: Edwin Mellen Press, 1984.

Brooks, Max. *World War Z: An Oral History of the Zombie War*. New York: Broadway Books, 2013.

Brooks, Peter. *The Melodramatic Imagination: Balzac, Henry James, Melodrama, and the Mode of Excess*. New Haven: Yale University Press, 1995.

———. *Reading for the Plot: Design and Intention in Narrative*. New York: Knopf, 2012.

Broverman, Neal. "Powerful Russian News Anchor: Gay Hearts Should Be Burned | Advocate.com." August 11, 2013. https://www.advocate.com/news/world-news/2013/08/11/powerful-russian-news-anchor-gay-hearts-should-be-burned.

Budraitskis, Ilya. "Putin Lives in the World That Huntington Built." Translated by Giuliano Vivaldi. *WDR Review*, July 18, 2017. http://wdwreview.org/desks/putin-lives-in-the-world-that-huntington-built/.

———. "'The Putinist Majority Could Fast Become Anti-Putinist.'" *openDemocracy*, July 25, 2017. https://www.opendemocracy.net/od-russia/ilya-budraitskis/putinist-majority-could-fast-become-anti-putinist.

Bugorkova, Ol 'ga. "Katastrofa MH17: Kak menialis' versii rossiiskikh SMI–BBS Russkaia sluzhba." *BBS. Russkaia sluzhba*, September 28, 2016. http://www.bbc.com/russian/features-37496581.

Burnosov, Iurii. "Moskva, dvadtsat' vtoroi." In *Besposhchadnaia tolerantnost'*, edited by S.V. Chekmaev. 2012. Electronic ed.

Bushkov, Aleksandr. *Beshanaia*. Moscow: Olma-Press, 1998.

———. *Na to i volki*. Moscow: Olma-Press, 1997.

Carnegie, Dale. *How to Win Friends and Influence People*. New York: Simon & Schuster, 2010.

Casula, Philipp. "Sovereign Democracy, Populism, and Depoliticization in Russia." *Problems of Post-Communism* 60, no. 3 (2013): 3–15.

Chalmers, David J. *The Conscious Mind: In Search of a Fundamental Theory*. Revised ed. New York: Oxford University Press, 1997.

Chaplin, Vsevolod. "Absoliutnaia tolerantnost' neizbezhno privedet k utrate svobody i individual'nosti cheloveka,—Prot. Vsevolod Chaplin." *Pravmir*, May 11, 2012. https://www.pravmir.ru/absolyutnaya-tolerantnost-neizbezhno-privedet-k-utrate-svobody-i-individualnosti-cheloveka-prot-vsevolod-chaplin/.

Chekmaev, S. V., ed. *Besposhchadnaia tolerantnost'*. Moscow: EKSMO, 2012.

———, ed. *Liberal'nyi apokalipsis*. Moscow: EKSMO, 2013.

———, ed. *Sem'i.net*. Moscow: EKSMO, 2014.

Chomsky, Noam. "ZCommunications Outrage." *Z Magazine*, August 24, 2014.

Cichlowas, Ola. "The Kremlin Is Trying to Erase the Memory of the Gulag." *The New Republic*. 2014. https://newrepublic.com/article/118306/kremlin-trying-erase-memories-gulag.

Coady, David, ed. *Conspiracy Theories: The Philosophical Debate*. Burlington, VT: Ashgate, 2006.

Cohen, Stanley. *Folk Devils and Moral Panics*. New York: Routledge, 2011.

Cohen, Stephen F. "The New Cold War and the Necessity of Patriotic Heresy." *The Nation*, August 12, 2014.

Coleman, John. *Conspirator's Hierarchy: The Committee of 300*. Carson City, NV: Bridger House, 1992.

Dashkova, Polina. *Priz*. Moscow: AST, 2004.

——. *Zolotoi pesok*. Moscow: AST, 2004.

Dawkins, Richard. *The Selfish Gene: Fortieth Anniversary Edition*. 4th ed. New York: Oxford University Press, 2016.

Debaty: Irina Prokhorova—N. Mikhalkov (Putin). https://www.youtube.com/watch?v= 8xVLEKnQTpg.

Decker, Erin, trans. "Russia's 'Gay Propaganda' Law." http://www.sras.org/russia_gay_ propaganda_law.

DeHaven-Smith, Lance. *Conspiracy Theory in America*. Austin: University of Texas Press, 2013.

Delany, Samuel R. "About 5.750 Words." In his *The Jewel-Hinged Jaw: Notes on the Language of Science Fiction*, 1–15. Middletown, CT: Wesleyan University Press, 1977.

Demolition Man. Directed by Marco Brambilla. 1993. Film.

Dennett, Daniel C. *The Intentional Stance*. Rev. ed. Cambridge, MA: MIT Press, 1989.

Dentith, M. *The Philosophy of Conspiracy Theories*. New York: Palgrave Macmillan, 2014.

Derrida, Jacques. "Signature Event Context." In *Limited Inc.*, edited by Gerald Graff, translated by Jeffrey Mehlman and Samuel Weber, 1–24. Evanston, IL: Northwestern University Press, 1988.

Devin, Isabelle. *Ulitsy razbitykh fonarei 1 sezon (1 seriia)*. Film.

Diachenko, Marina, and Sergei. *Armaged-dom*. Moscow: OLMA-Press, 2000.

Dick, Philip K. *Eye in the Sky*. Boston: Mariner Books, 2012.

Disch, Thomas M. *The Dreams Our Stuff Is Made Of: How Science Fiction Conquered the World*. New ed. New York: Free Press, 2000.

Disch, Thomas M., and John Thomas Sladek. *Black Alice*. New York: Carroll and Graf, 1989.

Dorofeev, Roman. "Pochemu Liza Lerer ushla s kanala "Rossiia'." August 6, 2015. http://www.colta.ru.

Dotsenko, Viktor. *Kremlevskoe delo Beshenogo*. Moscow: Vagrius, 2000.

——. *Liubov' Beshenogo*. Moscow: Vagrius, 2000.

——. *Ostrov Beshenogo*. Moscow: Vagrius, 2000.

——. *Pravosudie Beshenogo*. Moscow: Vagrius, 2000.

——. *Sled Beshenogo*. Moscow: Vagrius, 2000.

——. *Tridtsatogo Unichtozhit!* Moscow: Vagrius, 1998.

——. *Vozvrashchenie Beshenogo*. Moscow: Vagrius, 1998.

——. *Zoloto Beshenogo*. Moscow: Vagrius, 1998.

Duffy, Nick. "Russia: Newspaper Editor Fined under Anti-Gay Law for Printing 'Being Gay Is Normal.'" January 30, 2014. http://www.pinknews.co.uk.

Dugin, Aleksandr. *Ukraina: Moia voina. Geopoliticheskii dnevnik*. Moscow: Tsentrpoligraf, 2015.

Dunlop, John B. *The Moscow Bombings of September 1999: Examinations of Russian Terrorist Attacks at the Onset of Vladimir Putin's Rule*. New York: ibidem, 2014.

Dutsik, Diana. "Mediagramotnost': Itogi monitoringa rossiiskikh SMI za 2014 god." January 10, 2015. https://www.stopfake.org.

Dvorkin, A. L. *Sektovedenie: Totalitarnye sekty. Opyt sistematicheskogo issledova-niia.* 3rd ed. Nizhnii Novgorod: Izdatel'stvo Bratstva vo imia Sv. Kniazia Aleksan-dra Nevskogo, 2002.

Edsall, Thomas B. "The Paranoid Style in American Politics Is Back." *The New York Times.* September 8, 2016. https://www.nytimes.com/2016/09/08/opinion/campaign-stops/the-paranoid-style-in-american-politics-is-back.html.

Eggers, Dave. *The Circle: A Novel.* New York: Vintage, 2014.

Engström, Maria. "Contemporary Russian Messianism and New Russian Foreign Policy." *Contemporary Security Policy* 35, no. 3 (2014): 356–79.

Epstein, Mikhail. "Labor of Lust: Erotic Metaphors of Soviet Civilisation." In his *After the Future: The Paradoxes of Postmodernism and Contemporary Russian Culture,* 164–87. Amherst: University of Massachusetts Press, 1995.

Essig, Laurie. "'Bury Their Hearts': Some Thoughts on the Specter of Homosexuality Haunting Russia." *QED: A Journal in GLBTQ Worldmaking* (2014): 39–58.

——. *Queer in Russia: A Story of Sex, Self, and the Other.* Durham, NC: Duke University Press, 1999.

Fagan, Geraldine. *Believing in Russia: Religious Policy after Communism.* New York: Routledge, 2013.

Fenster, Mark. *Conspiracy Theories: Secrecy and Power in American Culture.* Rev. ed. Minneapolis: University of Minnesota Press, 2008.

Fish, Stanley. *There's No Such Thing as Free Speech: And It's a Good Thing, Too.* New York: Oxford University Press, 1994.

Flintoff, Corey. "Putin Gives Victory Speech, Charges of Flawed Voting." March 5, 2012. http:www.npr.org.

Foucault, Michel. "What Is an Author?" In *Language, Counter-memory, Practice: Selected Essays and Interviews by Michel Foucault,* edited by Donald F. Bouchard, 113–38. Ithaca, NY: Cornell University Press, 1980.

Friedman, Max Paul. *Rethinking Anti-Americanism.* New York: Cambridge University Press, 2012.

Friedman, Thomas L. "As Food Airlift Starts, Baker Hints U.S. Might Agree to Role in a Ruble Fund." *The New York Times,* February 11, 1992.

Frye, Timothy, Scott Gehlback, Kyle L. Marquardt, and Ora John Reuter. "Is Putin's Popularity Real?" *Post-Soviet Affairs* 33, no. 1 (2017): 1–15.

Fuller, Robert K. "AmerRuss." *Whole Evolution Quarterly* 53 (1986): no pp.

Galeotti, Mark. "Russia Has No Grand Plans, but Lots of 'Adhocrats.'" May 26, 2017. https://raamoprusland.nl/dossiers/het-kremlin/428-russia-has-no-grand-plans-but-lots-of-adhocrats.

Galvin, Olga Gardner. *The Alphabet Challenge.* Hoboken, NJ: ENC Press, 2003.

Gambarato, Renira Rampazzo, and Ekaterina Lapina-Kratasiuk. "Transmedia Story-telling Panorama in the Russian Media Landscape." *Russian Journal of Communica-tion* 8, no. 1 (2016): 1–16.

Garadzha, Nikita. *Liberaly o narode.* Moscow: Evropa, 2006.

Garner, James Finn. *Politically Correct Bedtime Stories.* New York: Macmillan, 1994.

Gasparov, Boris. "Introduction." In Iurii M. Lotman and Boris Uspenskii, *The Semiot-ics of Russian Culture,* 13–29. Ann Arbor: Michigan Slavic Publications, 1984.

Gelaev, Vladimir. "'Priamo so shkoly na granty 'sazhaiut' i uvoziat." June 24, 2015. https://www.gazeta.ru/science/2015/06/24_a_6852933.shtml.

Gessen, Masha. *Dead Again: The Russian Intelligentsia after Communism*. New York: Verso, 1997.

——. "Family Values: Mapping the Spread of Antigay Ideology." *Harper's Magazine* (March 2017): 35–40.

——. "Iskusstvo zhit' vezde." *Snob*, no. 6 (2009): no pp.

——. *Man without a Face: The Unlikely Rise of Vladimir Putin*. London: Granta, 2012.

Gogol, Nikolai. "A Bewitched Place." In *The Complete Tales of Nikolai Gogol*, vol. 1: 198–206. Translated by Constance Garnett, revised by Lawrence Kent. Chicago: University of Chicago Press, 1985.

Goldman, Russell. "Russia's RT: The Network Implicated in U.S. Election Meddling." *The New York Times*, January 7 2017.

Golovanov, Iaroslav. "Zametki vashego sovremennika. God 2000. Iz zapisnykh knizhek Iaroslava Golovanova." *Komsomol'skaia pravda*, February 22, 2001.

Gopnik, Adam. *Paris to the Moon*. New York: Random House, 2001.

Gorbachev, Mikhail S. *Perestroika: New Thinking for Our Country and the World*. New York: HarperCollins, 1987.

Gordon, Aleksandr. "Sobranie zabluzhdenii: Zakat Ameriki." *Sobranie zabluzhdenii*. ORT, May 25, 1999. Television.

Goscilo, Helena. "Playing Dead: The Operatics of Celebrity Funerals." In *Imitations of Life: Two Centuries of Melodrama in Russia*, edited by Louise McReynolds and Joan Neuberger. Durham, NC: Duke University Press Books, 2002.

——. "Russia's Ultimate Celebrity: VVP as VIP Objet D'art." In *Putin as Celebrity and Cultural Icon*, edited by Helena Goscilo. New York: Routledge, 2014.

Grant, Mira. *Feed*. London: Orbit, 2011.

Grant, Rob. *Incompetence: A Novel of the Far Too Near Future*. London: Gollancz, 2004.

Gularian, Artem Borisovich. "Ot eskhatologii k liberpanku: Evoliutsiia zhanra antiutopii v sotsial'noi fantastike." October 25, 2008. http://samlib.ru/g/gularjan_a_b/asha tolojy.shtml.

Gumenyuk, Nataliya. *The Luhansk "People"s Republic's Forbids Women to Enter Bars*. 2014. Film. https://www.youtube.com/watch?v=140dFQx8Wr8.

Gupta, Samarth. "Hidden Hypocrisy." *Harvard Political Review*. July 28, 2014. http://harvardpolitics.com/world/hidden-hypocrisy.

Hahn, Gordon. "Did Putin Really Tell Bush 'Ukraine Is Not Even as State'?" *Russian and Eurasian Politics*, January 26, 2015. https://gordonhahn.com/2015/01/26/did-putin-really-tell-bush-ukraine-is-not-even-a-state/.

Haldeman, Joe W., Bruno Marchand, and Marvano. *The Forever War*. New York: Nantier-Beall-Minoustchine, 1990.

Harper, Steven. "Interactive Timeline: Everything We Know about Russia and President Trump." August 21, 2017. https://billmoyers.com.

Hartley, L. P. *Facial Justice*. New York: Penguin, 2014.

Hautman, Pete, and 3M Company. *Rash*. e-book. New York: Simon & Schuster, 2012.

Healey, Dan. *Russian Homophobia from Stalin to Sochi*. New York: Bloomsbury, 2017.

Heer, Jeet. "Trump's Cult of Personality Takes Paranoia to the Next Level." *The New Republic*. January 26, 2018. https://newrepublic.com/article/146786/trumps-cult-personality-takes-paranoia-next-level.

Heinrich Boll Foundation, eds. *Anti-Gender Movements on the Rise? Strategizing for Gender Equality in Central and Eastern Europe*. Heinrich Bollstiftung Publication Series on Democracy, no. 38 (2015).

Heins, Volker. "Critical Theory and the Traps of Conspiracy Thinking." *Philosophy and Social Criticism* 33, no. 7 (2007): 787–801.

Hellekson, Karen. *The Alternate History: Refiguring Historical Time*. Akron, OH: Kent State University Press, 2000.

Hemment, Julie. "Nashi, Youth Voluntarism, and Potemkin NGOs: Making Sense of Civil Society in Post-Soviet Russia." *Slavic Review* 71, no. 2 (2012): 234–60.

Hersey, John. *White Lotus*. New York: Bantam Books, 1971.

Hofstadter, Richard, and Sean Wilentz. *The Paranoid Style in American Politics*. New York: Vintage, 2012.

Holmgren, Beth. "Bug Inspectors and Beauty Queens: The Problem of Translating Feminism into Russian." In *Postcommunism and the Body Politic*, edited by Ellen E. Berry, 15–31. New York: New York University Press, 1995.

Horvath, Robert. *The Legacy of Soviet Dissent: Dissidents, Democratisation and Radical Nationalism in Russia*. London: Routledge, 2014.

Howey, Hugh. *I, Zombie*. Mankato, MN: Broad Reach Publishing, 2012.

Hughes, Geoffrey. *Political Correctness: A History of Semantics and Culture*. Malden, MA: Wiley-Blackwell, 2011.

Hunter, Edward. *Brainwashing: The Story of the Men Who Defied It*. London: Forgotten Books, 2012.

Iablokov, Aleksandr. "Otravlennye pechen'ki Nuland." April 27, 2016.

Idicula, Thomas Sajan Titto. "There's Another Side to the Norway Episode." *The Hindu Business Line*, February 22, 2012. http://www.thehindubusinessline.com/opinion/theres-another-side-to-the-norway-episode/article2920383.ece.

Idiocracy. Dir. Mike Judge. 2007. Film.

Inozemtsev, Vladislav. "Neliberal'naia Rossiia." August 22, 2016. https://snob.ru.

Intergirl. Directed by Pyotr Todorovsky. 1989. Film

Interventsiia: Garvardsko-Khiustonskii proekt. Directed by Andrii Sviatynya. Film. https://imperiya.by/video/09ok57OEOlr/interventsiya-garvardsko_hyustonskiy-proekt-chast-2.html.

Invasion of the Body Snatchers. 1956. IMDb.

Irina Bergset marsh "V zashchitu detei" 2 marta. 2013. Film.

Iur'ev, Mikhail. *Tret'ia imperiia: Rossiia, kotoraia dolzhen byt'*. St. Petersburg: K. Tublin, 2007.

Ivanov, Anatolii. *Vechnyi zov*. Moscow: Molodaia gvardiia, 1981.

"Iznasilovanie devochki v FRG: Feik ili tendentsiia?" http://korrespondent.net/world/3620042-yznasylovanye-devochky-v-frh-feik-yly-tendentsyia.

Jameson, Fredric. *Archaeologies of the Future: The Desire Called Utopia and Other Science Fictions*. London: Verso, 2007.

———. "Cognitive Mapping." In *Marxism and the Interpretation of Culture*, edited by Cary Nelson, 347–57. Urbana: University of Illinois Press, 1990.

Jane, Emma A. *Modern Conspiracy: The Importance of Being Paranoid.* New York: Bloomsbury Academic, 2014.

Jarry, Alfred. *Ubu Roi.* Translated by Beverly Keith and G. Legman. Mineola, NY: Dover Publications, 2003.

Jeffords, Susan. *Hard Bodies: Hollywood Masculinity in the Reagan Era.* New Brunswick, NJ: Rutgers University Press, 1993.

Kachurovskaia, Anna. "Rodnaia grech'." *Kommersant*", May 22, 2006.

Kaganov, Leonid. "Dalekaia GeiParaduga." In *Besposhchadnaia tolerantnost'*, edited by S.V. Chekmaev. Moscow: EKSMO, 2012. Electronic ed.

Kak Nuland gosdepovskimi pechen'kami Evromaidan kormila. Accidents News. February 27, 2014. Film. https://www.youtube.com/watch?v=tp5wT7SWdls.

Kanygin, Pavel. "Golubye i politzakliuchennye—a razve eto nabolevshaia tema?" *Novaia gazeta*, August 29, 2016.

Kaplan, Robert D. *Balkan Ghosts: A Journey through History.* New York: Picador, 2005.

Kara-Murza, Sergei. *Manipuliatsiia soznaniem.* 3 vols. Moscow: EKSMO, 2004.

Kashin, Oleg. "Krovavyi nalet v efire 'pervogo kanala': Izvinitsia li Konstantin Ernst pered zriteliami." *Slon*, July 14, 2014.

Kayiatos, Anastasia. "Penile Servitude and the Police State." *All the Russias.* November 20, 2013. http://jordanrussiacenter.org/news/penile-servitude-police-state/#.W3Ht-JNKiu4.

Keeley, Brian L. "Of Conspiracy Theories." *Journal of Philosophy* 96, no. 3 (1999): 109–26.

Kharitonov, Mikhail. "Vsegda Koka-kola." In his *Morgenshtern*. Moscow: AST, 2004.

Khan, Shamus. "Not Born This Way: Other Liberation Movements Have Rejected the Idea That Biology Is Destiny. So Why Should Gay Rights Depend on It?" July 23, 2015. https://aeon.co/essays/why-should-gay-rights-depend-on-being-born-this-way.

Khor, Iurii. *TVN.* N.p. 2015.

Kirkman, Robert, and Charlie Adlard. *The Walking Dead.* Vol. 24. Portland, OR: Image Comics, 2005.

"Kiselev rasskazal ob alkogol'nykh motivakh Brexit." June 3, 2016. https://www.newstube.ru/media/kiselyov-rasskazal-ob-alkogolnyh-motivah-brexit.

Kishkovsky, Sophia. "Putin Backs Memorial to Gulags' Victims." *The Art Newspaper*, November 1, 2015.

Klimov, Grigorii. *Imia moe—Legion.* Krasnodar: Sovetskii Kuban, 1998.

———. *Kniaz' mira sego.* Krasnodar: Sovetskii Kuban, 1998.

———. *Krasnaia kabbala.* Krasnodar: Sovetskii Kuban, 1998.

———. *Protokoly sovetskikh mudretsov.* Krasnodar: Sovetskii Kuban, 1998.

Klimova, Lena. *Deti-404: LGBT-podrostki v stenakh molchaniia.* s.l.: Ridero, 2015.

Knight, Ben. "Teenage Girl Admits Making up Migrant Rape Claim That Outraged Germany." *The Guardian*, January 31, 2016.

Knight, Peter. *Conspiracy Culture: From Kennedy to The X Files.* New York: Routledge, 2013.

——. "Making Sense of Conspiracy Theories." In *Conspiracy Theories in American History*. 2 vols., 1: 15–25. Santa Barbara, CA: ABC-CLIO, 2003.

Knightley, Phillip. "Analysis: The Disinformation Campaign." *The Guardian*, October 4, 2001.

Koposov, Nikolay. *Memory Laws, Memory Wars: The Politics of the Past in Europe and Russia*. New York: Cambridge University Press, 2017.

——. *Pamiat' strogogo rezhima: Istoriia i politika v Rossii*. Moscow: Novoe literaturnoe obozrenie, 2011.

Kotkin, Stephen. *Magnetic Mountain: Stalinism as a Civilization*. Berkeley: University of California Press, 1995.

Kress, Nancy. *Probability Moon*. New York: Tor, 2002.

Kristof, Agota. *The Notebook*. New York: Grove Press, 1988.

Krylov, Konstantin. "Novyi mirovoi poriadok." n.d.

Kucherena, Anatolii. "Politkorrektnost': Totalitarizm dlia durakov." *Ekho Moskvy*. May 30, 2011. https://echo.msk.ru/blog/kucherena/779918-echo/.

Kundera, Milan. *The Book of Laughter and Forgetting*. Translated by Aaron Asher. New York: Harper Perennial, 1999.

Kuz'menkova, Ol'ga. "'Russkii mir' prishel v Berlin: Kak istoriia ob 'iznasilovannoi devochke' vzbudorazhila nemetskuiu stolitsu. Reportazh 'Meduzy.'" *Meduza*, January 25, 2016.

Kuz'mich, Anatolii. *Zagovor mirovogo pravitel'stva: Rossiia i "zolotoi milliard."* N.p., 1994.

Lacan, Jacques. *Écrits: A Selection*. Translated by Alan Sheridan. New York: W. W. Norton, 1977.

——, and John Forrester. *Freud's Papers on Technique, 1953–1954*. Edited by Jacques-Alain Miller. New York: W. W. Norton, 1991.

LaHaye, Tim, and Jerry B. Jenkins. *Left Behind*. Carol Stream, IL: Tyndale House, 1995.

Lapikura, Valerii. "'Beloe bratsvo': Zombie ili fanatiki?" *Rossiiskaia gazeta*, November 9, 1993.

Laruelle, Marlène. "Conspiracy and Alternate History in Russia: A Nationalist Equation for Success?" *Russian Review* 71, no. 4 (2012): 565–80.

——. "Negotiating History: Memory Wars in the Near Abroad and the Pro-Kremlin Youth Movements." In *Russian Nationalism, Foreign Policy and Identity Debates in Putin's Russia: New Ideological Patterns after the Orange Revolution*, edited by Marlène Laruelle, 75–105. Stuttgart: ibidem, 2014.

Leites, Nathan. *The Operational Code of the Politbiuro*. New York: McGraw-Hill, 1971.

Leont'ev, Mikhail. *Krepost' Rossiia: Proshchanie s liberalizmom*. Moscow: Iauza, 2005.

Lesko, M. "G.G.G., ili gorizonty grazhdanina Gordona." *Moskovskaia pravda*, October 16, 1999.

Levenchuk, Anatolii. "Liberpank." April 2, 2005. http://ailev.livejournal.com/295795.html.

Levintova, Hannah. "These US Evangelicals Helped Create Russia's Anti-Gay Movement." *Mother Jones* (February 2014).

Lévi-Strauss, Claude. *Structural Anthropology*. Rev. ed. New York: Basic Books, 1974.

"Libfag." *Urban Dictionary*. http://www.urbandictionary.com.

License to Harm: Violence and Harassment against LGBT People and Activists in Russia. December 15, 2014. https://www.hrw.org/report/2014/12/15/license-harm/violence-and-harassment-against-lgbt-people-and-activists-russia.

Lifton, Robert Jay. *Thought Reform and the Psychology of Totalism: A Study of Brainwashing in China*. Chapel Hill: University of North Carolina Press, 1989.

Lipovetskii, Mark, and Aleksandr Etkind. "Vozvrashchenie Tritona: Sovetskaia katastrofa i postsovetskii roman." *Novoe literaturnoe obozrenie*, no. 94 (2008): no pp.

Lipovetsky, Mark. "The Poetics of the ITR Discourse in the 1960s and Today." In his *Postmodern Crises: From Lolita to Pussy Riot*. Brighton, MA: Academic Studies Press, 2017.

Litvinova, Daria. "Sexual Assault Scandal Hits Elite Moscow School, Rocks Russian Intelligentsia." *The Moscow Times*, September 7, 2016.

Lotman, Iurii M., and B. A. Uspenskii. *The Semiotics of Russian Culture*. Ann Arbor: Michigan Slavic Publications, 1984.

Luk'ianenko, Sergei. *Osennie vizity*. Moscow: AST, 2010.

——. *Spektr*. Moscow: AST, 2010.

Luk'ianenko, Sergei, and Valerii Kukhareshin. *Kvazi*. Moscow: AST, 2016.

L'vov, Ruslan. *A zombi zdes' tikhie*. Izhevsk TK TNT-Novyi region, 2013. Television.

MacFahrquhar, Neil. "A Tug of War over Gulag History in Russia's North." *The New York Times*, August 30, 2015.

Makarov, Slava. "Opredeleniia liberpanka—zapiski o proiskhodiashchem poblizosti." http://slavamakarov.livejournal.com/183822.html.

Makarychev, Andrey S. "Politics, the State, and De-Politicization: Putin's Project Reassessed." *Problems of Post-Communism* 55, no. 5 (2008): 62–71.

Maksimov, Konstantin. *Vidiashchii smert'*. Moscow: Armada-Press, 1999.

Malov, Dmitrii. *Nikita Mikhalkov o plane Allena Dallesa po razvalu Rossii*. Film.

Mamikonian, Mariia. "'Sut' vremeni': 'Novyi nariad korolia,' ili o prodvizhenii tolerantnosti v massy." http://ulpressa.ru.

The Manchurian Candidate. Directed by John Frankenheimer. 1962. Film.

Marinina. Aleksandra. *Smert' radi smerti (Beskonechnost- zla)*. Moscow: Eksmo, 1998.

Marson, James. "Putin to the West: Hands off Ukraine." *Time*, May 25 2009.

McDaniel, Tim. *The Agony of the Russian Idea*. Princeton, NJ: Princeton University Press, 1998.

"Mediinyi Medinskii." *Izvestiia*, May 22, 2012.

Mendlesohn, Farah. *Rhetorics of Fantasy*. Middletown, CT: Wesleyan University Press, 2008.

Mettan, Guy. *Creating Russophobia: From the Great Religious Schism to Anti-Putin Hysteria*. Atlanta: Clarity Press, 2017.

"Mificheskii 'Plan Dallesa' po unichtozheniiu SSSR priznali ekstremistskim." *Meduza*, n.d.

"Migranty v Berline iznasilovali devochku iz sem'i rossiiskikh nemtsev." Lenta.ru, January 17, 2016. https://lenta.ru/news/2016/01/17/horror/.

Mijnssen, Ivo, and Jeronim Perović. *The Quest for an Ideal Youth in Putin's Russia I: Back to Our Future! History, Modernity, and Patriotism according to Nashi, 2005–2013*. 2nd ed. Stuttgart: ibidem, 2014.

Mikhalkov, Nikita. *Besogon: Rossiia mezhdu proshlym i budushchim.* Moscow: EKSMO, 2016.

"Millionaire Son Burns $245k Ferrari to Make Dad Buy New One." *Sputnik,* August 13, 2015. https://sputniknews.com/europe/201508131025683038/.

Milosz, Czeslaw. *The Captive Mind.* New York: Vintage, 1990.

Minakov, I. *A zombi zdes' tikhie.* Moscow: EKSMO, 2013.

Minkova, Yuliya. "The Squid and the Whale à la Russe: Navigating the Uncanny in Dmitry Bykov's *ZhD.*" *Russian Review* 72, no. 2 (2013): 285–302.

Mironov, Arsenii. *Tupik gumanizma.* n.p., 2004.

Misra, Ria. "Author Ken Liu Explains 'Silkpunk' to Us." July 14, 2015. http://io9.gizmodo.com/author-ken-liu-explains-silkpunk-to-us-1717812714.

Mogutin, Iaroslav. "Interv'iu s Grigoriem Petrovichem Klimovym, professorom satanovedeniia i vysshei sotsiologii, avtorom 'Kniazia mira sego' i drugikh knig." *Pechatnyi organ,* nos. 108–9 (1997): no pp.

Munipov, Aleksei. "Nartsiss v iantare/prem'era seriala 'Sobranie zabluzhdenii' na kanale ORT." *Izvestiia,* January 29, 1999.

Musafirova, Ol 'ga, and Viktoriia Makarenko. ""Mal'chika' ne bylo, no on zhivet." *Novaia gazeta,* July 14, 2015. https://www.novayagazeta.ru/articles/2015/07/15/64898-171-malchika-187-ne-bylo-no-on-zhivet.

Musgrave, Paul. "Donald Trump Is Normalizing Paranoia and Conspiracy Thinking in US Politics." *The Washington Post,* January 12, 2017. https://www.washingtonpost.com/posteverything/wp/2017/01/12/donald-trump-has-brought-us-the-american-style-in-paranoid-politics/?utm_term=.15cdebb1b389.

My New Orthodox Video. Directed by Anatoly Ulyanov. 2013.

"Na Ukraine opublikovali spisok zapreshchennykh v vvoz knig." Lenta.ru, August 11, 2016. https://lenta.ru/news/2015/08/11/antiukr/.

"'Nashistka' Sveta iz Ivanovo." December 6, 2011. https://www.youtube.com/watch?v=24XBX0Wkmpw.

Nazarenko, Mikhail. *Real'nost' chuda: O knigakh Mariny i Sergei Diachenko.* Vinnitsa: Tezis, 2005.

Nemenskii, Oleg. "Rusofibia kak ideologiia." *Voprosy natsionalizma* 1, no. 13 (2013): 26–65. http://www.russdom.ru/node/7732.

Nemtsov, Boris. *Zimniia olimpiada v subtropikakh.* May 29, 2013. http://nemtsov.ru/2013/05/zimnyaya-olimpiada-v-subtropikax/.

NewsFromUkraine. *Russian Parliament Applauds Trump's Victory.* Film.

Newton, Mark. "The Real, Parallel Universe Reason Why No One Says Zombie on The Walking Dead." October 17 2014. https://moviepilot.com/posts/2344816.

Night of the Living Dead. Directed by George Romero. 1968. Film.

Niven, Larry, Jerry Pournelle, and Michael Flynn. *Fallen Angel.* New York: Melia, 2004.

No Place for Fools. Directed by Oleg Mavromatti. 2015. Film.

Norka, Sergei. *Inkvizitor.* Moscow: Vagrius, 2004.

——. *Rus' okaiannaia.* Moscow: OLMA-Press, 2000.

——. *Zagovor protiv rossii.* Moscow: Vagrius, 2004.

Nosovskii, Gleb. *Khristos rodilsia v Krymu, tam zhe umerla Bogoroditsa.* Moscow: AST, 2009.

"Nuland: Ia razdavala na Maidane ne pechen'e, a sendvichi." RIA Novosti Ukraina, December 17, 2014. https://rian.com.ua.

Nyers, Peter. *Rethinking Refugees beyond States of Emergency.* New York: Routledge, 2005.

"O dostizhenii stepeni total'nogo nedoveriia i podozritel'nosti." *Nezavisimaia gazeta,* June 23, 2015.

O'Leary, Stephen D. *Arguing the Apocalypse: A Theory of Millennial Rhetoric.* New York: Oxford University Press, 1998.

Ostrander, Sheila, Lynn Schroeder, and Ivan T. Sanderson. *Psychic Discoveries behind the Iron Curtain.* New York: Bantam, 1971.

Oushakine, Serguei Alex. "(Post)Ideological Novel." In *Russian Literature since 1991,* edited by E. A. Dobrenko and M. N. Lipovetskii, 45–65. New York: Cambridge University Press, 2015.

Pagán, Victoria Emma. *Conspiracy Narratives in Roman History.* Austin: University of Texas Press, 2013.

"Palace Square: 100 Years After. A Film-Lecture '4 Seasons of Zombie.'" http://vimeo.com/241639647.

Parry, Hannah. "Norway 'Taking Foreign Children as It Has Highest Rates of Inbreeding.'" *The Daily Mail,* April 14, 2015.

Pelevin, Victor. *Homo Zapiens.* Translated by Andrew Bromfield. London: Penguin Books, 2002.

"Peskov priznal protsess unichtozheniia sanktsionnoi edy vizual'no nepriiatnym." Lenta.ru, August 6, 2015. https://lenta.ru/news/2015/08/06/eda/.

Pesmen, Dale. *Russia and Soul: An Exploration.* Ithaca, NY: Cornell University Press.

Petrov, K. P. *Tainy upravleniia chelovechestvom.* Moscow: Akademiia upravleniia, 2009.

Petrov, Nikolai. *From Managed Democracy to Sovereign Democracy.* PONARS Policy Memo no. 396 (2005).

Pidgen, Charles. "Popper Revisited, or, What Is Wrong with Conspiracy Theories?" In *Conspiracy Theories: The Philosophical Debate,* edited by David Coady, 17–44. Burlington, VT: Ashgate, 2006.

Piekalkiewicz, Jaroslaw, and Alfred Wayne Penn. *Politics of Ideocracy.* Albany: State University of New York Press, 1995.

Pillar, Paul R. "Malaysia Airlines Flight 17 and Iran Air Flight 655." *The National Interest,* July 24, 2014.

"Plan Dallesa—entsiklopediia KOB." http://wiki.kob.su.

Platonov, Andrei. *Chevengur.* Translated by Anthony Olcott. Ann Arbor: Ardis, 1978.

——. *The Foundation Pit.* Translated by Robert Chandler, Elizabeth Chander, and Olga Meerson. New York: New York Review Books Classics, 2009.

Plokhy, Serhii. *The Gates of Europe: A History of Ukraine.* New York: Basic Books, 2017.

Pomerantsev, Peter. *Nothing Is True and Everything Is Possible: The Surreal Heart of the New Russia.* New York: PublicAffairs, 2014.

Pomerantsev, Peter, and Michael Weiss. *The Menace of Unreality: How the Kremlin Weaponizes Information, Culture, and Money.* New York: Institute of Modern Russia, 2014.

Popper, Karl R., Alan Ryan, and E. H. Gombrich. *The Open Society and Its Enemies.* New one-volume ed. with a new introduction by Alan Ryan and an essay by E. H. Gombrich. Princeton, NJ: Princeton University Press, 2013.

The Protocols of the Learned Elders of Zion. https://en.wikisource.org/wiki/The_ Protocols_of_the_Learned_Elders_of_Zion.

Powers, John. "The Political Economy of Zombies." *The Airship.* http://airshipdaily. com/the-political-economy-of-zombies/.

Prokhanov, Aleksandr. *Gospodin Geksogen.* Moscow: Ad Marginem. 2002.

Putin, Vladimir. "Meeting of the Valdai International Discussion Club." September 19, 2013. http://en.kremlin.ru/events/president/news/19243.

Puzina, Lelia. "Telepuziki: Kto oni?" *Telenedelia,* May 20, 2001. http://www.tele7.ru/ 21_01.html#raz.

Ramsay, Julius. "Them." *The Walking Dead.* February 15, 2015. Television.

Rancour-Laferriere, Daniel. *The Slave Soul of Russia: Moral Masochism and the Cult of Suffering.* Revised ed. New York: New York University Press, 1995.

Rand, Ayn. *Atlas Shrugged.* Centennial ed. New York: Signet, 1996.

"Rasporiazhenie Administratsii Prezidenta RF ot 17.08.95 no. 1495 'O'napisanii naz-vanii gosudarstv—byvshikh respublik SSSR i ikh stolits.'" August 17, 1995. https:// zakonbase.ru/content/base/15656.

Ray, Lada. "Why Ukraine Radicals Marked Maidan Coup Anniversary by Attacks on Russian Banks." *Futurist Trendcast,* February 20, 2016. https://futuristtrendcast. wordpress.com.

Reuter, Ora John. "Is Putin's Popularity Real?" PONARS Eurasia Policy Memos (2015).

Riabchuk, Mykola. "Two Ukraines?" *East European Reporter* 5, no. 4: no pp.

———. "'Two Ukraines' Reconsidered: The End of Ukrainian Ambivalence?" *Studies in Ethnicity and Nationalism* 15, no. 1 (2015): 138–56.

———. "Ukraine: One State, Two Countries? With Comments." *Transit Online,* no. 23 (2002). http://www.iwm.at/transit/transit-online/ukraine-one-state-two-countries/.

Riabov, Nikolai, and Tatiana Riabova. "The Decline of Gayropa?" *Eurozine,* February 2, 2014.

Ribuffo, Leo P. "Policy Series: Donald Trump and the 'Paranoid Style' in American (Intellectual) Politics. H-Diplo. June 13, 2017. https://issforum.org/roundtables/ policy/1-5an-paranoid.

Ries, Nancy. *Russian Talk: Culture and Conversation during Perestroika.* Ithaca, NY: Cornell University Press, 1997.

Rittersporn, Gábor. *Anguish, Anger, and Folkways in Soviet Russia.* Pittsburgh: University of Pittsburgh Press, 2014.

Robin, Ron Theodore. *The Making of the Cold War Enemy: Culture and Politics in the Military-Intellectual Complex.* Princeton, NJ: Princeton University Press, 2003.

Rosenfeld, Gavriel. "Why Do We Ask 'What If?' Reflections on the Function of Alternate History." *History and Theory* 41, no. 4 (2002): 90–103.

Rossoliński-Liebe, Grzegorz. *Stepan Bandera: The Life and Afterlife of a Ukrainian Nationalist. Fascism, Genocide, and Cult.* Stuttgart: ibidem, 2014.

Roth, Philip. "The Story behind 'The Plot Against America.'" *The New York Times,* September 19, 2004.

"Rusofobiia kak ideologiia." *Perspektivy*, July 9, 2015. http://www.perspektivy.info/book/rusofobija_kak_ideologija_2015-09-07.htm.

Russ, Joanna. *The Country You Have Never Seen: Essays and Reviews*. Liverpool: Liverpool University Press, 2005.

"Russia Takes Down Steve Jobs Memorial after Apple's Tim Cook Comes Out as Gay." *NBC News*, November 13, 2014. http://www.nbcnews.com/news/world/russia-takes-down-steve-jobs-memorial-after-apples-tim-cook-n239956.

"Russian Actor Wants to Put All Homosexuals 'in the Oven'." *The Guardian*. December 16, 2013. https://www.theguardian.com/film/2013/dec/16/russian-actor-ivan-okhlobystin-oven-homosexuals-burned-alive.

"Russian Government Spends Almost 2 Million Rubles Researching How 'Russophobia' Threatens National Security." *Meduza*, August 9, 2016. https://meduza.io/en/news/2016/08/09/russian-government-spends-almost-2-million-rubles-researching-how-russophobia-threatens-national-security.

"Russian Lawyers Say Harry Potter Character Dobby Is Based on Putin." *The Guardian*, January 30, 2003.

"Russian 'Scrubs' Actor Tells Putin to Make Homosexuality Illegal." *The Moscow Times*, January 10, 2014. https://themoscowtimes.com/articles/russian-scrubs-actor-tells-putin-to-make-homosexuality-illegal-30943.

Rybakov, Viacheslav. *Na budushchii god v Moskve*. Moscow: AST, 2003.

Ryzhenkova, Iuliia. "Demonkontrol'." In *Besposhchadnaia tolerantnost'*, edited by S. V. Chekmaev. Moscow: EKSMO, 2012. Electronic ed.

"Sandwiches Are Symbol of Sympathy to Ukrainians at Maidan: Nuland—Sputnik International." *Sputnik*, August 22, 2017.

Sanger, David E. "Putin Ordered 'Influence Campaign' Aimed at US Election, Report Says." *The New York Times*, January 6, 2017.

Savitskii, Georgii. *Posle boia: Slomannyi trezubets*. Moscow: Eksmo, 2009.

Scheffler, Samuel. *Death and the Afterlife*. Edited by Niko Kolodny. New York: Oxford University Press, 2013.

Schneider-Mayerson, Matthew. "What Almost Was: The Politics of the Contemporary Alternate History Novel." *American Studies* 50, nos. 3–4 (2009): 63–83.

Schwirtz, Michael. "Russia Seeks to Cleanse Its Palate of U.S. Chicken." *The New York Times*, January 19, 2010.

Shafarevich, Igor. *Rusofobiia*. Moscow: Algoritm, 20117.

Shaidakova, Svetlana. "Telepuziki privivaiut rossiiskim detiam buddizm?" *Komsomol'skaia pravda*, April 19, 2001.

Shelepin, Il 'ia. "Dmitrii Kiselev: 'Teper' Ukraina—virtual'naia strana, a nash portal nastoiashchii!'" *Slon*, May 15, 2014.

Sherlock, Thomas. "Confronting the Stalinist Past: The Politics of Memory in Russia." *The Washington Quarterly* 34, no. 2 (2011): 93–109.

Shnirel'man, Viktor. *Porog tolerantnosti: Ideologiia i praktika novogo rasizma*. Moscow: Novoe literaturnoe obozrenie, 2014.

"Siuzhet 'Pervogo kanala' o zverstviakh ukrainskikh voennykh." https://www.youtube.com/watch?v=_-SxR16JCCY.

Slezkine, Yuri. *The Jewish Century*. Princeton, NJ: Princeton University Press, 2006.

Smirnov, Ilya. "Liberastiia." http://screen.ru/Smirnov/.

Smith, Mark, and Conflict Studies Research Centre (Great Britain). *Sovereign Democracy: The Ideology of Yedinaya Rossiya*. Camberley: Defence Academy of the United Kingdom, Conflict Studies Research Centre, 2006.

Smolchenko, Anna. "Putting Words in Albright's Mouth." *The Moscow Times*, November 7, 2007.

Snyder, Timothy. *Bloodlands: Europe between Hitler and Stalin*. New York: Basic Books, 2012.

Sobolev, Sergei. "Programmnyi sbornik esse pro liberpank, iz starogo." December 28, 2008. http://velobos.livejournal.com/146887.html.

Sokolov, Mikhail. "Irina Prokhorova: Podoshli li 'dukhovnye skrepy' Rossii?" *Radio Svoboda*, February 3, 2014. https://www.svoboda.org/a/25251258.html.

Sokolova, Natalia. "Co-Opting Transmedia Consumers: User Content as Entertainment or 'Free Labour'? The Cases of S.T.A.L.K.E.R. and Metro 2033." *Europe-Asia Studies* 64, no. 8 (2012): 1565–83.

——. "'Eto Vashe shou!' Massovye kreativnye praktiki v transmediinykh proektakh." *Digital Icons*, no. 6 (2011): 1–33.

Sorokin, Vladimir. *Day of the Oprichnik*. Translated by Jamey Gambrell. New York: Farrar, Straus, and Giroux, 2012.

——. *Goluboe salo*. Moscow: AST, 2018.

——. "Russia Is Pregnant with Ukraine." *The New York Review of Books*, July 24, 2014.

Sperling, Valerie. *Sex, Politics, and Putin: Political Legitimacy in Russia*. New York: Oxford University Press, 2014.

"Spetsial'nyi korrespondent: Efir ot 28.11.2014." November 28, 2014.

Stahl, Jeremy. "How Trump and His Allies Exploited the Killing of 'Beautiful Kate' to Stoke Anti-Immigrant Fear." *Slate Magazine*. August 10, 2017.

Starikov, Nikolai. *Lakonizmy: Politika. Vlast'. Obshchestvo*. St. Petersburg: Piter, 2016.

Stephens, Bret. "The G.O.P.'s Bonfire of the Sanities." *The New York Times*, January 26, 2018. https://www.nytimes.com/2018/01/26/opinion/republicans-paranoia-mueller-trump.html.

Stone, Oliver. *The Putin Interviews*. New York: Hot Books, 2017.

Sturken, Marita. *Tourists of History: Memory, Kitsch, and Consumerism from Oklahoma City to Ground Zero*. Durham, NC: Duke University Press Books, 2007.

Sunstein, Cass R. *Conspiracy Theories and Other Dangerous Ideas*. New York: Simon & Schuster, 2014.

"Surrounded by the Undead Deep beneath Moscow: A Russian Illustrator Maps out a Subway Survival Scheme for the Zombie Apocalypse." *Meduza*, August 9, 2017 https://meduza.io/en/shapito/2017/08/09/surrounded-by-the-undead-deep-beneath-moscow.

"Swedish Paper Slams Norway's Child Welfare." *The Local*, May 12, 2015. https://www.thelocal.no/20150512/norways-child-welfare-slammed-by-swedish-press.

Tal'kovskii, Dmitrii Vikent'evich. "Zhizn' i smert' Generala Petrova." http://samlib.ru/t/talxkowskij_d_w/istorijaipolitika-14.shtml.

Taylor, Kathleen. *Brainwashing: The Science of Thought Control*. New York: Oxford University Press, 2017.

Taylor, Philip M. *War and the Media: Propaganda and Persuasion in the Gulf War*. Rev. ed. Manchester: Manchester University Press, 1998.

"Territoriia zabluzhdeniii." *Territoriia zabluzhdeniii*. February 6, 2016. Television.

Timofeeva, Oxana. "Manifesto for Zombie Communism." *Mute*, January 12, 2015. http://www.metamute.org/community/your-posts/manifesto-zombie-communism.

Toler, Aric. "The Weird World of MH17 Conspiracy Theories." August 7, 2015. https://www.bellingcat.com.

Tolstaia, Tati'iana. "Politcheskaia korrektnost'." In her *Ne Kys'*. Moscow: EKSMO, 2013.

Tolstoy, Leo. *How Much Land Does a Man Need? and Other Stories*. Edited by A. N. Wilson. Translated by Ronald Wilks. New York: Penguin, 1993.

Torbakov, Igor. "History, Memory and National Identity. Understanding the Politics of History and Memory Wars in Post-Soviet Lands." In *Russian Nationalism, Foreign Policy and Identity Debates in Putin's Russia: New Ideological Patterns after the Orange Revolution*, edited by Marlène Laruelle, 41–74. Stuttgart: ibidem, 2014.

Tsygankov, Andrei. *Russophobia: Anti-Russian Lobby and American Foreign Policy*. New York: Palgrave MacMillan, 2009.

Tsyrlina-Spady, Tatyana, and Michael Lovorn. "Patriotism, History Teaching, and History Textbooks in Russia: What Was Old Is New Again," In *Globalization, Ideology, and Politics of Educational Reforms*, edited by Joseph Zajda, 41–58. Berlin: Springer, 2016.

Tuller, David. *Cracks in the Iron Closet: Travels to Gay and Lesbian Russia*. Boston: Faber and Faber, 1996.

"Ukraine Crisis: Transcript of Leaked Nuland-Pyatt Call." *BBC News*, February 7, 2014.

"V 'LNR' ob'iasnili slova ob areste devushek za pokhod v kafe." *TV-Rain*. November 6, 2014.

Vasil'ev, Vladimir. *A zombi zdes' tikhie*. Moscow: Eksmo, 2013.

Vasserman, Anatolii. *Ukraina i ostal'naia Rossiia*. Moscow: AST, 2013.

Vinnik, Nikolai. "O 'zaprete' slov 'otets' i 'mat'' Sovetom Evropy: Anatomiia odnoi utki." September 16, 2010.

Voennaia taina s Igorem Propkopenko. January 16, 2016; June 25, 2016; October 13, 2015 (episode 729). Television.

Volodikhin, Dmitrii. "Bol'shaia sobaka: Liberpank-pritcha." In *Besposhchadnaia tolerantnost'*, edited by S. V. Chekmaev. Moscow: EKSMO, 2012. Electronic ed.

"Vorwurf Der Vergewaltigung: Mutter Bleibt Bei Lisas Version Des Tathergangs." *RP ONLINE*. https://rp-online.de. July 26, 2016.

Ward, Jane. *Not Gay*. New York: New York University Press, 2015.

White, Stephen. *Russia Goes Dry: Alcohol, State, and Society*. New York: Cambridge University Press, 1995.

Whitehouse, John A. "Historical Thinking and Narrative in a Global Culture." In *Nation-Building and History Education in a Global Culture*, edited by Joseph Zajda, 15–28. Berlin: Springer, 2015.

"Why Russia Is Not Rising Up against the Destruction of Parmesan." *Sputnik*, August 10, 2015. https://sputniknews.com/analysis/201508101025585137/.

Wimsatt, William K., and Monroe Beardsley. "The Intentional Fallacy." In *The Verbal Icon: Studies in the Meaning of Poetry*, edited by William K. Wimsatt. Lexington: University of Kentucky Press, 2015. Electronic ed.

Witkiewicz, Stanislaw Ignacy. *Insatiability*. Translated by Louis Iribarne. Evanston, IL: Northwestern University Press, 2012.

Wyspianski, Stanislaw. *The Wedding*. Translated by Noel Clark. London: Oberon Books, 1999.

Young, Cathy. "The Sci-Fi Writers' War." *Slate*, July 11, 2014.

Zajda, Joseph, ed. *Globalisation, Ideology and Politics of Education Reforms*. Berlin: Springer, 2017.

Zervas, Nikos. *Deti protiv vol'shebnikov*. Moscow: Lubianskaia ploshchad', 2004.

Zhurzhenko, Tatiana. "The Myth of Two Ukraines: A Commentary on Mykola Riabchuk's 'Ukraine: One State, Two Countries'?" *Eurozine*, September 17, 2002.

Zviagintsev, Vasilii. *Odissej pokidaet itaku*. Moscow: EKSMO, 2005.

Zygar, Mikhail. *All the Kremlin's Men: Inside the Court of Valdimir Putin*. New York: PublicAffairs, 2016.

INDEX

White, Hayden, *Metahistory,* 23
Wilde, Oscar, 154
Wimsatt, William K., 244n12
Witkiewicz, Ignacy, *Insatiability,* 189
women's studies, 144. *See also* feminism;
  gender ideology
world building, 9, 23
World War I, 57
World War II (Great Patriotic War), 2,
  23, 57, 97, 118, 215–17, 232
World War Z, 182
Wurst, Conchita, 251n23
Wyspianksi, Stanislav, *The Wedding,* 204

xenophobia, 84, 101, 120, 159, 177,
  246n14
The X-Files (television show), 43–44, 74,
  94, 245n3(ch.1), 246n9

Yakovlev, Alexander, 248n14
Yakovlev, Dima, 152
Yanov, Alexander, 123
Yeltsin, Boris, 60–61, 129
Yeltsin era, 6–7, 108–9, 230; liberalism
  and, 134, 136, 171 (*see also*
  liberalism); post-Yeltsin era, 87–88
youth, 91–92, 97

YouTube, 196–99
Yugoslavia: collapse of, 119, 128–29,
  206–7; NATO bombings of, 76,
  119–20, 128–29, 133
Yuriev, Mikhail, 209; *The Third Empire,*
  13, 244n11

Zamyatin, Yevgeny, *We,* 13, 24
Zavtra (newspaper), 83, 208, 240
Zhdanov, Andrei, 25, 169
Zhurzhenko, Tatiana, 208
Zionism, 21, 117
Žižek, Slavoj, 115
zombies: in popular culture, 180–82;
  postsocialist, 182–87, 191–92;
  revolution and, 183–84
zombification, 28–29; alien subject
  position and, 44; brainwashing and
  mind control, 185–94; cults and,
  190–93; media and, 181–200;
  paranoia and, 52; subjectivity
  and, 181–82, 185, 200. *See also*
  brainwashing; mind control
zoophilia, 166, 174
Zvyagintsev, Vasily, *Odysseus Leaves
  Ithaca,* 71, 76, 126
Zygar, Mikhail, 250n8

CPSIA information can be obtained
at www.ICGtesting.com
Printed in the USA
FFHW021038160319
51078873-56490FF